MAR   2007

An Arkansas History for Young People

An Arkansas History for Young People

THIRD EDITION

T. Harri Baker
and Jane Browning

THE UNIVERSITY OF ARKANSAS PRESS • FAYETTEVILLE 2003

To our next generation:

Kyle Chatman, Rick Hunter, Sarah Chatman,

Pierce Hunter, and Cari Lou Hunter

and

John William Browning IV and Paul Cornelius Browning

CONTENTS

PREFACE

Many minds and hands have contributed to this book. Altogether, it has been an effort to tell a story about what life has been like for all of the people who have lived in Arkansas down through the ages. The experiences of the Native Americans and the men and the women who later came here from Europe, Africa, and other lands are all valuable subjects of study. We hope to have highlighted the many different contributions that collectively have created our shared but diverse and extremely rich heritage.

We believe it is important for young people to have a sense of belonging to a place and its cultural heritage and to have a pride in their own history. The Arkansas experience has been brutal and painful at times, but it has been colorful and exciting and is well worth knowing.

It is equally important to understand the relationship of one's home place to the rest of the world. Arkansas history is an ideal subject of study for examining the ways in which global economic and political forces shape the lives of people everywhere, in prehistoric times as well as today. We hope this book adequately reflects Arkansas's place in the large stream of human events.

With its companion teacher's guide, this book is intended for classroom use as a text for students. We hope that people of all ages may also find this book a source of enjoyment in their personal reading for pleasure.

Arkansas is unique among the states in its production of diamonds, and the diamond is an appropriate emblem for this unique state. A diamond is born in volcanic violence; a rarity; a thing of the earth. It is prized for its beauty but equally for its supreme durability and superior strength. It can be an extravagance of vanity; it can be an industrial tool. A diamond is like Arkansas and its multi-faceted population: beautiful, earthy, and—above all—enduring.

Our heartfelt thanks go to the following individuals and institutions, whose generous assistance made this book possible: the Arkansas Humanities Council (formerly the Arkansas Endowment for the Humanities); the Butler Center, Central Arkansas Library System; Carolyn P. Baker; Tom Baskett; Swannee Bennett and Lana Nunly, Arkansas Territorial Restoration; Marian Berry, Old State House; Diane Blair and David Sloan, University of Arkansas, Fayetteville; Charlie Bolton, Jerry Hanson, Carl Moneyhon, C. Fred Williams, and LeRoy Williams, University of Arkansas at Little Rock; Judy Butler, Arkansas Department of Education; Andrea Cantrell and Michael Dabrishus, U of A Special Collections; Hester Davis, State Archeologist; Tom Dillard, Butler Center, CALS; Jan Eddleman; Donald Holley and William Shea, University of Arkansas at Monticello; Denyse Killgore, Arkansas Historical Association; George Lankford, Lyon College; Foy Lisenby, University of Central Arkansas; John McFarland, Arkansas Geology Commission; Johnnie Gentry and Mary McGimsey, University Museum, UAF; Dan and Phyllis Morse, Arkansas Archeological Survey; Linda Pine, UALR Archives; Scot Danforth, David Sanders, Debbie Self, and Miller Williams, University of Arkansas Press; Calvin Smith and Michael Dougan, Arkansas State University; Elizabeth Jacoway Watson; and special thanks to Bill Stricklin.

T. Harri Baker and Jane Browning
1991

PREFACE TO THE THIRD EDITION

We'd like to thank for their valuable comments all the students, teachers, and curriculum administrators who have used this book. We have enjoyed their occasional praise, and we have profited from their constructive critiques. The changes in this edition, especially the addition of material to make the book more useful to students, are largely a result of their comments.

As always, we are indebted to the skill and dedication of the people of the University of Arkansas Press, especially director Larry Malley, managing editor Brian King, production manager John Coghlan, designer Ellen Beeler, and business manager Rosalyn Carr.

—THB and JB
2003

HOW TO USE THIS BOOK

This book is designed to help you learn the fascinating history of our state and its people.

It's divided into eleven chapters. Each is about the same number of pages, but they cover longer or shorter periods of time, depending on how much is going on in that period.

Each chapter has features designed to help you make the most of it. At the beginning is a section called "What to Look For," showing you the most important things to come. At the end is a list of vocabulary words. If a word or phrase is in boldfaced type in the book, **like this**, it is in the vocabulary list for that chapter. Also at the end is a list of study questions, which is a way of helping you focus on important points. These questions or comments will help you think about what happened, and also about how and why it happened.

In each chapter there are several "sidebars," sections set off from the rest of the narrative by a green background. These sections usually deal with some special story, to help you see history in more depth. Often these sections are in the words of real people who lived at that time.

The pictures and their captions will also help you understand what people were like in the past. And maps are included to help you see certain developments.

Your teacher has a teacher's guide that contains suggestions for additional reading, special projects you may wish to do, and a list of Arkansas history web sites.

An Arkansas History for Young People

1

The First Arkansas People

The Beginning to 1541

What to Look for in Chapter 1

This first chapter looks like it covers a lot of time, from the earliest formation of the land and the earliest human settlements, to the first major European exploration in 1541. But you'll see that we know very little about many things that happened in that period, so this chapter touches just a few important topics.

The first important topic is the land that became Arkansas. Some of the terms you'll be introduced to here, like "Ozarks" and "Delta," will be used throughout the book. Then you'll meet the earliest residents, the Native Americans. Using the terms archeologists use, you'll learn about the Archaic, Woodlands, and Mississippian traditions. Although those terms at first may seem complicated, you'll see that they are just ways of describing how people lived and worked.

By 1500, Europeans travelers came to Arkansas, leaving written records about the land and the Native Americans. So the Historic period (history based on written records) began for Arkansas. You'll learn about the major tribes living here when the Europeans came: the Quapaw, the Caddo, and the Osage.

THE FIRST PEOPLE

Tough big-game hunters were the first Arkansans, living and working long, long ago where we do now. The hunters tracked game in small bands, and they depended on their intelligence as well as their pointed stones to catch their prey. One of the most impressive animals they hunted was the **mastodon**, a huge, shaggy ancestor of the modern elephant. Killing a **mastodon** would provide food for weeks and clothing for cold winter months. We do not know very much about them, except that they were the ancestors of today's American Indians, and they were here as long as 12,500 years ago.

Actually, the story of Arkansas begins long before that. Maybe 600 million years ago, the land that would be called Arkansas was covered by water. Slowly, the movement of the earth's land masses forced up mountains.

By about 230 million years ago, parts of the flat plain of the southwest and what would later become the **Delta** of the Mississippi gradually started to become dry land. At one time, dinosaurs roamed here, and they left

*This is an artist's recreation of a **mastodon**, as one might have looked in early Arkansas.* (Courtesy of the University Museum of the University of Arkansas, Fayetteville)

their footprints in mud that would become rock.

But the dinosaurs disappeared, and the once warm and swampy earth turned cooler and entered a series of Ice Ages. Far to the north, glaciers formed, moved south, then melted back to the north. The glaciers never quite reached Arkansas, but they did make the climate colder.

During the most recent advance of the glaciers, perhaps 40,000 years ago, a bridge of land connected what is now Russia with Alaska. The first human beings probably came to North America over this land. Whole tribes of men, women, and children traveled together, perhaps with their dogs, following the herds of wild animals upon which they depended for food and clothing. As they spread through North America, some came to

the land that would be called Arkansas. They must have had many different names for themselves, but we call them all the Indians. Christopher Columbus, the European explorer who gave us our name for them much later when he came to America, thought he had reached the East Indies, some islands off the coast of Asia.

We know, because we can date the remains of tools, weapons, and burials, that Indians reached Arkansas by about 10,000 B.C. (10,000 years before the birth of Jesus). We can only guess that these people marked the passage of time by observing the sun, the moon, the seasons, and the movement of animals, or by recalling important events in their tribal memories.

We wish we knew more about these early people. They could speak to each other, but they apparently did not have written languages. We must look at the evidence they left of their lives and try to imagine them. The study of what they left behind is called **archeology.**

Indians lived by hunting animals and gathering wild plants. They probably shared the land with large animals such as the woolly mammoth, the **mastodon,** the giant beaver, the sloth, the musk ox, and the tapir. They also hunted smaller animals, birds, and fish. The people had to be strong and sturdy to live, and they must have known how to work with each other on the hunt.

They probably lived in groups of about twenty men, women, and children. They moved frequently, following the animals, and they may have had dogs as pets. Although they did not have a lot of material things we

have today, these early Indians did have important skills. They knew about fire, so they could keep warm and cook their food. They could make tools of stone, like their spear points and knives, and probably used wood and animal bones for tools, too. The word "paleo" means long ago, and we call these people the Paleo-Indians.

THE ARKANSAS LAND

By the time the first Paleo-Indians arrived, the land we now call Arkansas looked very much as it does today. One big difference was that it had a drier climate then, with less rainfall each year. Then as now, the land was divided into three regions that are very different from each other, the Uplands (consisting of the

This **mastodon** skull, with a tusk still attached, was found in the Red River area of Arkansas. (Photo by Frank Schambach, courtesy of Arkansas Archeological Survey)

These are fluted points from the Paleo period. Much skill and patience was required to chip out the point and the edges. The other picture is a modern re-creation of the technique. (Courtesy of the University Museum of the University of Arkansas, Fayetteville)

Ozarks, Ouachitas, and the Arkansas River valley), the Gulf Coastal Plain, and the Mississippi **Alluvial** Plain.

Almost all of northwestern Arkansas occupies the southern portion of the Ozark Plateau, which stretches into southwestern Missouri. This is the oldest land form in the state. Eroded into the Ozark Plateau region are the rugged and lovely Boston Mountains. The Buffalo, Kings, and White rivers carve through the Ozark Plateau, where they have created fertile river valleys. The trees are mostly hardwoods, such as oak and hickory, walnut and maple.

To the south of the Ozarks are the Ouachita (pronounced WASH-ih-taw) Mountains, the westernmost reach of the Appalachian Mountain range. These are among the oldest mountains in North America. When they were new, they were possibly as tall and craggy as the Rocky Mountains are now. Millions of years of water and weather have worn them down and smoothed their edges. In the Uplands are softwood evergreen trees, including pines. In the valleys are hardwood trees, such as tupelo,

oak, hickory, cottonwood, and gum. Several rivers run through these mountains, including the Maumelle, the Fourche LaFave, and the Ouachita rivers. The Ouachita Mountains are rich in underground mineral resources. The Indians knew how to quarry some of these minerals, called chert, for making spear points, arrowheads, and other tools. An unusual rock is **novaculite**, which the Indians also used for making tools and which is still used for sharpening metal tools and knives. A later age of industry would value the region's barite, antimony, and mercury.

Across the southern part of the state is the flat area called the Gulf Coastal Plain. This area is crossed by several rivers, including the Ouachita, Saline, and Red rivers, all flowing toward the south. The river valleys create narrow strips of rich, fertile soil, which is suitable for farming, but much of the rest of the Gulf Coastal Plain is timberland. Pine forests grow there, but it is poor soil for farming.

Crossing the state from northwest to southeast is the mighty and beautiful Arkansas River, one of America's major rivers. The

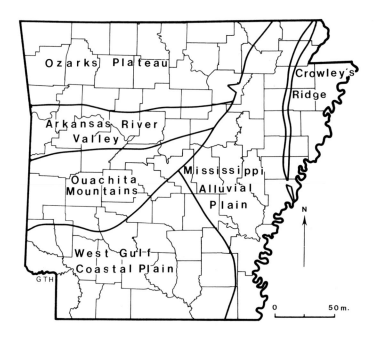

These are the major geographical regions of Arkansas. (Courtesy of Gerald T. Hanson)

Arkansas begins high in the Colorado Rocky Mountains and travels across a third of the continent to join the Mississippi River in the southeast corner of Arkansas.

The Arkansas River has always brought good times and bad times to Arkansans. Its long valley contains good farmland, but it can also flood frequently. Before the railroad and the automobile, the river offered the primary avenue of travel into the state.

All along the eastern part of Arkansas is the Mississippi **Alluvial** Plain, a broad, flat area of rich soil. "**Alluvial**" refers to soil left behind by rivers. This is the area often called the Mississippi **Delta**, because it was formed by the waters of the Mississippi River.

Almost all flat, the **Delta** is some of the best farmland in America. Part of it, the Grand Prairie between the White and St. Francis rivers, is a natural grassland. This is the location of what are now Prairie and Arkansas counties.

Running north to south in the upper part of the **Delta** is a long, narrow area of high ground called Crowley's Ridge. Long ago, the Ohio River flowed down one side of Crowley's Ridge, and the Mississippi River flowed down the other side. The water washed away the

Artist Dan Kerlin imagined that a typical family scene in the Archaic period might look like this. The men, women, and young people are busy gathering wild plants, hunting animals, and fishing in the river. And they have a pet dog. (Courtesy of the University Museum of the University of Arkansas, Fayetteville)

*This is a modern recreation of an **atlatl**, or throwing stick, showing its construction and use with a spear. The device works like a lever to increase the speed and force of the spear.* (Courtesy of the University Museum of the University of Arkansas, Fayetteville)

soil of the river valleys, but left the tall ridge in the middle.

The ridge is covered by wind-blown dirt, which is called "**loess**." Crowley's Ridge offers high ground, safe from the Mississippi River floods that can put the **Delta** land under water.

THE ARCHAIC TRADITION

Major changes in the climate made for changes in the lives of the Indians. As the **glaciers** retreated for the last time, the climate became warmer and drier. Large animals more suited for the colder weather, such as the **mastodon**, died out or moved far to the north, leaving the Arkansas forests filled with smaller animals, such as bears, deer, elk, wolves, raccoons, rabbits, and squirrels.

Man, the most adaptable animal, prospered too. The Indians became more numerous and more widespread. Their tools and

weapons were more efficient. Instead of traveling all the time on the trails of the animals, Indians could settle down part of the year. These new conditions are what **archeologists** call the Archaic tradition, beginning about 8,000 B.C.

Frequently, the Archaic Indians selected ridges along the river banks or other kinds of high ground for their homes. The Indians dug pits in the ground for garbage dumps. To bake a kind of bread made from wild grains, they surrounded the dough with clay balls then built a fire over the balls. The clay balls would heat up just like an oven and bake the bread without burning it. From the streams the Indians collected mussels and crayfish to eat.

The Indians of this time buried their dead with care, in individual graves.

Indians still traveled to the lowlands for big hunts or to areas where nuts and berries could be harvested in the fall. There, groups of Indians would meet each other and

History: How Do We Know What We Know?

Learning about the past is based on gathering evidence and studying it.

"History" usually means the study of the written records made by people in past times and still in existence. "Historians" think of questions about the past, gather written evidence, judge its value, and draw conclusions from the evidence. The more records we have from different sources, the better we can understand the past.

The word "prehistory" usually means the time before people learned to write. Writing was invented at different times in different places, but the earliest writing dates from about five thousand or six thousand years ago. To gather evidence about the lives of people who did not write, **archeologists** and anthropologists look for any kind of physical evidence that might have survived, such as tools, weapons, bones, art, and parts of houses and other buildings. This kind of evidence is hard to judge, and it cannot tell us all we want to know. But a lot of what we know about the early Indians in America and Arkansas is based on such physical evidence.

Sometimes almost all of our written evidence comes from one side, as when the first European explorers met the American Indians. This means we have to be careful studying this evidence and remember that it might reflect the biases and prejudices of the people who wrote it. Someday, a long, long time from now, people will want to know about how we lived in this time. What sort of evidence do you think they will have about us, and what kind of things will that evidence tell them?

exchange ideas and ways of doing things. Thus, new tools spread quickly.

A kind of tool called an **atlatl**, or throwing stick, made a spear go farther and faster. The **adze**, like an axe with the blade crosswise to the handle, allowed them to dig the wood out of a log to make a canoe. Some of their handmade objects, such as beads and little statues carved from stone, had either decorative or religious purposes.

THE WOODLAND TRADITION

We call the next period, beginning about 1,000 B.C., the Woodland tradition. The most important change at that time was the widespread practice of agriculture. The Arkansas Indians either learned for themselves or borrowed from others the idea that seeds, planted in the ground and cared for, would grow and provide a secure source of food.

The first crops in Arkansas were gourds, squash, and weedlike grains that we no longer eat, with names like goosefoot, marsh elder, and sumpweed. The people still hunted, fished, and gathered wild berries and nuts, but at times the crops they grew must have made the difference between hunger and comfort.

Farming was responsible for many important changes. The tribe now had to stay in one place to protect and cultivate the crops. A more secure food supply meant that tribal government had to have more power, deciding when and what to plant.

In hundreds of places along the Arkansas River valley and in the Ozark Mountains, Indian artists drew pictures on rocks. Using paint made of clay or powdered rock, or carving into the face of the rock, they drew stylized images of animals or fish. Many of these pictures can still be seen.

Some of the carvings are spiral designs, with circles inside of circles to a point in the middle. The sun or the moon probably shone on different parts of the design at different times of the year, so these drawings may have been a kind of calendar, which helped the Indians predict the seasons and the movements of animals.

In the Ozark Mountains, the Woodlands Indians made their homes on the ledges in the cliffs, where the rocky overhang of the cliff walls protected them from wind and rain. They built fires to warm themselves and cook the food they gathered or hunted. They used different kinds of grasses to weave baskets to hold their food. They could make moccasins from woven grass, too.

Some of their bluff shelters were so dry and protected that a few of the objects they made and stored in their shelters have lasted more than a thousand years for us to see. The museum at the University of Arkansas in Fayetteville has a collection of them on

During the Woodland tradition, or perhaps even earlier, Indians in Arkansas expressed themselves by drawing on rock. This example is the stylized version of an animal. (Courtesy of the Arkansas Archeological Survey)

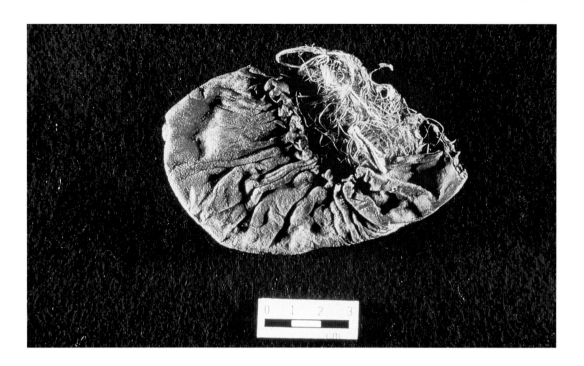

This baby's moccasin dates from the Woodland tradition in Arkansas. Someone—probably a loving mother or father—has carefully filled the moccasin with grass to warm a baby's foot. (Courtesy of the University Museum of the University of Arkansas, Fayetteville)

Long after the mounds at the Indian city we now call Toltec were abandoned, an artist drew their remains. Still visible were parts of the wall and **moat**, *and some of the mounds, overgrown with trees.* (Courtesy of the Smithsonian Institution)

display. Among them is a pair of soft leather shoes for a baby. The shoes are still lined with a fine, soft grass that was tucked in them to keep a baby's feet warm during a cold winter long ago. We also know that the some of the Indians of this period began to set aside one section of their settlement as a burial place for their dead. The graves were covered with earth, forming small hills or mounds. Important items were sometimes placed in the graves.

Toltec Mounds State Park near Little Rock is one of the largest existing Woodlands tradition sites, and visitors can see the remains of the burial mounds, along with films and displays. The name "Toltec," by the way, is one example of how our knowledge of Arkansas Indians has changed and grown. When white men first discovered the mounds, they assumed that the Indians must have learned mound-building skills from more distant cultures, like the Toltec Indians of Mexico. We know now that the mound-building cultures in Arkansas and elsewhere in the Mississippi Valley developed out of the local Indians' own efforts.

Trade among various Indian groups seems to have increased during the Woodland tradition. In some years, Indians may have had surplus food to exchange. Arkansas Indians also had rocks, minerals, and salt sought by other tribes. **Hematite**, a mineral containing

B.C., A.D., Who Cares? What Year Is It?

The world has many different calendars, or ways of marking the passage of years. In this book, we are using the Western calendar, which is based on Christian tradition.

In that calendar, all years are dated before and after the birth of Jesus. Thus the year 1541, when De Soto came to Arkansas, is 1,541 years after the birth of Jesus. Sometimes that is written A.D. 1541. A.D. stands for Anno Domini, Latin for "in the year of the Lord." The length of a year itself is measured by the earth's passage around the sun.

The years before the birth of Jesus are marked B.C., "before Christ," and are counted backwards. Thus the year 5,000 B.C. comes before 3,000 B.C.

In this chapter we have used the Western or Christian calendar to date events in the lives of the Indians, even though they did not use that method themselves.

We do not know what kinds of calendars Indians used. They surely could measure the passage of a single year by observing the position of the sun at different times of the year. They probably dated the years by great events in the history of their tribe. Many such groups of people selected a wise man to remember the group's history, repeat it to the people, and pass it on to the next generation.

We have also used the word "generation" to describe the passage of time. It means the amount of time between the birth of parents and the birth of their children. You, for example, are the second generation after your grandparents, and the third generation after your great-grandparents. It is not a precise period of time, but a generation is usually considered to be twenty or twenty-five years.

iron, could be used as weights for fishing nets; **novaculite** could be made into tools with a fine edge; and quartz crystal was always in demand. In return, Arkansas Indians might get seashells from the Gulf Coast or copper from Indians from Missouri, Tennessee, or even from as far away as Wisconsin.

Another important addition to the Indian culture at this time was the making of pottery. At first, the clay pots had straight sides, like flower pots today. Later, the Indians began to decorate their pots with lines carved into the wet clay. The presence of pottery is important to our knowledge of Indians. Since well-made clay pots, or pieces of them, can last a long time; their remains give us a way of measuring the Indians' cultural stages and their contacts with other pottery-making Indians.

THE MISSISSIPPIAN TRADITION

The Arkansas Indian culture had grown into what we call the Mississippian tradition by about the year 700. (In the Christian dating system, this was the year 700 A.D., or 700 years after the birth of Jesus.) The number of people grew very large, living for the most part in villages or farmsteads. In the center of the villages would be a large open field or **plaza.** At one end of the **plaza** would be a mound, or several mounds, built not for burials but as a place for public buildings. The buildings on the mounds were connected with religious practices, but they also housed something like government functions and served as home sites for the chiefs.

Artist Dan Kerlin shows a ceremony at a city center in the Mississippian tradition. The focus of the ceremony is on the temple at the top of the mound. The smoke comes from the part of the ceremony that involves burning symbols of the last year so the new year can start fresh.
(Courtesy of the University Museum of the University of Arkansas, Fayetteville)

This is an effigy vessel from the Mississippian tradition. An effigy vessel is one designed to look like something else—in this case, clearly a turtle. (Courtesy of the University Museum of the University of Arkansas, Fayetteville)

Another effigy vessel from the Mississippian tradition. Modern people have nicknamed this one "Big Boy." (Courtesy of the University Museum of the University of Arkansas, Fayetteville)

This King's Creek Bowl from the Poverty Point site in Arkansas is the oldest example of graphic art found so far in the United States. The color photograph shows the remains of the bowl. The other drawings show what the complete bowl would have looked like and a reproduction of the design on the inside of the bowl. (Courtesy of the Arkansas Archeological Survey)

The **plaza** and the temple mounds were used for special occasions, when all the people from the surrounding village would gather for a meeting, a harvest festival, or a religious service. In some cases, the **plaza** and mounds were surrounded by wooden and earthen walls and by ditches like **moats.** The walls and ditches made the area look like a fort, and they were probably used for protection against other tribes. One of the largest temple mound cities in Arkansas was at Parkin.

During the Mississippian tradition, the Indians' technical skills continued to increase. By about the eighth century A.D., Arkansas Indians were using the bow and arrow, cer-tainly for hunting and possibly for protection or warfare.

Another great advance for Indian culture was the growing of corn, an extremely useful food and a crop originally grown only in the Americas that eventually spread throughout the world. Babies could now switch from milk at a much earlier stage and be fed a sort of corn gruel as baby food. Children were big helpers in an agricultural society because they could help plant the seeds and care for the growing plants. But corn contains more starch than the earlier diet of the Indians, and they began to suffer from tooth decay and other nutrition problems.

A Nodena head pot from the Mississippian tradition. (Courtesy of the Hampson Museum, Wilson, Arkansas)

Pottery became sturdier when the Indians began mixing crushed and burned mussel shell, which contained lime, with the clay, making the pots lighter and stronger so they could be larger and more carefully shaped. Much of the pottery of this period is truly beautiful, with complex designs and intricate shapes. Some pieces are even shaped like animals. University museums at Fayetteville, Jonesboro, and Arkadelphia today have especially good collections of such pottery.

During this period in southwest Arkansas, one can recognize tools, pottery, and houses made by the ancestors of today's Caddo Indians. The Caddo way of life was spread over a large region covering parts of what is now Oklahoma, Texas, Arkansas, and Louisiana.

The Caddo built mounds, too, where important leaders were buried and temples were built. But the Caddo lived on small family farms rather than sharing their fields with the whole group. Each household had an outdoor fireplace for cooking with a garden nearby. The Caddo grew tobacco, which they smoked on special occasions.

The Caddo in Arkansas also had an important industry, making salt. The Indians poured water through sand to dissolve the salt out and then boiled the water to evaporate all the moisture. When the water boiled off, little chunks of usable salt remained. They traded the salt widely.

Although we can piece together an account of the early Indians of Arkansas based on nothing more than the few objects that survive, there is still so much we do not know and probably never will. All the important questions about what these people thought about themselves, the other people they met, and the larger world around them are closed to us.

This account of the Indians covers more than ten thousand years in the lives of Arkansas people over hundreds of generations. Our knowledge of these fascinating people expanded when European explorers and settlers begin to appear in their country, but as a consequence we generally see the Indians through the eyes of European culture.

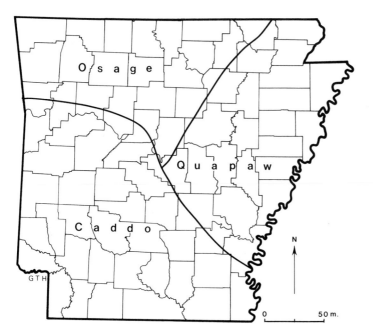

As Europeans began to come to Arkansas, the major Indian tribes were located in these general areas. For the Quapaw and Caddo, the land was home; for the Osage, northwest Arkansas was part of a larger hunting range. (Courtesy of Gerald T. Hanson)

THE HISTORIC INDIANS

The first explorers began to come to Arkansas from Europe soon after the year 1500 A.D. In the next chapter we will explain who these visitors were and what they were doing, but for now we can describe the Indian tribes as the Europeans saw them. This is called the Historic period, because we have written records from the European travelers to supplement the physical remains Indians left behind.

By 1500, the Indians living in Arkansas were organized in distinct tribes, for each of which the Europeans recorded a name. In the Red River and Ouachita valleys of the southwest lived the Caddo, who had productive farms. In the eastern part of Arkansas, where they would be the first to be "discovered" by Europeans, were the Quapaw, the inheritors of the temple mound traditions. Sometime later, possibly after 1700, the Osage would come to dominate the northwest part of Arkansas.

The Caddo had a large and complex farming culture. There may have been as many as eight thousand of them, organized into tribes and larger groups. Excellent farmers, the Caddo produced large crops of corn and beans, and they did some hunting, too.

Their houses were shaped like cones, made by setting long poles in the ground in a circle and tying them together at the top. The Caddo would cover that frame with a thick

The Caddo Indians in what is now southwestern Arkansas had a distinct way of making and decorating their pottery. Notice the vase or pot standing on its own three legs. (Courtesy of the University Museum of the University of Arkansas, Fayetteville)

This is an artist's rendering of a deer mask, used in some of the Caddo ceremonies.
(Courtesy of the University Museum of the University of Arkansas, Fayetteville)

This is an actual photograph of a Caddo farmstead. The photograph dates from the late 1860s or the early 1870s when the Caddo were living in eastern Oklahoma. (Courtesy of the Smithsonian Institution)

thatch made out of grass. Men wore tanned deerskins, sometimes adorned with fringes and small seeds. Women wore skirts made of woven grass or a kind of cloth made from plants. Caddo men and women apparently thought that tattoos and body paint made them more attractive.

Some researchers believe that the Quapaw may have begun as a branch of the large Sioux language group of Indians of middle North America. They think that at least 350 years ago, and possibly earlier, part of this group moved south down the Ohio River valley, then down the Mississippi to the mouth of the Arkansas River.

Others believe the Quapaw to be the descendants of the great Mississippian tribes described by De Soto's expedition in 1542. In any case, they were the "Downstream People,"

in their own language, the Quapaw. Others called them the Arkansas.

The Quapaw lived in the river valleys of eastern Arkansas, especially near the mouth of the Arkansas River. They grew squash, beans, and corn, and they did some hunting and fishing. Their houses, usually shared by several families, were long rectangles with curved roofs, made of wood and covered by bark.

Because the Quapaw lived along the Mississippi and Arkansas rivers, they were usually the first Arkansas Indians seen by the European explorers. Almost always, the explorers described the Quapaw as a tall and handsome people, friendly and peaceful.

The Osage were a hunting tribe. They did not actually live in Arkansas. Their home villages were in what is now southern Missouri. Although they did some farming in the

As late as 1820, an Osage village in southwestern Missouri looked like this. The artist has shown one house under construction, so the framework of poles can be seen under the thatch, and has also shown several activities related to the Osage hunting culture. (From Ingenthorn, *Indians of the Ozark Plain*)

Artist Charles Banks Wilson, after thorough research on features and dress, suggests that an adult male Quapaw of about 1700 would have looked much like this. (Courtesy of the University Museum of the University of Arkansas, Fayetteville)

The Quapaw built their houses long and narrow, with curved walls and a roof covered in bark. (Courtesy of the Arkansas Archeological Survey)

home villages, they still relied on hunting for much of their food. They considered northern Arkansas to be their hunting lands, and their hunting parties sometimes attacked the Quapaw and Caddo settlements.

The Osage dressed in animal skins: breechcloths and leggings for the men; shirts and dresses for the women. At home they lived in villages based on family ties. Their houses were rectangles made of small tree trunks covered with animal skins or mats woven out of brush. Each house was home to several families.

But it was in the lands of the Quapaw in this future state of Arkansas that the first contact between the Indian and the European cultures began.

VOCABULARY

adze (ADZ) a tool similar to an axe, with the blade attached crosswise to the handle. Used for carving a canoe out of a whole log.

alluvial (uh-LOO-vee-uhl) left behind by streams and rivers. Alluvial soils are those deposited by a river as it carries soil from upstream to downstream. The Mississippi Alluvial Plain covers much of eastern Arkansas and is referred to in Arkansas as "the Delta."

archeologists (ARE-kee-AH-luh-jists) scientists who carefully uncover objects left behind by earlier people. Archeologists are able to judge how people lived and when they lived by putting together the physical clues—like pieces of pottery made in a certain way—that they find. Their study is archeology.

atlatl (AT-uh-LAT-uhl) a tool used by the early Indians for throwing spears.

delta in one meaning, the land around the mouth of a river built up by the river as it deposits silt, or soil, as it empties into the sea. In Arkansas and Mississippi, the entire flatland region of alluvial soil on either side of the Mississippi River is called "the Delta."

glacier (GLAY-shur) a sheet of snow and ice that never completely melts, even in the middle of summer. During the Ice Ages, huge glaciers covered North America as far south as the Great Plains states. Their advances and retreats during the Pleistocene era created much of North America's current topography, such as lakes, hills, and valleys.

hematite (HEE-muh-tite) a stone native to Arkansas that is especially heavy because it contains iron.

loess (LOH-uhs) wind-borne soil. The soil of Crowley's Ridge in northeastern Arkansas is chiefly loess that was carried there and deposited by the wind thousands of years ago. It is especially fragile soil, and it is subject to erosion.

mastodon (MASS-tuh-dahn) an ancestor of the modern elephant that lived in the Pleistocene era, or during the Ice Ages.

moat a water-filled circular ditch surrounding a building or set of buildings, usually designed to protect the buildings from attack.

novaculite (no-VA-kyuh-lite) a stone native to southwestern Arkansas that is a natural sharpening tool. Known to prehistoric Indians and traded widely among the Indian tribes of the eastern United States, novaculite is still very much in demand today.

plaza an open area, like a park, surrounded by buildings.

STUDY QUESTIONS

1. Where did the first people to live in what is now Arkansas come from? How did they survive?

2. Name five geographic regions in Arkansas and describe how they are different from one another.

3. What are some of the plants, animals, and minerals that existed in prehistoric Arkansas? Name at least two of each.

4. Name and describe two inventions of the Archaic Indians.

5. What was the most important change in Indian life during the Woodland tradition?

6. Name two important changes that came about because of agriculture.

7. What kinds of things did the various Indian tribes trade among their groups? Name at least five.

8. Describe a Mississippian tradition village. What were the mounds used for?

9. The introduction of corn had good and bad effects. What were they?

10. What were the three historic Indian tribes of Arkansas? How were they alike? How were they different?

2 Arkansas Becomes a Part of the European World

1541–1803

What to Look for in Chapter 2

This chapter deals with the effect that European explorers and settlers had on the Native Americans and on Arkansas from 1541 to 1803. The chapter encourages you to see the events of this period as part of a broad picture. All over the world, Spain, France, and England were competing with each other to dominate newly discovered lands and peoples. One major area of this rivalry was North America, including the Mississippi Valley where Arkansas lies.

As this chapter focuses one by one on the Spanish, the French, and the English, notice the different ways each tried to dominate, or colonize, the land and how far each succeeded.

The chapter ends with the creation by revolution of a new nation, as the English colonies in North America become the United States of America. The leaders of the new United States understood the value of the land that all those other nations had struggled over. So through the Louisiana Purchase, Arkansas and the rest of the western half of the Mississippi Valley became part of the United States.

THE FIRST EXPLORERS

About the year 1500, the Europeans began expanding their way of life all over the world. On the other side of the Atlantic Ocean from Europe were the Indian cultures, including those in the land that would one day be called Arkansas. Without knowing it, the Indians were about to become players in a huge struggle for the control of North America.

The people of Europe were forming new ideas and new ways of doing things. The burst of creative activity that we call the **Renaissance** had made people curious about the world. Technology was changing rapidly: ship design and tools for navigation allowed longer voyages, firearms made for easier conquests, and the printing press spread news quickly. Nation-states such as Spain, France, and England emerged with unified populations and strong kings. They were now able to organize and carry out large-scale plans to explore and colonize the **New World.**

These nations competed with each other for power and influence. Differences in religion between Roman Catholic and Protestant nations heightened the rivalry. Trade, the buying and selling of goods for a profit, was growing more important as a way for people and their nations to become rich.

This was the world of Christopher Columbus. An Italian skilled in ship handling and **navigation**, he was convinced that he could open a new trade route to the Indies by sailing straight west from Europe. He thought he could sail around the world to the coast of India and China.

The rulers of Spain, Ferdinand and Isabella, backed his voyage, and in 1492 his three ships touched what we now know as the islands of the Caribbean. Columbus was con-vinced he had found the Indies (so he called the new people he met Indians) and made several more voyages trying to find the mainland of Asia.

Columbus, of course, had made a more amazing discovery than he realized. He had found two entire **continents**, never before known to Europeans. The European explorers wanted to extend the power of their nations, spread their religion, and find wealth for themselves and their kings. So for glory, for God, and for gold, explorers from the European nations began to move through the Americas.

Spain was the first nation to benefit from the New World. By the early 1500s, not long after the voyages of Columbus, Hernando Cortés had **conquered** the Aztecs of Mexico,

This is an eighteenth-century French artist's view—possibly somewhat fanciful—of Arkansas Indians hunting buffalo. Notice the spectators in a stand at the left rear, and the framework for smoking meat in the right rear. (Courtesy of the Library of Congress)

and Francisco Pizarro had **conquered** the Incas of Peru. The abundant gold of those empires encouraged other explorers. In the 1540s, Francisco Vasquez de Coronado traveled north of Mexico through the American southwest as far as Kansas.

Meanwhile, the French explorer Jacques Cartier explored the St. Lawrence River valley of Canada, establishing a French claim in the northern part of North America. Sailing in the service of the English, John Cabot cruised along the Atlantic Coast. The rivalry for domination of North America had begun.

Although the explorers were curious about the Indians they encountered, Europeans were unwilling or unable to value fully the richness of Indian cultures. Because the Indians lacked the technology of Europeans,

were not Christians, and had a different economic system, the Europeans called them all savages. To the Europeans that meant they could take the Indians' lands and goods if they wanted to, and they sometimes made slaves of Indians and even killed them.

However, the Europeans' most deadly impact on the Indians was disease. Smallpox, measles, and **influenza** (the "flu") had been common diseases in Europe for centuries, and the people there had some natural resistance to them. These diseases had been unknown in the Americas, however, and the Indians had no defenses against them.

The Quapaws of Arkansas, for example, may have numbered in the tens of thousands when they first met Europeans. Two hundred years after that first contact, there were only

Long before the first European, De Soto, saw the hot springs, Indian tribes believed the water could heal and refresh. Here an artist imagines Indians bringing their sick and weary to "take the waters." (Courtesy of the J. N. Heiskell Historical Collection, UALR Archives and Special Collections)

FERNANDO DE SOTO.

Hernando de Soto. His signature is below the picture. (Courtesy of the Chicago Historical Society)

ARKANSAS BECOMES A PART OF THE EUROPEAN WORLD

about fifteen hundred Quapaw, and when they left Arkansas for good another hundred years later, the tribe had only five hundred members. Although many other things affected them, European diseases probably took the most lives.

DE SOTO COMES TO ARKANSAS

The Spanish, moving from their bases in the Caribbean Sea and Florida, were the first Europeans to visit Arkansas. In 1539, Hernando de Soto left Florida with six hundred men (some of whom were black), two hundred horses, a drove of hogs, and a pack of fighting dogs.

They had a long, hard journey. De Soto and his men often dealt with the Indians ruthlessly. They fought with some tribes and killed at least four thousand Indians in battle. They took captives whenever they needed laborers. Through warfare, disease, and accident, De Soto's group grew smaller as the trip grew longer.

Two years after they started, in 1541, De Soto and his men reached the banks of a huge river. De Soto called it in Spanish the *Rio Grande,* the Great River. Later it would take the Indian name that means "father of waters," the **Mississippi River.** De Soto stood on the east bank, in what is now the state of Mississippi. Across the broad and swift river was what is now Arkansas.

De Soto ordered his men to build rafts for the crossing. As the Spaniards were working, Indians came from the other bank in a fleet of two hundred canoes and showered them with arrows, no doubt increasing the Spaniards' fear about what lay ahead. But De Soto's men finished their four big rafts and, after a rough crossing of the fast-running river, made it to the other side, Arkansas. It was June of 1541.

Waiting for De Soto were the Indians of Arkansas, thousands of them living in great settlements. Exactly who they were is one of

Whatever You Call It, Can You Eat It?

As the European explorers moved through the Americas, they were amazed to find many kinds of plants and animals that did not exist in Europe.

Here is the way a man traveling with Hernando de Soto described a fish that the Indians caught in the waters of Arkansas:

> There was a fish which they called bagres; the third part of it was head, and it had on both sides the gills, and along the sides great pricks like very sharp awls. Those of the kind that were in the lakes were as big as pikes; and in the river there were some of a hundred and of a hundred and fifty pounds weight and many of them were taken with the hook.

Recognize it? De Soto and his followers had just met their first catfish.

Sarah M. Fountain, *Authentic Voices: Arkansas Culture, 1541–1860* (Conway: University of Central Arkansas Press, 1986), p. 9.

the unsolved mysteries of Arkansas history. The Spanish records describe these natives in ways that make them seem much like the temple mound builders of the Parkin site. If so, those Indians must have moved or died out from exposure to European diseases within a hundred years after the Spanish visit. The next European visitors, the French, met the Quapaw Indians. Whether the Quapaw Indians moved downstream from the Ohio valley into a deserted countryside or were the remnants of the temple mound builders themselves may never be known for sure.

Another mystery is exactly where De Soto crossed the Mississippi. There are four different accounts of his journey, three of them written by men who traveled with him. Each describes land features and Indian towns which have to be matched with geography and physical remains after almost 450 years of floods and erosion. In 1939, a group of researchers argued that the most likely site was

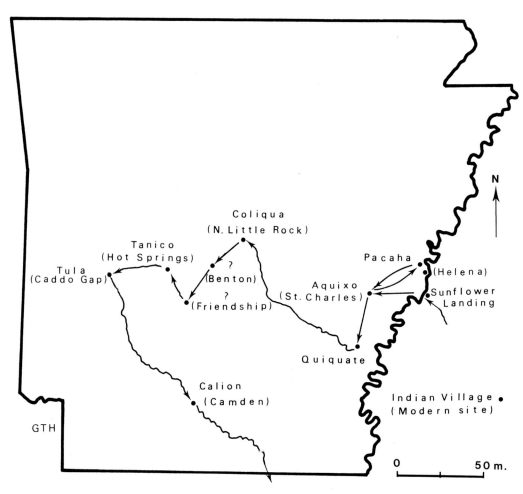

*Although the exact route of the De Soto **expedition** is still debated, a 1939 state commission decided on this version. The names of settlements are the Indian names De Soto used, with their modern versions in parentheses. Another version has De Soto entering the state at Commerce Landing, about halfway between Helena and Memphis, and moving into the northeast part of the state before heading west to the little rock and hot springs. (Courtesy of Gerald T. Hanson)*

Artist Dan Kerlin reproduces the moment when Hernando de Soto and his men raised a Christian cross in an Arkansas Indian village. (Courtesy of the University Museum of the University of Arkansas, Fayetteville)

Sunflower Landing, just south of modern Helena. Modern evidence places the location near Commerce Landing, south of what is now Memphis.

After the canoe attack, De Soto must have been pleased to get a friendly reception from the first Indians he met on the Arkansas side of the **Mississippi River.** Following the Indians' directions to a great town, and hoping the gold he was looking for would be there, he moved north past large villages and fields of corn. After a time, he came to the home of the chief of what De Soto's chroniclers called the Casqui. Here was a group of Indians living around a temple mound settlement like the one at Parkin.

De Soto stayed for three days in the chief's house, located high on one of the mounds.

When the chief asked De Soto if his god could make it rain, De Soto built a Christian cross as tall as a tree on one of the mounds. The Roman Catholic priests with him conducted a religious service, while, according to one of the accounts of De Soto's men, fifteen thousand Indians watched. The Spaniard who wrote about this episode claimed that it did rain a few days later.

ON TO SOUTHWEST ARKANSAS

Still hunting for gold, De Soto explored eastern Arkansas to a point north up the White River, then moved west. Some modern historians and archeologists have supposed that

Hernando de Soto might have looked like this as he led his men into Arkansas. (Courtesy of the University Museum of the University of Arkansas, Fayetteville)

his route went deep into the Ouachita Mountains and then circled back to the Arkansas River. It used to be thought that De Soto's **expedition** spent the winter somewhere near Camden, but it is more likely that De Soto and his men were really closer to what is now Little Rock.

At winter's end, they followed the Arkansas downriver. On May 21, 1542, De Soto died. Afraid of what the Indians might do if they learned that their chief was dead, the Spaniards hid his body and carried it with them until they reached the **Mississippi River,** probably at a location near present-day Helena. There, they secretly slipped De Soto's coffin into the great river he had discovered.

Taking over as leader, Luís de Moscoso tried to march the remaining army overland to Mexico. Traveling through Caddo Indian country, they had many battles with those fierce and crafty warriors. According to modern evidence, the Spaniards followed the Red River south. They were probably prevented from continuing by the Great **Red River Raft** —a hundred miles of trees and other debris that had been piling up in the river for centuries—and turned west.

From there, they went deep into Texas, about as far as Dallas. But the country was barren and empty, and they had trouble finding enough food to survive. Instead of going on to Mexico, they retraced their steps all the way back to the Mississippi around Helena. There, they built crude boats and escaped downriver to the Gulf of Mexico.

After three years of travel including a summer and winter in Arkansas, the men of the **expedition** were tired, sick, and frustrated. Only three hundred men and twenty horses were left of the original group. They had seen towns of four hundred houses and thousands of Indians, warehouses brimming with grain, and natural wonders like the hot springs, but they had not discovered gold.

The Spaniards left no permanent settlements in Arkansas or anywhere else in the

This Spanish bell was found in Arkansas. If it is not the result of later trade with the Spanish, it may be one of the few physical survivals of De Soto's journey through the state. (Courtesy of the Arkansas Archeological Survey)

Mississippi valley. They almost certainly had introduced European diseases among the Indians. And, according to legend, some of their pigs got loose in the woods and became ancestors of the Arkansas wild razorback hog.

THE FRENCH IN ARKANSAS

It would be another 130 years before Europeans again visited Arkansas. In the meantime, European rivalry for the North American continent grew more intense. The Spanish continued to hold Mexico, the Southwest, Florida, and parts of the Gulf Coast. The French expanded their control over Canada, founding Quebec in the early 1600s. Along the Atlantic Coast, the English, in the race for North America, began creating colonies in Virginia in 1603 and in New England in 1620.

The French pattern of settlement involved small bands of men who were soldiers, priests, traders, and trappers. Too few in number to be **conquerors**, the French tried to make friends with the Indians. They used these friendships to tap the fur trade.

In 1673, two Frenchmen in Canada planned a voyage down the **Mississippi River.** Father Jacques Marquette was a Roman Catholic priest, sincerely intent on converting the Indians to the Christian faith. Louis Joliet was a fur trapper and trader, interested in new

Father Jacques Marquette.
(Courtesy of the Chicago
Historical Society)

Louis Joliet. (Courtesy of the Chicago Historical Society)

*Marquette, in priest's robes with a cross at his waist, raises his **calumet** (or ceremonial pipe) as a sign of peace as he approaches an Indian village on his trip down the **Mississippi River.*** (Courtesy of the University of Central Arkansas Archives)

trade options. Both also hoped, like many of the early explorers, to find gold or a water route through North America to the Indies.

In two big canoes, with five other men and a supply of food, Marquette and Joliet set out down the river. The Illinois Indians gave the Frenchmen a long-stemmed pipe made of red stone, called a **calumet**, or "peace pipe," that would serve as a passport and a guarantee of safe travel. Marquette and Joliet showed it several times as they made their way downstream.

When they reached Arkansas, they were met by Quapaw, possibly in the same towns De Soto had visited much earlier. The Quapaw were friendly, sharing their abundant food with the Frenchmen. By that time, the Quapaw had European hatchets, knives, and beads, acquired in trade from other Indians, but they did not have guns. Marquette and Joliet learned that they were only about ten or twelve days from the mouth of the Mississippi. They realized that the Mississippi did not empty into the Pacific Ocean or the Gulf of California, and that they were very close to Spanish lands, which might be dangerous for Frenchmen.

Arkansas: How Do You Spell It and How Do You Pronounce It?

The name of the state came originally from the Quapaw Indians by way of the French. When Marquette and Joliet visited the Quapaw in 1673, their interpreter was a young man living with the Quapaw who spoke the languages of both the Quapaw and the Illinois Indians. When Marquette asked who these people were, the interpreter translated from the Quapaw language to the Illinois language and then to the French language. Marquette recorded the answer as "Arkansea." That may have been the Illinois Indian word for "downriver people."

Because spelling was not as standardized then as it is now, people tended to write words the way they sounded to them. So there came to be many ways of writing that word, perhaps as many as seventy, including Akamsea, Acansa, Arkansa, Arkanssas, Axkanzas, Arkinsaw, and Arkansaw.

The act of Congress in 1819 that officially created the Territory of Arkansas used the spelling "Arkansaw." Eventually the spelling "Arkansas" became the accepted version for both the land and its major river, partly because the new *Arkansas Gazette*, established in 1819, consistently used that version.

And that led to a debate on how to say the name. The accepted version came to be AR-kan-SAW or AR-ken-SAW, which is probably pretty close to the way the French heard it from their interpreter. (The French do not pronounce the "s" at the end of a word.) It is a bit confusing that the name Kansas, which looks similar, is pronounced KAN-zass. But the state of Arkansas is never Ar-KAN-zass.

The Arkansas River, which runs from the Rockies to the Mississippi, is pronounced AR-kan-SAW in Arkansas, but Ar-KAN-zass in all the other states it runs through.

And to make things worse, there has always been a debate on what to call the people who live in Arkansas. Most today call them Arkansans (in this form it is pronounced Ar-KAN-zans), but they have also been called Arkansians and Arkansawyers.

Marquette and Joliet decided to go back to Canada. After the long trip paddling upstream, they prepared a map and wrote a report of their trip. The report was done from memory because Marquette lost his notes when his canoe tipped over. Their report fixed a name on the future state. They called the people they had met and their land "Arkansas" after the Illinois Indian word for the Quapaw.

Marquette and Joliet's journey inspired another Frenchman to greater things. René Robert de La Salle had been born into a wealthy family in France, but he had come to Canada as a young man to enter the fur trade. He had a vision of a large **expedition** that could secure all of the Mississippi valley for France and even challenge Spain for control of the mouth of the river.

With fifty men, La Salle headed down the Mississippi in 1682, nine years after Marquette and Joliet. The force included La Salle's lieutenant, Henri de Tonti. (De Tonti was an Italian by birth, and sometimes his name is spelled "Henry de Tonty.")

La Salle, too, came to the same Arkansas towns visited by De Soto and Marquette and Joliet, and to the same friendly reception. La Salle solemnly informed the Indians that he claimed the entire **Mississippi River** valley in the name of the king of France. That must have either amused or baffled the Indians, especially when the foreigners left behind as a symbol of their rule only a tall pole with the king's **coat-of-arms** on it.

From the Arkansas towns, with two Quapaw Indians as his guides, La Salle went all the way to the mouth of the Mississippi. There La Salle repeated his claim of all the river valley

*Robert Cavelier, Sieur de La Salle, and the **Mississippi River** valley he explored for France. The painting was done in the 1930s.*
(Courtesy of the Chicago Historical Society)

*This is an artist's fanciful version of La Salle on his trip down the **Mississippi River** in 1682, formally declaring that all the Mississippi Valley belongs to the king of France. La Salle called the land "Louisiana" in honor of the French King Louis XIV. One wonders what the Indians thought of this sort of ceremony.* (Courtesy of the Chicago Historical Society)

for his king. He had proved that the Mississippi emptied into the Gulf of Mexico, removing any hopes he still might have had of a water route to the Indies.

With grand notions of founding a city at the mouth of the Mississippi to control the river, La Salle went back to France to prepare an even larger **expedition** for 1684. He planned to sail by ship to the mouth of the Mississippi and then head up the river. His assistant De Tonti would at the same time go down the river from Canada to meet him.

To the great misfortune of La Salle, and of France, he missed. His ships passed the mouth of the Mississippi, went on to the Texas coast, got caught in a storm, and ended up wrecked along the coast. La Salle went ashore with the idea of getting back to the **Mississippi River**

Parades, Guns, and Hymns: La Salle Takes Possession of Louisiana

The European explorers assumed they had a right to take possession of the lands they visited. Although they sometimes paid attention to claims from other European countries, they seldom considered that the Indians had any rights to the land.

This is how Robert Cavelier, Sieur de La Salle, claimed the land for the king of France, Louis XIV, while visiting the Quapaw in Arkansas in 1682. La Salle first promised the Quapaw that France would protect them against their enemies, like the Osage. In return, he asked the Quapaw to allow him to place the seal of the king of France on their land. To La Salle, that meant the king of France would own the land.

To complete the bargain, La Salle arranged a ceremony. First he formed his fifty men into two companies, one headed by himself and the other headed by his assistant Henri de Tonti. Then the two companies marched to the plaza, or central area, of the village, carrying with them a tall pole bearing a cross and the **coat-of-arms** of Louis XIV. They marched around the plaza three times, singing hymns and psalms. They stopped, fired their guns, shouted *"vive le roi"* ("long live the king"), and planted their pole in the ground.

Then La Salle, speaking in French, made the long formal announcement:

> On behalf of the very high, very invincible, and victorious prince Louis the Great, by the grace of God, King of France and of Navarre, the fourteen of this name, today, the 13th of March, 1682, with the consent of the nation of the Arkansas assembled at the village of Kappa and present in this place, in the name of the king and his allies, I . . . have taken possession in the name of His Majesty . . . of the country of Louisiana and of all the nations, mines, minerals, ports, harbors, seas, straits, and roadsteads, and of everything contained within the same.

The French shouted some more, fired their guns again, and it was done. By their standards, the French owned Arkansas and all of Louisiana. The Quapaw, who probably did not understand a word of La Salle's speech in French, must have thought it was all great fun and totally meaningless.

Morris S. Arnold, *Unequal Laws Unto a Savage Race: European Legal Traditions in Arkansas, 1686–1836* (Fayetteville: University of Arkansas Press, 1985), p. 3.

by land. But as his small party headed east, some of the men, weary and frightened, murdered La Salle.

THE FOUNDING OF ARKANSAS POST

De Tonti, waiting near the site that would later be St. Louis, was worried after hearing nothing from La Salle for two years. De Tonti set out to find his commander. Getting as far as the Quapaw towns where the Arkansas River meets the **Mississippi River**, De Tonti decided to settle down there until La Salle showed up. La Salle had given his lieutenant the right to take for himself a large amount of land, so De Tonti decided to claim the land around the mouth of the Arkansas River.

In 1686 De Tonti established his fort and trading post at the mouth of the Arkansas and named it Arkansas Post. Finally De Tonti gave up on La Salle and headed back to Canada, and eventually he returned to France. But he left six of his men at Arkansas Post. That slim beginning here in Arkansas was the first permanent European settlement on the west bank of the **Mississippi River.**

De Tonti did not find out what happened to La Salle until he got back to France. In the meantime, the few survivors of the La Salle group had made it overland from Texas to the **Mississippi River**, arriving by chance at Arkansas Post.

Henri de Tonti. (Courtesy of the Arkansas History Commission)

Lacking a man of La Salle's vision and ambition, and occupied by war in Europe, France did not press its claim to the Mississippi valley or send over large numbers of settlers. Like moving pieces on a checkerboard, the French did try to limit Spanish and English claims by forming towns along the Gulf coast, such as Mobile in 1702 and New Orleans in 1718. The French founded St. Louis, upstream from Arkansas, in 1764 as a trading post.

ARKANSAS IN THE EUROPEAN RIVALRY

For its first hundred years, Arkansas Post remained a thinly settled French outpost in Europe's rivalry for North America. The main French settlements were far to the north in Canada. Only scattered trading posts existed in the **Mississippi River** valley, which the French called Louisiana, after their king Louis XIV. The Spanish focused on maintaining their **colonies** in Mexico and the Southwest, with posts in Florida and along the Gulf coast. Along the Atlantic coast, the British extended their settlements from New England to Georgia.

These various **colonies** differed in ways that were important for the future of North America. The Spanish sent over a few soldiers, farm managers, and priests to control the thousands of Indians and African slaves who worked the farms and mines for them. Although some French settlers were farmers, most continued to be traders and trappers, the *coureurs des bois,* or woods runners. The French continued their policy of making allies and trading partners of the Indians, instead of fighting them. The British sent whole families of permanent settlers to remove or kill the Indians and take the land for farming.

French traders on the inland rivers stop on the bank to rest, smoke, and prepare a hot meal. (Courtesy of the Library of Congress)

The French and Spaniards in the New World tended to think of themselves as temporary residents who would go home as soon as they got rich. The British in the American **colonies**, however, came to think of this land as their new home.

The French colony at Arkansas Post, hundreds of miles from the main settlements, never attracted many Europeans. But thanks to one man, John Law, it got a brief burst of publicity in Europe. Law, a Scotsman who was working with the French king, was a real estate **speculator**, a person who buys land cheaply and sells it at a higher price. Law convinced the French king to give him the right to sell land in Louisiana, then tried to get settlers to go there and buy the land from him. He also hoped people in Europe would buy stock, or shares, in his business company at a profit to him.

Looking at a map, Law picked the site of Arkansas Post as one of the main areas to be **colonized.** Although he knew nothing about the land there, he thought prospective buyers and settlers would see the location as suitable for both trade and farming. Beginning in 1717, he recruited settlers by describing Arkansas as a beautiful land where no one would have to work hard because gold and silver were easily had in the mines there. Others with more knowledge of Arkansas and less interest in trying to sell land or stock pointed out that so far no one had discovered gold or silver in Arkansas. Many hopeful but uninformed people, however, wanted to believe that Arkansas held the promise of instant wealth.

John Law. (Courtesy of the Chicago Historical Society)

This drawing shows part of the settlement at Arkansas Post, with a house, picket fence, and cross on the far bank. The drawing probably idealizes the early settlement. (Courtesy of the Arkansas History Commission)

In 1721, about eighty of Law's French colonists arrived at the site of De Tonti's settlement. The Quapaw were friendly to the new arrivals, as usual, but there were no white men to greet Law's settlers. De Tonti's original settlers had gone long before, leaving behind only one log house. The colonists thought Law was going to help them get started. But even before they had arrived in Arkansas, John Law went bankrupt, and his grand scheme fell apart. The colonists were on their own.

Through much of the rest of the 1700s, the population at Arkansas Post was about thirty to fifty people, mostly traders, hunters, and trappers, and their families. Usually a small band of French soldiers was stationed at the Post. For example, in 1749 there were thirty-one white people and fourteen black slaves, counting all the men, women, and children. They had among them three horses, twenty-nine bulls and steers, sixty cows, and twenty-nine pigs. Not until the late 1700s did the population approach three hundred people.

The settlement itself also moved several times as the colonists tried to find a location that would be free from floods but still close enough to the Mississippi to serve traders. The original location, where the De Tonti and Law colonists lived, was on the Arkansas River about twenty-seven miles from its meeting with the Mississippi.

In the mid-1700s the settlers moved upstream to the higher ground of the *Ecores Rouges,* or Red Bluffs. After a while they moved downstream closer to the Mississippi, then back up to the Red Bluffs. (Today's Arkansas Post State Park is at the Red Bluffs site.)

Arkansas Post remained the only actual French settlement in Arkansas. The French decided to concentrate their resources down-river, closer to the mouth of the Mississippi. They also blocked trade with the Spanish to the west, so the chances Arkansas Post had to grow were limited.

However, French explorers continued to visit. In 1719 Benard de La Harpe traveled the Arkansas River. Because he hoped to find gold or precious stones, he was extremely careful to look for large rock formations. He made a note in his journal about the site we know as Big Rock, calling it "French Rock." He stopped there and climbed to the top to admire the view, looking out over the area that would one day become Little Rock. Legend has it that La Harpe gave it the name Little Rock, but there is no proof for this.

LIFE AT ARKANSAS POST

On any Saturday night at the Arkansas Post settlement, one might have found logs blazing in the two open fireplaces of the dogtrot house. The house was two square rooms, with an open porch—where the dogs could trot—in between them. As darkness fell, the neighbors would begin to arrive. The single men would come alone or in groups; the families brought their children.

As they greeted each other, most of the talk was in French. Soon one man would take up his fiddle, and the dancing would begin. With a line of men facing a line of women, they began a lively **reel**. There were always more men than women, so the men took turns or sometimes danced with each other. In the other room, people could be found drinking, eating, or playing cards. A favorite card game, called *loo,* resembled bridge. If the children got sleepy, they made a bed wherever they could, but the party went on.

That is the kind of entertainment the pioneers at Arkansas Post made for themselves, far away from larger settlements. There was no school and no church, although a French priest sometimes visited. Some of the traders operated stores for the other settlers, as well as for the Indians.

The people lived, for the most part, in the

Let's Speak French Now: Say Smackover

The French, who tried to dominate Arkansas for almost one hundred years, left the sound of their language on our land.

French explorers—and their mapmakers—gave us the names we still use for many geographical features. The L'Anguille (eel in French) River twists around like an eel. In Nevada County there is Terre Rouge (red earth) Creek, and in Clark County a Terre Noir (black earth) Creek.

Some townships are probably named for French settlers: Baugine and Bogy in Jefferson County, and Darysaw (a phonetic version of the French *Desruisseaux*) in Grant County.

There is a place in South Arkansas that the French called the covered way, *Chemin Couvert.* Although it seems far-fetched, an English-speaking American, after hearing the French words, might very well spell out the name of the town Smackover.

log house village itself, staying close together for safety. The Quapaw living near the settlement were friendly and were also brave and effective warriors offering good protection. But they were becoming fewer in number each year, probably because of the white settlers' diseases. The pioneers feared raids from the Osage to the north and west and the Chickasaw to the east across the **Mississippi River.** During one attack by 150 Chickasaw warriors, six men were killed and eight women and children were taken as slaves.

Most of the people at Arkansas Post had a little bit of land, and they tried to raise some food for themselves and their livestock. But hunting and fishing still provided much of their food. Their clothing came from hunting, too. Almost everyone wore **buckskins,** tanned deer skin garments.

Trading with the Indians was the major business of the settlers of Arkansas Post. Traveling by canoe up the Arkansas, White, and St. Francis rivers, the traders sought out the Indians in order to exchange goods. For the French, the most desired trade goods were animal furs and skins. They preferred deer skins, but would also accept bear, buffalo, beaver, mink, and muskrat. The traders collected bear oil, too, to use in cooking and in lanterns. Bear oil came from melting a bear's fat, often in big troughs. There is still a town in Arkansas named Oil Trough.

In return for animal skins and furs, the Europeans gave the Indians knives, hatchets, hoes, plows, animal traps, cloth, glass, metal cooking pots, bells, and beads. The visiting British traders sold guns to the Indians, though the French traders, perhaps because

A party in a French village in early Arkansas might have looked like this. The French dance to fiddle music while the Indians look on. (Courtesy of the Illinois State Historical Library)

they had to live among the Indians, did not approve of their having firearms. The government of France tried to stop the trading of whiskey to the Indians, but people did it anyway.

When a trader had collected enough furs, he headed by canoe or raft down the Mississippi River to New Orleans, a trip that took ten or twelve days from Arkansas Post. From there, the furs and skins were shipped to Europe. Many a man of fashion in Paris or London wore a fine beaver hat that came from the wilds of Arkansas.

The Arkansas trader collected his fee in money or, more often, in goods. He needed salt, sugar, guns, powder, and many other things not available in the woods. He also brought back items to remind himself of home in Europe and to make life a little better for his family, perhaps a set of fine china dishes or a few bottles of wine.

We know less about life for the slaves at Arkansas Post. Europeans discovered Africa at about the same time they discovered the Americas, and the enslaved black Africans were an important part of the process of settling the New World. De Soto had slaves on his expedition, and the settlers at Arkansas Post always had slaves, who sometimes made up as much as a third of the total population. Probably each slave-owning white man had just one or two slaves, or perhaps a family of slaves. The slaves did the household chores and the hard labor.

There were some mixed marriages among whites, blacks, and Indians. Sometimes a white father would free his children by a mixed marriage, so there were some free blacks at Arkansas Post. Free and slave blacks both faced uncertainty and sometimes cruelty in their lives as part of the Arkansas pioneer life. Free blacks were uncertain of their status—they could suddenly find themselves "slaves" and defenseless before the law. Cruelty could range from daily humiliations to beatings to the sale of black slaves away from their families.

THE AMERICAN NATION

All this time, the great nations of France, Spain, and Britain steadily tried to gain the advantage over one another, with North America as one of the prizes in their game. In the early 1700s, while Arkansas Post was struggling along, the European nations fought a series of wars with each other. Always in these wars, Britain challenged France for control of the **colonies** all over the world.

The greatest war for empire was the Seven Years' War, from 1756 to 1763. In America, where British colonists such as Colonel George Washington of the Virginia Militia faced the French and their Indian allies, the colonists called this war the French and Indian War. When it was over, the British had beaten the French all over the world and could take what they wanted. In Paris, where the peace treaty was signed, important men on both sides sat around a table, studied maps, and decided the future of North America, including Arkansas.

The **continent** was divided at the **Mississippi River.** Great Britain got all the land east of the river, where the original thirteen **colonies** were, and Canada in the north. Spain got all the land west of the river, including Arkansas. France lost all its land and claims in North America and had to abandon the descendants of their settlers like those at Arkansas Post.

The people of Arkansas Post probably did not even know what had happened for some time. It was five years after the treaty before a Spanish army officer showed up at Arkansas

Post to take over. He changed very few things. The big changes would come later, after the American Revolution.

The end of the French and Indian War was also the beginning of the events that led to the American Revolution. The British, now with a larger empire to govern, wanted more control over the **colonies** and more tax revenues from their successful **colonies,** including those in America. The American colonists, freed of the threat of the French at their backs, wanted things to stay as they were. Americans liked being largely in control of their own internal affairs while accepting Britain's very light trading regulations.

The conflict swirled out of control, through the Stamp Tax argument of 1765, the Boston Tea Party and the Intolerable Acts of 1773 and 1774, and the outbreak of fighting at Lexington and Concord in 1775. The Americans declared their independence in July of 1776, in Thomas Jefferson's ringing words. The War for American Independence was underway. France and Spain, eager to get back at Britain, also declared war against the British. Far-off Arkansas Post, now a Spanish possession, was on the side against the British, but it was not "American" in the sense of being one of the thirteen English **colonies** in North America.

One brief episode of the war occurred in Arkansas. A daring British supporter, James Colbert, began a series of raids against Spanish trade in the Mississippi Valley. Colbert was a trader who had lived among the Indians, and his force was made up primarily of Chickasaw Indians. In April of 1783, Colbert's raiders crossed the Mississippi south of Arkansas Post and surprised the settlers there with an early morning attack. The raiders killed "two soldiers, the one belonging to the hunters and the other a negro of the neighborhood," as the Spanish commander wrote

to his superior. Colbert's raiders also captured a few Spanish soldiers and some of the settlers.

The Spanish commander, Captain Balthazar de Villiers, refused to surrender. He ordered his cannon to fire at the attackers, then charged against them. Colbert and the Chickasaw retreated, and the only Revolutionary War battle west of the Mississippi River was over. In fact, so was the American Revolution, although the news had not reached the Mississippi valley. The British had surrendered at Yorktown, and peace had already been declared in January of 1783.

The fight at Arkansas Post was not much of a battle, but it meant that later, as Americans began to move west, they would face weak Spanish posts instead of strong British posts.

THE LOUISIANA PURCHASE

The new United States of America did not at first include Arkansas. The new country's western boundary was the **Mississippi River,** and Arkansas was still in Spanish territory. While most Americans still lived along the eastern coast, they created a new government under the Constitution that established a procedure for admitting new states into the Union.

When the Revolutionary War was over, Americans began to move west into the land between the Appalachian Mountains and the **Mississippi River** in increasing numbers. These new Tennesseans and Kentuckians looked to the **Mississippi River** as their hope for future economic success. If they were to sell their crops to outside markets, they would have to transport them down the river. The major threat to this **commerce** was Spain, with its bases along the west bank of the **Mississippi River,** like Arkansas Post. More important, Spain governed New Orleans, which controlled the mouth of the river and therefore the outlet to ocean-going ships. The American government knew that it was not likely to maintain the loyalty of the westerners unless it could guarantee them the use of the **Mississippi River.**

Once again, the affairs of Europe were to determine the future of Arkansas and the United States. Just twenty years after the end of the American Revolution, Emperor Napoleon Bonaparte had taken over France. Dreaming of glory, very much like La Salle and John Law before him, he hoped to create a great French empire. An important part of his plan was Louisiana, as the French called the land between the **Mississippi River** and the Rocky Mountains, including Arkansas. In Europe, Napoleon had conquered most of the other nations, including Spain. He forced Spain to return Louisiana to France.

Napoleon lost interest in the project before it really got started, even before the new French soldiers and governors had time to replace the Spanish in Louisiana. In Europe, his war with Britain was about to begin again. In the Americas, France lost its rich colony of Santo Domingo when the slaves there rebelled and established their own free nation, the first black republic in the New World. Napoleon decided to cut his losses and sell Louisiana.

The United States was the most likely buyer. President Thomas Jefferson had already sent Robert Livingston and James Monroe to

This monument marks the spot from which all the land in Arkansas and most of the northern part of the Louisiana Purchase was measured. Located where Lee, Phillips, and Monroe counties meet, it is today the Louisiana Purchase Historical Monument. The land is still swampy, so visitors view the monument from a deck and boardwalk built by the state Department of Parks and Tourism. (Courtesy of A. C. Haralson, Arkansas Dept. of Parks and Tourism)

France to buy New Orleans at the mouth of the river. When Napoleon asked if they would like to have all of Louisiana, they at first were not sure they had heard correctly. But the Americans did not hesitate about accepting the offer, and the deal was made. Louisiana became a part of America, for about fifteen million dollars. No one was very clear about the exact boundaries, but it surely included both banks of the **Mississippi River,** from its source to its mouth, along with the place called Arkansas.

In 1802, the year before the Louisiana Purchase, a French traveler who clearly measured all societies by the standards of Paris described Arkansas Post this way:

> The inhabitants, almost all originally French **emigrants** . . . are hunters by profession, and grow only corn for the nour-ishment of their horses and of a small number of oxen used in plowing. More than half the year one finds in this village only women, children, and old people. The men go to hunt deer, the skins of which are less valued than those from the northern country; buffalo which they salt for their use; and some beaver which they still find at a little distance. On their return they pass their time in playing games, dancing, drinking, or doing nothing, similar in this as well as in other things, to the savage peoples with whom they pass the greater part of their lives, and whose habits and customs they acquire.

First Indian land, then French, briefly Spanish, Arkansas was now American. Soon American society would transform the wilderness into a farming frontier.

VOCABULARY

buckskins soft, suede-like leather, usually made from deer hide; an outfit of clothing made from buckskin.

calumet (CAL-yoo-MET) Indian pipe made of stone and signifying peaceful intentions.

coat-of-arms pictorial symbols forming a design that represents an individual or family, usually royalty. They are generally displayed on a shield or embroidered onto a flag or piece of clothing.

colony a territory claimed as belonging to another, "mother," country and usually settled by people coming to the colony from the other country. Often taken by force from the original inhabitants and operated as a source of wealth for the mother country.

commerce (KAHM-erss) the exchange of surplus goods, services, or money for goods and services from some other source, as between countries. Business; trade.

conqueror (KONK-er-or) one who overcomes an opponent by force. Also a verb, to conquer.

continents the great land masses of the globe. There are seven continents.

coureurs des bois (KOO-ROOR-day-BWAH) "woods runners"; French trappers and traders who traveled by canoe throughout the streams, rivers, lakes, and woods of North America.

emigrant (EH-mih-gruhnt) one who leaves one location or country to live in a different location or country.

expedition a large, well-equipped body of people set out upon a specific mission, such as climbing a mountain, exploring unknown territory, conducting a search, or attacking a military target.

influenza (IN-floo-ENZ-uh) an acute, highly contagious viral disease with fever, severe aches and pains, and respiratory distress;

in early times, often called "ague" or "the grippe."

loo short for "lanterloo"; an old card game involving money staked on the winning hand, and involving the taking of card tricks (four cards of the same suit, such as hearts) as in whist, bridge, or pinochle.

Mississippi River the largest river in North America. "Mississippi" is an Indian word meaning "father of waters."

navigation (NAV-ih-GAY-suhn) the act of getting ships from one place to another; the method of determining position, course, and distance traveled.

New World the Western Hemisphere: North, Central, and South America.

Red River Raft a huge tangle of logs, mud, and brush that accumulated over the centuries in the Red River of southwest Arkansas that greatly impeded travel until its removal in the mid-nineteenth century. Usually, the Great Red River Raft.

reel a rhythmic tune for dancing, usually played on a fiddle; also used to refer to the dance itself.

Renaissance (REHN-uh-sahns) "rebirth"; a surge of creativity in Europe resulting in artistic, scientific, and literary achievement, brought on in part by rediscovery of Greek and Roman cultures and accomplishments. Stemming from around 1400 in Italy through the Elizabethan era of the early 1600s in England.

speculator (SPECK-yoo-LATE-er) a person who tries to get land (or some other type of property) cheaply in hopes of selling it at a higher price.

STUDY QUESTIONS

1. What were some of the reasons the European explorers had such a low opinion of the Native American population of the New World?

2. What was the single greatest cause of death among Native American populations after contact with Europeans? Why?

3. What was De Soto looking for?

4. Describe the different approaches to North American colonization taken by the British, the French, and the Spanish.

5. What were some good and bad points about the location of Arkansas Post? What happened as a result of the problems?

6. How did Great Britain manage to win in the European struggle for domination of North America?

7. How did the British lose the American colony? Why is Canada a separate country from the United States?

8. Whose side was Arkansas on during the American Revolution and why?

9. How did Arkansas become a part of the United States?

10. The land that became the state of Arkansas belonged to four different groups or nations. Name these groups

3 The Territorial Period

1803–1836

What to Look for in Chapter 3

This chapter covers the period from the Louisiana Purchase in 1803 until Arkansas became a state in 1836. During this time, Arkansas was first a county in the Territory of Missouri, and then a territory itself. That means it was in a preliminary status before statehood, with a government appointed by the president of the United States.

You'll learn about the early explorations, the first transportation methods, and the beginning of farming. You will also see how the United States measured land, and why land was so important to settlers in Arkansas.

In 1819 and 1820, a lot of things happened very quickly. Missouri became a state. The Missouri Compromise made Arkansas a slave area. And Arkansas became a territory. A group of men called the "the Family" dominated the politics of Arkansas.

During this period, the national government carried out a policy called Indian Removal. The last of the Native American tribes in Arkansas were moved west. Tribes east of the Mississippi River were also forced to move west, some through Arkansas, on the long "Trail of Tears."

THE AMERICAN EXPLORATIONS

President Thomas Jefferson moved very quickly to find out more about the new lands of the Louisiana Purchase. The most famous expedition he supported, led by Meriwether Lewis and William Clark, went to the sources of the Missouri River and beyond from 1803 to 1806. At the same time, Jefferson commissioned William Dunbar of Mississippi, a farmer, scientist, and diplomat, to explore the Ouachita River in Louisiana and Arkansas. With George Hunter, a medical doctor, Dunbar spent 1804 and 1805 traveling up the Ouachita as far as the hot springs.

In 1806 and 1807, Zebulon Pike led another government expedition west from St. Louis to the mountain he named Pike's Peak, then through part of the Spanish Southwest. When Pike crossed the Great Bend of the Arkansas River in the future state of Kansas, west of Arkansas, the party split up. Pike assigned army Lieutenant James B. Wilkinson and three other members of his expedition to float down the river by canoe to Arkansas Post near the mouth of the river.

These official exploring parties prepared maps and reports on the land, animal life,

53

The famous naturalist John James Audubon traveled extensively in western lands. Near Arkansas Post in April 1822, the artist made this watercolor of a bird, the Traill's Flycatcher. (Courtesy of the New York Historical Society)

and natural resources. They also commented on the location and nature of the Indians, and on the few white settlements that existed. For pioneers planning to move west, the new government reports paved the way.

Later Arkansas attracted the attention of two private explorers, Henry R. Schoolcraft and Thomas Nuttall. Schoolcraft, a writer and geologist, entered Arkansas in 1818 at Mammoth Springs in the northeast. He traveled through the valleys of the Spring, Black, and White rivers. He went as far as the settlements at Calico Rock and Poke Bayou (later Batesville) on the White River.

Nuttall, an Englishman and a biologist, started at Arkansas Post in 1819 and went up the Arkansas River to Fort Smith. Both men were trained observers and skilled writers, and each published a book about his trip in 1821. Still good reading today, their accounts helped publicize Arkansas to the rest of the United States. By all these accounts, Arkansas was a scenic land, rich in animal and plant life and natural resources, but thinly settled.

In those first years of the nineteenth century (the 1800s), Arkansas was hard to get to and not on the way to anywhere. Americans moving westward tended to move straight west, going to land that would grow the same crops as the land they left. But settlers coming from Tennessee or Mississippi faced a major barrier in the swampy lowlands of eastern Arkansas.

In addition, Arkansas was not on any of the major paths for expansion to the Far West. Beyond Arkansas was Texas, still a Spanish possession, and Oklahoma, already reserved by the national government as Indian land on which whites were not allowed to settle.

The Great Red River Raft was mile after mile of piled-up logs, swept into the river over years of floods. Note the two men standing on the logs in the middle of the drawing. The steamboat on the right is equipped with derricks to lift out the logs. (Courtesy of the Historic Arkansas Museum)

Overland travel was very difficult for wagons carrying household goods, so the Arkansas River was the major avenue into Arkansas. The Red River and the Ouachita River in the southwest part of Arkansas were also routes for migration. The Red River, however, was blocked for much of its length by the Great Red River Raft.

People traveled on the rivers by canoe, **flatboat**, or **keelboat**. The **flatboat** was usually nothing more than a crude raft, useful only for going downstream at the rate of the current. The **keelboat**, with a rounded bottom and a keel to help keep it going straight, could move upstream, but it was a slow process. The **keelboat** was either pushed along by poles against the bottom of the river, or pulled by horses or men walking along the bank. Ten miles a day was a good speed for a **keelboat.**

On land, travelers either walked or rode horseback. The **Southwest Trail**, an old Indian path, ran from Ste. Genevieve in southeast Missouri, through central Arkansas, and on through the Red River settlements to Texas. It was, however, no more than a path through the forest. After Arkansas became part of the United States in 1803, the **Southwest Trail** was the first "road" to be chosen by the national government for improvement. Another major trail followed the north bank of the Arkansas River from Arkansas Post to Crystal Hill, just above Little Rock.

The remote position of Arkansas helped it become known as a haven for people who wanted to get lost. Stories spread that a lot of the early settlers in Arkansas were men who had gotten in trouble with the law "back in the states." They fled to Arkansas because they were fairly sure no sheriff was going to find them in its wilderness. There almost certainly were some **fugitives** among the early Arkansas settlers, but there probably never were as many outlaws in Arkansas as some of the stories said.

A flatboat could only go downstream with the current, guided by poles, but it could carry a whole family and everything that family owned. (Courtesy of the University of Arkansas, Fayetteville, Special Collections. From John Hugh Reynolds, *Makers of Arkansas History* [1911])

This is one of many paintings based on the legend of the Arkansas Traveler. The city slicker on horseback always tries to match his wits with the settler, and he always loses. But when the settler discovers that the traveler knows the "Arkansas Traveler" fiddle tune, the traveler is welcomed to stay a spell. (Courtesy of the Arkansas History Commission)

THE EARLY SETTLEMENTS

By 1810, when a special census was taken, there were a little more than a thousand people in Arkansas, not counting the Indians. About three-fourths of them lived in the Arkansas River valley, including villages at Arkansas Post, Pine Bluff, Little Rock, Crystal Hill, and Cadron. Most of the rest were scattered along the Mississippi River, especially at St. Francis (later Helena) and Hopefield (later West Memphis).

Other pioneers were in the valleys of the Red and Ouachita rivers in the southwest, in villages such as Blakely Town (later Arkadel-

phia) and Ecore á Fabri (later Camden). There were also people living in the White River valley in the north, where Poke Bayou (later Batesville) was the main settlement.

In these early years, there were two different types of settlers, the hunters and the farmers. The hunters, many of them single men but some with families, tended to live in the more remote areas. They hunted and trapped for animal skins and traded with the Indians. Although a hunter's family might sometimes have a garden to provide some variety to a diet of wild game, the hunters did not think of themselves as farmers.

For the hunters, Arkansas in those days

This is a painting of a typical log cabin, at Cane Hill. With one roof and two rooms exactly alike separated by an open space, it's what the settlers called a double-log or two-pen house; later the style would be called a dogtrot house. The smaller log house on the left is the kitchen. (Courtesy of the Historic Arkansas Museum)

The Wolf House, with its two stories, porch, and second-floor gallery, is bigger and grander than most early Arkansas log cabins. (Courtesy of the University of Central Arkansas Archives)

was rich in animal life, very much the "natural state." There were herds of buffalo, as Arkansans and all Americans called the American **bison.** However, the pressure of hunting and the clearing of land for farming seemed to be thinning them out. The land teemed with deer, elk, beavers, bears, panthers, wildcats, and wolves, all valued for their hides or furs. One hunters' trick, learned from the Indians, was to burn off the underbrush each year over a wide area to make the hunting easier.

Overhead were birds in abundance, including the Carolina parakeet and huge flocks of **passenger pigeons**, also soon to be wiped out.

"All the luxuries of life that a new country could afford."

Writing more than fifty years after he came to Arkansas, John Billingsley described what life was like for the early white settlers.

My father, with two other families moved from Middle Tennessee . . . six in each family, made eighteen persons. That was in 1814. We came to the Post of Arkansas in a flatboat. There we found a French and Creole village. The Quapaw Indians lived on the south side of the river. There we exchanged our flatboat for a keelboat with an old Indian trader. . . . We made our way the best we could until we got to the Cadron; there we found one of my father's brothers that had moved from Kentucky in an early day. We stayed there one year. . . . Then we moved to Big Mulberry. In 1816 we made up about thirty families and lived there two years in all the luxuries of life that a new country could afford, such as buffalo, bear, deer, and elk and fish and honey; we had pound cake every day, for we beat all the [corn] meal we ate in a mortar, and the first year our corn gave out about six weeks before roasting ears came in. Our substitute for bread was venison dried by the fire and then pounded in the mortar and made up in small cakes and fried in bear's oil. . . .

Well, the way we clothed ourselves—this is, the men and boys—was by dressing buckskins and wore full suits of the same. The French came up the river in large canoes and supplied us with domestic and checks and earthing ware [dishes] and calico. . . . This was all paid for in bear skins and deer skins and coon skins and bear oil, some beaver and otter skins and bees wax and that in abundance. For we had honey in any amount.

Note: this document serves as an example of some of the symbols used in writing history. This is a direct quotation from the original, taken from a book that reprints many documents from Arkansas history. The ellipsis points (. . .) mean that we left something out of the original, in this case to make the quotation shorter. The brackets mean we added something to make items within the quotation clearer.

C. Fred Williams, S. Charles Bolton, Carl H. Moneyhon, and LeRoy T. Williams, *A Documentary History of Arkansas* (Fayetteville: University of Arkansas Press, 1984), pp. 18–19.

EARLY AGRICULTURE

For the farmers, Arkansas had fertile land and a long growing season. From the last spring freeze to the first fall frost was 220 to 240 days. Rainfall averaged about 45 inches a year, enough to water the crops. There were plenty of trees for fuel, fences, and log cabins.

Most parts of Arkansas had soil and climate conditions that were suitable for growing cotton, corn, or wheat. Cotton was most common in the Arkansas River valley and along the Mississippi River in the southeast, where the rivers allowed easy transport to the markets in New Orleans. Wheat, **milled** into flour, was generally grown and used locally, and corn provided food for the farm family and its horses, cows, and pigs.

Many small farms would also grow some vegetables and fruit trees for the family's use. Some early Arkansans also planted rice, tobacco, **hemp** (for rope), **indigo** (for a blue dye), and grapes (for wine). None of these, however, became important crops in the early years, because each of them required a skill or a market lacking in Arkansas.

The weather could be harsh and hard to predict. Heavy rains often flooded the rivers, usually in the late winter or early spring, when the crops were newly planted. Or the rains could fail in the hot summer, bringing a drought like the one that ruined the crops in 1818.

One of Arkansas's early problems was being known as an unhealthy place to live. Arkansans suspected some connection between the weather and disease, but in those days before knowledge of germs and insect carriers of germs they did not know exactly what the connection was. We now know that the heavy rainfalls and frequent floods left large areas of standing water. The standing water became the breeding ground for the kinds of mosquitoes that carry **malaria** and **yellow fever.**

The settlers frequently complained about the "ague," "bilious fever," or the "chills and fever," all of them names for **malaria.** Common in the hot summer months, when mosquitoes flourished, the disease was marked by chills, followed by a fever and often frequent vomiting. For many, the "**ague**" caused death. For others, attacks of the disease could recur for years.

Yellow fever, also carried by mosquitoes, had an even higher death rate than **malaria. Yellow fever** was not always present, like **malaria,** but swept through in **epidemics.** It tended to spread up the Mississippi River valley into Arkansas, as it did in 1818.

THE NEW MADRID EARTHQUAKE

Arkansas had a major earthquake in 1811 and 1812, probably the most severe and long-lasting earthquake ever to take place in what is now the United States. It happened, luckily, in a sparsely settled area and had little direct effect on people. **New Madrid** (pronounced MAD-rid) is a town in southeast Missouri, near the Mississippi River and just north of the Arkansas border. A great geologic fault, a place where the earth's underlying plates come together, runs northeast to southwest deep in the earth under **New Madrid.** When those plates slipped, the earth moved and shook in what is called the **New Madrid** earthquake.

The earthquake began in December of 1811, and shocks continued for almost four months until March of 1812. The most severe shocks were along a line from **New Madrid** to near where Parkin, Arkansas, is today. The **tremors** from the earthquake were felt as far away as Canada and Massachusetts. A man in

Louisville, Kentucky, kept a careful record of almost two thousand separate **tremors** over the four-month period.

One witness described the ground heaving up in swells "resembling waves, which increased in elevation as they advanced, and when they had attained a certain fearful height the earth would burst and vast columns of water and sand and pit coal were discharged, as high as the tops of trees, leaving large crevices or chasms where the ground had burst."

The Mississippi River for miles looked like "a boiling cauldron," and some swore that it ran backwards for several days. The earthquake totally altered much of the land, creating new lakes such as Reelfoot Lake in Tennessee. The earthquake may have pushed parts of northeast Arkansas even lower than they had been, making the swamps larger.

There was very little permanent settlement in that area then, perhaps a few hundred Indian and white hunters. Apparently no one was killed in Arkansas, but the earthquake may have put the fear of God into some of the settlers. The traveling Methodist preachers in the region reported a membership increase of almost 50 percent that year.

Children in Territorial Arkansas

Many of the settlers of early Arkansas were hunters and trappers who lived isolated lives in remote parts of the country. Henry Rowe Schoolcraft, a New Yorker who toured Arkansas in 1819, was disturbed by the effect of this kind of life on the hunters' children. This is the way he described them:

> Schools are . . . unknown, and no species of learning cultivated. Children are wholly ignorant of the knowledge of books, and have not learned even the rudiments of their own tongue. Thus situated, without moral restraint, brought up in the uncontrolled indulgence of every passion and without a regard of religion, the state of society among the rising generation in this region is truly deplorable.
>
> In their childish disputes, boys frequently stab each other with knives, two instances of which have occurred since our residence here. No correction was administered in either case, the act being rather looked upon as a promising trait of character. They begin to assert their independence as soon as they can walk, and by the time they have reached the age of fourteen, have completely learned the use of rifle, the arts of trapping beaver and otter, killing the bear, deer, and buffalo, and dressing skins and making mockasons [sic] and leather clothes.

Note: *Sic* is Latin for "thus" or "just so." Historians have to reproduce quotations exactly like the original source. If the source has a mistake in it, or a word that appears to be misspelled, the historian uses the term *sic* to indicate that it was that way in the original.

Henry R. Schoolcraft, *Journal of a Tour into the Interior of Missouri and Arkansaw* . . . (London: Printed for Sir Richard Phillips and Co., 1821), pp. 49–50.

THE FIRST GOVERNMENTS

Although the early settlers of Arkansas were self-sufficient in many ways, they did need government to do things they could not do for themselves. These things included making laws, operating courts, building roads, and dealing with the Indians. The U.S. Constitution and national laws provided an orderly process for new lands to develop government by stages: new lands first became territories and then moved on to statehood.

When Arkansas and the rest of the Louisiana Purchase became part of the United States, the national government divided it into two big sections. In the north was the Territory of Louisiana, which included present-day Arkansas; in the south was the Territory of Orleans. In 1806, Arkansas was named a **district** within the Territory of Louisiana.

When the southern Territory of Orleans became a state in 1812, it took the name Louisiana, so the name of the northern **territory** was changed to Missouri. In 1814, the lands of Arkansas became a county of the Territory of Missouri.

As the number of settlers grew, Arkansas itself split into more **counties.** In 1815 the Missouri legislature divided it into two **counties,** Arkansas County in the south and Lawrence County in the north. In 1818 three more **counties** were created out of Arkansas County: Clark, Hempstead, and Pulaski. Each **county** had its own sheriff and justices of the peace, and each sent a **delegate** to the Missouri legislature.

The War of 1812, in which the United States again fought Great Britain, speeded westward migration. One of the biggest battles of the war was fought in the West. Britain sent a major military force in an attempt to gain control of the mouth of the Mississippi River. General Andrew Jackson assembled a force of Indians, free blacks, pirates, and Kentucky and Tennessee soldiers. They soundly defeated the British at the Battle of New Orleans in January of 1815. Jackson, a Tennessee frontiersman himself, quickly became a national hero and a possible candidate for president.

After the end of the war in 1815, Americans had a new sense of national pride, a growing population, and a prosperous economy. All of this encouraged people to move west. In addition, men who had served in the army during the War of 1812 were given a **veteran's bonus** in the form of free land in

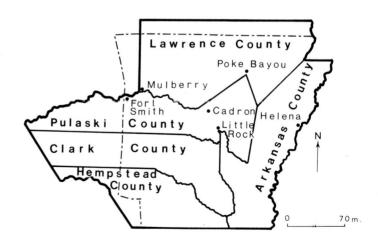

*In 1819, when Arkansas officially became a **territory** of the United States, it was divided into these **counties.** The modern western and northern boundaries of the state, established later, are shown in a dotted line.*
(Courtesy of Gerald T. Hanson)

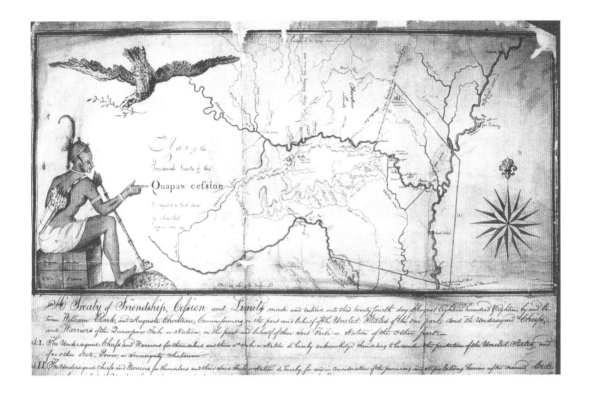

The first page of the **Treaty** of 1818 between the Quapaw Indians and the U.S. government includes this decoration. Because it was drawn by an army officer who had visited the Quapaw, the painting is considered an accurate representation of a Quapaw Indian. The map, centered on the Arkansas River, shows the land the tribe was giving up to the government for white settlement. (Courtesy of the Old State House Museum)

the West. The government set aside two million acres of land in Arkansas to be given to veterans. A veteran could either settle the land himself or sell it to someone else. People who lost land in the **New Madrid** earthquake were also given replacement land in Arkansas.

By that time, too, the land in Arkansas was beginning to be **surveyed**, or measured out, in lots for sale. In 1815 the deputy **surveyor** of the Missouri Territory, William Rector, started the process of creating **townships** and **sections.**

One team of **surveyors** marked a line north from the mouth of the Arkansas River, and another team marked a line west from the mouth of the St. Francis River. The place

where the two lines met was the starting point for measuring all land in Arkansas and the rest of the northern part of the Louisiana Purchase. (Today that point, about fifteen miles northwest of Marvell, is the Louisiana Purchase Historical State Park.) **Surveying** is difficult work, and the process of measuring all the land moved very slowly. But starting the **survey** further encouraged settlement in Arkansas.

After 1815 the population of Arkansas began to increase rapidly. In 1818 there were probably around three thousand white and black settlers in Arkansas. Only two years later, the U.S. census showed 14,273 white and black persons. The increase in numbers

Townships and Sections: The American Survey System

Almost all of America is measured out in the **survey** system designed by Thomas Jefferson and put into effect even before the Constitution was written.

The **survey** system starts with a base line, running east and west, and a principal meridian, running north and south. Along those the land is marked off in **townships**, each 6 miles on a side. Each **township** is then divided into 36 **sections**, each of them 1 mile on a side. A **section** is 1 square mile or 640 acres.

A **section** could then be divided into quarter **sections**, 160 acres, or blocks of land of 40 acres each.

Surveyors actually measured off the lines on the ground, and land was sold by those measurements. The deeds to the land describe the **townships** and **sections** by number.

If you fly over America, or even look down from a place like Petit Jean Mountain or Mount Magazine in Arkansas, you can see the **section** lines. At one place, a **section** line might be a fence line or a road, but everywhere the land is laid out in straight lines and squares.

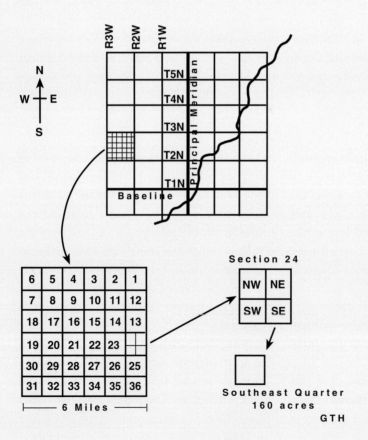

*This diagram shows how the U.S. government **survey** in Arkansas and most of the rest of the United States was done. Starting with an east-west base line and a north-south principal meridian, the **surveyors** created a **township** that was divided into numbered **sections**. Each **section**, in turn, was divided into quarters of 160 acres.* (Courtesy of Gerald T. Hanson)

encouraged Arkansans to think about becoming a **territory** separate from Missouri.

Meanwhile, the people of Missouri Territory applied to Congress for statehood. They asked for a boundary that included the "bootheel" area around **New Madrid**, but did not include the five **counties** of Arkansas. In Arkansas, the people responded by asking Congress for status as a **territory**.

SLAVERY AND THE MISSOURI COMPROMISE

The two requests, Missouri's to be a state and Arkansas's to be a **territory**, suddenly created a serious debate in Congress over **slavery**. Many Congressmen thought that **slavery** should be outlawed in both the proposed **ter**ritory of Arkansas and the proposed state of Missouri.

Slavery, the institution of owning human beings as property, had come to the Americas with the Europeans. Although there were attempts to enslave the Indians, American **slavery** almost always involved the enslavement of people of African descent.

Slavery was a labor system, a way of assuring a large supply of workers. But it also became a social system, a way the whites could keep the blacks under control. Most white people at the time believed that blacks were actually inferior to whites in basic and permanent ways.

Throughout much of the world, people were rethinking the system of **slavery**, and it was slowly dying out. In 1776, **slavery** had existed in all parts of this country. But as early

$105 REWARD.

RAN AWAY from the subscriber, living on the Mississippi river, 15 miles above Columbia, Chicot county, Arkansas Territory, on Thursday night, 8th August (inst.),

A negro man named **Pleasant**, about five feet 7 or 8 inches high, some of his fore teeth out, a scar on the top of his head, and has some scars on his arm, from his shoulder to his hand, occasioned by a burn. He took with him a rifle gun, the property of James Russell. I will pay a reward of SEVENTY-FIVE DOLLARS for his apprehension and delivery to me, at my residence.

Also—A negro man named **Peter**; he is about five feet high, and about thirty years of age. I will give FIFTEEN DOLLARS reward for his apprehension and delivery to me at my house.

Also—A yellow woman named **Tenez**, about thirty-five years of age, about five feet high. She is the property of Mr. William Gozey. I will give FIFTEEN DOLLARS for her apprehension and delivery to me at my residence.

JOHN FULTON.

Chicot county, August 26, 1833.   39-3*w*

Notices like this one appeared regularly in Arkansas newspapers. To gain their freedom, African American men and women often ran away from **slavery** *even though the punishment was harsh if they were captured. (Courtesy of the University of Arkansas, Fayetteville, Special Collections)*

as 1777, Vermont abolished **slavery**, and by 1800 all the northern states had done the same. In 1787, Congress passed the **Northwest Ordinance**, which outlawed **slavery** in the land north and west of the Ohio River. By 1808, the international slave trade had been outlawed.

The invention of the **cotton gin** (short for "engine") in 1793 delayed the natural death of **slavery**, however. The new machine made growing cotton extremely lucrative, and cotton growing demanded large numbers of laborers. Cotton growing was well suited to the southern states. Before long, the South committed itself to cotton as its chief cash crop, and to black **slavery** as a means of making the crop possible.

Southern states adopted, promoted, and defended black **slavery** just when the northern states wanted to end it. For one thing, the North did not depend on large-scale farming, so **slavery** was not as important there.

At the time Arkansas applied to become a **territory**, about 12 percent of its people were African American, all but a very few of them slaves. Ten existing states were slave-holding

James Miller. (Courtesy of the Arkansas History Commission)

The First Governor Arrives: "I'll Try, Sir!"

The first governor of Arkansas Territory, General James Miller, was very proud of his military reputation, and he made sure Arkansans remembered it when he arrived in the territory.

A regular army officer, General Miller was best known for his heroism at the Battle of Lundy's Lane, fought during the War of 1812 against the British. His commanding officer asked if Miller and his three hundred men could capture a British battery of seven cannon on a hill above the battlefield. Miller replied concisely, "I'll try, Sir!" He succeeded and gave the nation a popular slogan.

When he was appointed governor of Arkansas, General Miller traveled seventy days from Pittsburgh by the Ohio, Mississippi, and Arkansas rivers. His **keelboat**, big enough to carry **militia** supplies, Indian goods, and twenty people, had the word "Arkansas" painted in large letters on both sides. And flying from the cabin was a flag bearing the words, "I'll try, Sir!"

Someday, if you read Nathaniel Hawthorne's novel *The Scarlet Letter,* you will run across General Miller again. After he left Arkansas, General Miller became the collector of the U.S. Custom House in Salem, Massachusetts. Hawthorne, who worked in the Custom House, admired General Miller and describes him favorably in the preface to *The Scarlet Letter.*

southern states, and ten were northern states where **slavery** was banned. Would Missouri and Arkansas be "slave" or "free"?

The issue of **slavery** in Arkansas was settled in March of 1819 when Congress, by narrow margins in both houses, approved Arkansas as a **territory** without banning **slavery**. The next year, 1820, Congress approved statehood for Missouri in the **Missouri Compromise**.

The **Missouri Compromise** had three parts. Missouri would become a slave state. At the same time, Maine, which had been a part of Massachusetts, would come into the Union as a free state. This would maintain the even balance between slave and free states. Except in Missouri itself, slavery would not be allowed in any **territories** or states created out of the rest of the Louisiana Purchase north of the 36°30´ line of latitude. This was the border between Arkansas and Missouri.

The debate over **slavery** died down as quickly as it had flared up, but wise men saw that compromise on such an important moral and economic issue might not always be possible. It was "like a firebell in the night" to Thomas Jefferson. "I considered it at once as the knell of the Union."

THE NEW TERRITORY

Arkansas Territory came into existence on July 4, 1819, with its **capital** at Arkansas Post. It had its own government: a governor, a secretary, and three judges, all appointed by the president of the United States. The people of the **territory** elected their own legislature as well as a **delegate** to the U.S. Congress.

President James Monroe named James Miller of New Hampshire to be the first governor of the Arkansas Territory. The governor also supervised Indian affairs in the **territory** and commanded the **militia**, the territory's part-time army. Miller, a general in the U.S. Army and a hero of the War of 1812, was in no hurry to take up his new position. Miller did not leave for Arkansas until October of 1819. It was December, the day after Christmas, before his boat got to Arkansas Post.

In the meantime, Robert Crittenden, the man appointed secretary, had arrived in Arkansas and seized control. Just twenty-two years old, Crittenden was a veteran of the War of 1812, a lawyer, and a member of a leading Kentucky family.

He ordered an election in November of 1819 to create the first General Assembly. It had a legislative council of five men, one from each **county**, and a house of representatives of nine men, chosen from the **counties** on the basis of population. The people also elected James Woodson Bates to be Arkansas's **delegate** to Congress. After some grumbling, Miller accepted Crittenden's actions.

The leaders of the **territory** wanted a **capital** with a more healthy climate and a more central location than Arkansas Post. The Cadron settlement on the Arkansas River was a possible site, but nearby Little Rock won out. Although Little Rock at the time had only a few settlers, the site was owned by two groups of men who had some influence with the legislature. Later, the two groups of land speculators claimed to own exactly the same land in Little Rock. When the territorial

Robert Crittenden. (Courtesy of the Arkansas History Commission)

William Woodruff (in the foreground) *came to Arkansas by boat, bringing with him the newspaper press that he would use for the first issue of the* Arkansas Gazette. (Courtesy of the University of Arkansas, Fayetteville, Special Collections. From John Hugh Reynolds, *Makers of Arkansas History*, [1911])

Superior Court finally decided in favor of one group, the other group picked up its buildings in the middle of the night and moved them off the land.

When the government moved from Arkansas Post to Little Rock in 1821, so did the territory's first newspaper. This was the *Arkansas Gazette,* owned by William Woodruff. Woodruff was born in New York state, where he learned the printing trade. He had moved west in 1818, first to Louisville and then to Nashville.

When he heard about the creation of Arkansas Territory, the twenty-four-year-old printer decided to start a newspaper and printing business there. With a secondhand wooden press and cases of type, he traveled by **keelboat** and canoe to Arkansas Post. There, the first edition of the weekly *Arkansas Gazette* appeared on November 20, 1819. Woodruff became a major figure in Arkansas, and the newspaper he started lasted until 1991.

Secretary Crittenden was the most important man in politics in Arkansas for ten years. Governor Miller sometimes worked hard at his job, with special attention to Indian affairs, but he never adjusted to the frontier. His wife and family never moved to Arkansas. He took longer and longer trips to visit them in New Hampshire, and he finally resigned in 1824, pleading bad health.

President John Quincy Adams appointed George Izard of South Carolina as the new governor. Izard, who really wanted to be an **ambassador**, was not pleased with his new post and was often absent. So Crittenden, who was able, ambitious, and usually on the job, continued to dominate the new government.

THE "FAMILY" IN POLITICS

A group or faction of men finally formed to oppose Crittenden and his supporters. Called the "Family," it consisted of members of the Conway, Sevier, Johnson, Rector, and Ashley families. They were all related to each other by birth or marriage. Many had family ties to politicians in Tennessee and Missouri, just as Crittenden was related to an important Kentucky family.

The differences between the Crittenden group and the Family seem to have been based primarily on personal viewpoints and ambition, rather than on any issues of public policy.

The growing feud came out in the open in the election of 1827 for Arkansas's **delegate** to Congress. Crittenden supported one of his friends, Robert C. Oden. The Family backed Henry W. Conway. It was a mean and dirty campaign, with many personal charges on both sides. Conway won the election by a large margin, but that was not the end of it.

Crittenden believed that he had been insulted during and after the election, so he challenged Conway to a duel. The two met across the Mississippi from the mouth of the White River and exchanged pistol shots at a distance of thirty feet. Crittenden's shot wounded Conway, who died three days later.

Ambrose Sevier, like Conway a part of the Family, won the special election for a new **delegate** to Congress. Although he would try for years to come, Crittenden never regained power in Arkansas, and he died of a stroke at the age of thirty-seven.

Soon the political divisions in Arkansas began to reflect the divisions in national politics. The members of the Family were strong supporters of Andrew Jackson, who was elected president of the United States in 1828. When Jackson's supporters became the **Democratic Party**, the Family became the leaders of that party in Arkansas. The Crittenden group in Arkansas joined the party opposing Jackson, which came to be called the **Whig Party**.

Honor on a Sandbar: Dueling

Arkansans did not invent the **duel**, but they became some of its most eager practitioners.

A **duel** is a formal fight conducted with rules and the very real possibility of death. Dueling was a custom of men who considered themselves gentlemen, with a code of honor demanding that almost any sort of insult be met with a challenge to a **duel.**

Pistols were the usual weapons. Each duelist chose a "second," a close friend. The "seconds" agreed on the rules and conducted the **duel.** Often a doctor and other witnesses were present. The two duelists faced each other across a specified distance—it could be anywhere from ten feet to ten yards—and fired on a signal. Even if both missed, the duelists could declare that their honor was satisfied. If one or both were hit, death was often the result.

Dueling was common in early America. In 1804 the vice president of the United States, Aaron Burr, killed the first secretary of the treasury, Alexander Hamilton, in a **duel.** Andrew Jackson's many **duels** were campaign material in the presidential election of 1828, and the stories about his dueling probably helped him with the voters as much as they hurt him.

Many realized that dueling was both stupid and harmful to public order. The first Arkansas legislature made dueling illegal, which is why Arkansans went just outside the **territory** to fight, to places like sandbars in the Mississippi River or to Indian country.

Perhaps more importantly, influential men realized that real honor and bravery consisted of not playing such a foolish game. William Woodruff, editor of the *Gazette,* for one, refused to give or accept a challenge.

But there were many other **duels** in addition to the Conway-Crittenden duel mentioned in the text. For example, Andrew Scott and Joseph Selden, both judges of the Arkansas Superior Court, in 1824 got into an argument during a game of cards. Feeling their honor was involved, they went across the Mississippi from Helena and fired away. Scott killed Selden with a bullet to the heart on the first shot. Scott and Selden, like Conway and Crittenden, were public officials charged with enforcing the laws, including the law against dueling.

Often, prominent men got into less formal fights. In 1828 the same Andrew Scott lost an election to Edmund Hogan, once a general in the Arkansas militia. The two quarreled. Scott called Hogan a liar; Hogan started a fist fight right there. The 250-pound Hogan knocked the 150-pound Scott to the ground. Scott pulled out his sword cane and stabbed Hogan four times, killing him. It was ruled self-defense.

With Jackson as president, the Family's control of Arkansas became even stronger. Izard died in 1828. The appointment of a new governor was delayed until Jackson took office in 1829. Jackson's man for governor was John Pope of Kentucky. Pope had campaigned for Jackson in 1828 even though Jackson's opponent, John Quincy Adams, was Pope's brother-in-law. (Pope, like Izard, thought he deserved a better appointment; he wanted to be attorney general of the United States.)

Jackson also dismissed Crittenden as secretary of the territory and replaced him with William S. Fulton. A native of Maryland who had moved to Tennessee, Fulton had been Jackson's military aide in one of the general's early campaigns, the Indian wars in the Southeast. Then, in 1835, Jackson appointed Fulton to replace Pope as governor.

In those days newspapers were expected to choose sides in political disputes, and each party hoped to have its own newspaper. Woodruff of the *Gazette* sided with the Family. The **Whigs** in 1829 started a new newspaper in Little Rock, the *Arkansas Advocate*. In 1835 the *Advocate* was taken over by Albert Pike, a skilled writer who became a leader of the **Whig Party** in Arkansas.

THE POPULATION GROWS

The same year Arkansas became a **territory**, 1819, the United States had a national economic crisis. Encouraged by the growth of the nation, many people had borrowed too much money to start businesses or to buy land. When they could not pay back their loans, the Panic of 1819 hit the country, as banks and businesses failed and people lost their money. The Panic and its aftermath slowed the movement westward for several years, but by the late 1820s good times seemed to be returning.

In Arkansas people became more numerous and more settled. From 1820 to 1830 the non-Indian population almost doubled, from 14,273 to 30,388. About one-third of the people moving to Arkansas came from Tennessee. Most of the rest came from Missouri or from the southeastern states of Mississippi and Alabama.

This schoolhouse near Winslow, Arkansas, was built in 1832. Albert Pike taught there for a while. (Courtesy of the University of Central Arkansas Archives)

Clear the floor, strike up "Arkansas Traveler" on the fiddle and banjo, and early Arkansans are ready to jig and whirl the night away. (Courtesy of the J. N. Heiskell Collection, UALR Archives and Special Collections)

Travel began to get easier. The national government paid to build a road from Memphis to Little Rock, and later on to Fort Smith. Called the **Military Road**, it was supposed to be twenty-four feet wide and cleared of trees, with sturdy bridges across the rivers and creeks.

The first part, from Memphis to Little Rock, opened in 1828. However, tree stumps remained in the road until they rotted away, and the bridges were often washed out by floods. Sometimes a horse-drawn coach could go only about three miles an hour.

The national government also began mail service. By the 1820s most of the larger towns in Arkansas had mail every week or two, and connections could be made from Little Rock to Memphis, St. Louis, and Monroe, Louisiana.

The big news in travel was the arrival of the steamboat. For the western waters, Americans had invented a unique new vessel. It was really a big raft with a steam engine and one or two **paddlewheels.** On top of that was the cabin,

which was one, two, or even three decks high with fanciful wooden decorations. The steamboat could float in very shallow water.

The first steamboat had gone down and then back up the Mississippi River in 1811 and 1812. (It was on its way to New Orleans when the **New Madrid** earthquake occurred.) In 1820 the *Comet* became the first steamboat to call at Arkansas Post, and two years later the *Eagle* made the first steamboat landing at Little Rock.

Little Rock was as far as steamboats could go up the Arkansas River, except during the high water period in the spring when steamboats could get all the way to Fort Smith and beyond. Fast and comfortable, the steamboats could carry people and goods much more cheaply than any form of overland transport. They were also dangerous, frequently blowing up, catching fire, or running aground.

By the 1830s steamboats were running scheduled routes on the Arkansas River. They were also beginning to run on the lower parts

Life in the State Capital: Parties, Fights, and Ticks

Hiram Whittington came to Little Rock from Boston in 1827 to work as a printer on William Woodruff's *Gazette.* He was young, unmarried, and delighted with being in the Wild West. He clearly enjoyed writing about his experiences to his brother back home. This is part of one of his first letters:

> Of the female part of the community I have not much to say, as there are five grown girls in the township and they are as ugly as sin and mean as the devil. It is a famous place for parties. I have been to three since I have been here, where they have a violin and dance all night. . . . The men get drunk and generally have a fight before they get home. Last Sunday I saw two French ladies walking out, each with a young [rac]coon in her arms; they are used instead of lap dogs. The bushes in the woods, likewise in the town, are covered with ticks, which are the greatest curse I have yet discovered. . . . If the girls feel a tick biting them, and even if they are on the floor dancing, they immediately stop and unpin and scratch themselves until they find it; it would do your heart good to see how expert the dear little good-for-nothing creatures are at catching ticks.

Hiram worked his way up to foreman at the *Gazette,* moved to Hot Springs, and became a storekeeper and **county** government official. He later married one of those "dear good-for-nothing creatures" from Little Rock and lived the rest of his long life in Arkansas. The brother to whom this letter was addressed also came to Arkansas.

Letters of Hiram Abiff Whittington, *An Arkansas Pioneer from Massachusetts, 1827–1834,* edited by Margaret Smith Ross (Little Rock: Pulaski County Historical Society, 1956), p. 2.

of the White, Black, St. Francis, Red, and Ouachita rivers. Steamboat pilots had to worry about the constantly changing river levels and about the snags and **"sawyers." Sawyers** were whole trees caught on the river bottom and capable of tearing a hole in a steamboat's hull. Captain Henry Shreve invented a boat to pull snags out of the rivers, and in the 1830s he began work at government expense on clearing the Arkansas River. His **snag boats** also began to chew away at the Great Red River Raft.

INDIAN REMOVAL

The increase in white settlement meant the removal of the Indians from Arkansas. The U.S. government's Indian policy was simple. Pressured by white settlers, the government in a solemn **"treaty"** would force a tribe of Indians to leave their homes to go to new land, "reserved" for them. When settlement caught up with the new land, the Indians were moved again. For most, the final removal was to the Indian Territory of Oklahoma, west of Arkansas.

The removal of the Quapaw illustrates the process. These Indians, who had been the Europeans' first friends in Arkansas, were forced to leave their lands along the south bank of the Arkansas River. They were made to join the Caddo in the Red River Valley. Neither the Caddo nor the Quapaw were happy about the arrangement, but the Quapaw tried for a

By the 1830s, these were the major roads and trails in Arkansas. (Courtesy of Gerald T. Hanson)

A typical small steamboat on the White River looked like this in the nineteenth century. She's the Mary Woods II, *carefully preserved and today moored on the White River at Jacksonport State Park. The lower deck holds the steam boiler and the engines. The second deck is the cabin deck and above everything is the pilot house.* (Courtesy of A. C. Haralson, Arkansas Dept. of Parks and Tourism)

This is a dramatic artist's view of the Cherokee leader George Guess, better known as Sequoyah, who gave his people the gift of literacy by developing a written language for them. His alphabet, or more exactly, syllabary, is a set of symbols that represent the sounds or syllables of the Cherokee language. Part of it is on the scroll in his left hand. (Courtesy of the University Museum of the University of Arkansas, Fayetteville)

time to make a go of it and planted their fields. But the Red River flooded and washed away their new crops not once but twice in the first spring, and the displaced Quapaw nearly starved.

One group of Quapaw refused to stay, and they came back home to their Arkansas River land. Others followed, but they were not allowed to stay. In 1833, when only about five hundred Quapaw remained, the government moved them to a small **reservation** in northeast Oklahoma. The Caddo were moved two years later to a **reservation** in Texas.

In the meantime, northern Arkansas continued to be a hunting ground for the Osage and home for some newcomers, the Cherokee. In their homelands in the American southeast, the Cherokee had been one of the "five civilized tribes," tribes that were made up of skilled farmers. Shortly after the American Revolution, some Cherokee began moving to Arkansas on their own. By the 1820s about 3,500 Cherokee, about a third of the whole tribe, had followed. They lived in the St. Francis River Valley and around the site of present-day Russellville. For a time Sequoyah, the inventor of the alphabet for the written Cherokee language, lived among them.

A Protestant group started Dwight Mission near Russellville in 1820 to bring the Christian faith to the Cherokee. The Reverend Cephas Washburn and his wife Abbe Woodward Washburn ran a school and a hospital, as well as a church. They stayed for eight years, as long as the Cherokee remained in Arkansas.

The farming Cherokee and the hunting Osage often fought each other over their adjoining lands. In an effort to control them, the U.S. Army in 1817 established Fort Smith at the western edge of Arkansas. A small detachment of soldiers was supposed to keep the Indians from fighting each other. They also tried to keep the whites from trading in illegal goods with the Indians or settling on Indian land. It was not a popular job with anyone.

The government finally moved the Osage and the Arkansas Cherokee to Oklahoma, too. The Osage went by stages ending in 1825, and the Cherokee went in 1828. Arkansans witnessed one last sad scene in this story. In the 1830s, the national government decided to force all of the "five civilized tribes" to leave their homes in the Southeast and go to Oklahoma.

Over a period of several years, the Choctaw, Chickasaw, Creek, Seminole, and the Cherokee East tribes migrated to Oklahoma under the guidance of the U.S. Army. Some went by boat up the Arkansas River. Most walked over several different trails through Arkansas. Perhaps eighteen thousand men,

The Cherokee were gifted at designing and making brightly colored clothing. This is a beaded sash and a bag. (Courtesy of the University Museum of the University of Arkansas, Fayetteville)

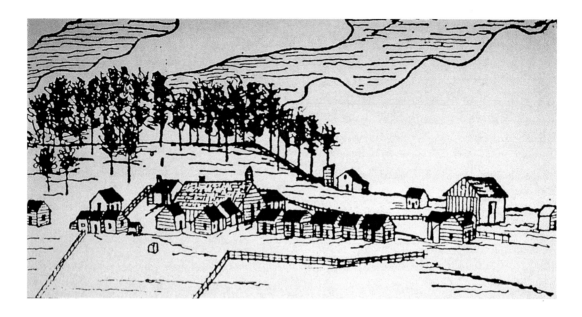

Dwight Mission, in the Cherokee country near Russellville, looked like this to a visiting artist. Centered on the combination church and school building, the settlement included cabins for school-children and the outbuildings of a working farm. (Courtesy of the Arkansas History Commission)

*This dramatic painting by Robert Lindneux captures the **Trail of Tears** as U.S. Army soldiers take Indians on the path to the West. Later, the long trail and harsh weather would be very hard on the Indians.* (Courtesy of the Woolaroc Museum, Bartlesville, Oklahoma)

Constantly in use since 1836 and lovingly preserved through the years, the Old State House looks like this today. It is now a museum emphasizing nineteenth-century Arkansas history. The cannon on the lawn dates from the Civil War and Reconstruction period. (Courtesy of the Old State House Museum)

women, and children started on the journey. About four thousand died along the way. The Indians called it the **Trail of Tears**.

THE BEGINNING OF PROGRESS

By the mid-1830s the nation and Arkansas were off on another boom period of expansion and growth. More people were coming to Arkansas all the time, and the territory was beginning to look civilized too. In 1835 a Tennessee newspaper editor who had read too much bad publicity about Arkansas visited Little Rock and was surprised. "Instead of a rude backwoods village," he said, "we found a handsome flourishing town, built up and refined. The citizens . . . were moral, polite,

and hospitable, and the ladies pretty, accomplished and amiable."

As a symbol of progress, a new **capitol** building was under construction in Little Rock. With the profit from the sale of ten sections of public land donated by Congress, Governor Pope set out to build one big building to house all the functions of government.

Pope selected a Kentuckian, Gordon Shyrock, to be the architect, and construction began in 1833. Shyrock chose the popular Greek Revival style, lining the front of the building with tall round columns. Americans in this period liked their public buildings to look like those of ancient Greece, because Greece was the birthplace of democracy. As the new building began to take shape, it became the background for the next major step for Arkansas, the application for statehood.

VOCABULARY

ague (uh-GYOO) another name for malaria or flu.

ambassador (am-BASS-uh-dohr) one who is appointed to represent one nation to another.

bilious fever (BILL-yuss FEE-ver) another name for malaria.

bison (BY-suhn) a wild, cow-like creature known in America as the buffalo.

bootheel the name given—on the basis of its shape—to the land south of 36°30' (the Arkansas/Missouri border elsewhere) which belongs to Missouri.

capital the city that is the seat of government in a county, state, etc.

capitol the building that houses a state's legislature.

cotton gin (KAH-tuhn JIHN) a machine that removes seeds from cotton.

county a governmental subdivision of a district within a territory or a state.

delegate (DEHL-uh-guht) one elected to represent others; for instance, a member of the U.S. Congress.

Democrats the political party founded by Thomas Jefferson that became known as the Democratic Party under the leadership of Andrew Jackson.

district a governmental subdivision of a territory.

duel a fight between two men in response to an insult, to settle a matter of honor.

epidemic (EH-pih-DEHM-ik) a major outbreak of a contagious disease.

flatboat a raftlike boat used for floating downstream.

fugitives (FYOO-jih-tihvz) outlaws on the run from justice.

hemp a type of grass that produces material suitable for making rope.

indigo (IHN-dih-goh) a plant that yields a dark blue dye.

keelboat a boat with rounded bottom and a keel to help it move straight that could be pulled upstream by men on horses or pushed along with poles.

malaria (muh-LAIR-ee-uh) a mosquito-borne chronic illness characterized by chills and fever.

Military Road built by the U.S. government to traverse Arkansas from Memphis to Fort Smith.

militia (mih-LIHSH-uh) a part-time, citizen army.

milled ground by a large stone wheel that was turned by animal or water power, turning wheat or other grains into flour.

Missouri Compromise (MIHZ-oo-ree CAHM-pro-mize) the 1820–21 U.S. congressional prohibition of slavery north of 36°30' latitude except in Missouri, which was admitted as a slave state to balance Maine's admission as a free state.

New Madrid Fault (nyoo MAD-rihd FAWLT) a major geologic formation where the earth's underlying plates come together; it is located in northeast Arkansas and southeastern Missouri.

Northwest Ordinance a 1787 act of the U.S. Congress prohibiting the practice of slavery in the land north and west of the Ohio River (not including the Louisiana Purchase, which came later).

paddlewheel a wheel made of horizontal blades powered by a steam engine that moved steamboats up and down America's rivers.

passenger pigeons a once-plentiful breed of bird in North America that became extinct during the 1800s from excessive hunting.

reservation land areas set aside, or "reserved," for Indians to live on.

sawyers (SOY-erz) entire trees caught on a river bottom that could "saw" a boat into pieces; similar to a snag.

section a measurement of land equal to one square mile; there are thirty-six sections per township.

slavery the practice of owning human beings as laborers.

snag boat a boat designed to remove snags from river channels; used to remove the Red River Raft.

Southwest Trail the main thoroughfare to Spanish settlements in the southwest, starting at Ste. Genevieve, Missouri, and traversing Arkansas into Texas and beyond.

survey the act of measuring areas of land and dividing them into townships and sections.

territory an area of newly acquired land administered by the U.S. government preparatory to statehood.

township a measurement of land equal to thirty-six square miles.

Trail of Tears the migration route of southeastern Indian tribes forcibly removed from their native land to Oklahoma Territory.

treaty an agreement between the U.S. government and an Indian tribe defining land ownership.

tremors (TREH-merz) shaking of the ground that occurs during earthquakes.

veteran's bonus a reward in the form of free land given to soldiers who fought on behalf of the U.S. government.

Whigs the political party formed in opposition to Jackson's Democratic Party.

yellow fever a lethal mosquito-borne disease that swept through the south periodically.

STUDY QUESTIONS

1. Describe the early efforts to explore Arkansas.

2. Explain the importance of transportation to the people of Arkansas.

3. Give the location of some of the first settlements.

4. Describe agriculture in this period: the size of farms, the crops grown.

5. What was the effect of the War of 1812 on Arkansas?

6. Explain the Missouri Compromise, with emphasis on the part that applied to Arkansas.

7. Explain how territorial government worked.

8. Tell why the territorial capital was moved from Arkansas Post to Little Rock.

9. Explain the role of the Family in territorial politics.

10. Why did Indian Removal and the Trail of Tears occur?

4

Arkansas Becomes a State

1836–1860

What to Look for in Chapter 4

This chapter starts when Arkansas became a state in 1836 and goes to 1860, just before the Civil War.

After a debate over becoming a state that involved slavery and national politics as well as local conditions, the people of Arkansas wrote a state constitution and applied for statehood. Congress made Arkansas a state in 1836. Statehood meant Arkansas had to have a new elected state government, with parties echoing the national Democratic and Whig parties. An attempt to create state banks failed, leaving a lot of bitterness.

The population grew in both number and prosperity. While most white Arkansans were small farmers, a few became planters, owners of many slaves and large amounts of land. For the African American slaves, life was hard. Through these years, the issue of slavery also became more controversial.

You'll also see the role of town life and religion in this period.

Arkansans participated in the Mexican War. When that war ended in 1848, the argument over the expansion of slavery put Arkansas and the nation on the path toward secession and civil war.

THE DECISION FOR STATEHOOD

By the spring of 1835, an air of excitement spread through Arkansas. All the talk was about the chance of becoming a full-fledged state of the Union, and almost every Arkansan had an opinion.

Statehood rallies took place all over the territory that spring and summer. An unofficial, territory-wide vote that August came out 1,942 in favor of statehood and 908 against.

Ambrose Sevier, Arkansas Territory's lone delegate to Congress, had introduced Arkansas's bid for statehood into Congress in 1833. In the debate that followed, the question of statehood involved national politics as well as Arkansas's own affairs.

The states of the Union—twenty-four of them in 1835—were divided half and half between **free states**, in which slavery was illegal, and **slave states**, in which it was allowed. Along with the Missouri Compromise of 1820 had come the idea that new states would come into the Union in pairs, one

83

slave and one free. That would maintain the even balance.

This balance was vital to the **slave states**, because an equal vote in the Senate gave them the strength to fight any proposed laws they deemed harmful to slavery. The Michigan Territory, which would be a free state, had applied for statehood. If Arkansas did not pair itself with Michigan, the Florida Territory might. It then might be many years before another non-slave area would be ready for statehood.

The election of the next president played a part, too. Andrew Jackson did not run in 1836. Instead, the Democrats nominated his vice president, Martin Van Buren of New York. Van Buren was a good man, but he was not the vote-getter that "Old Hickory" was.

The national Democrats wanted all the help they could get. As a state, Arkansas would have votes in the election, and the Family—the strongest faction in Arkansas politics—would certainly deliver them to Van Buren.

A territory had an appointed state government and national funding for almost all its needs. A state, however, could elect its own officials, but it would have to tax itself for many of its needs. Arkansas had the minimum number of people required for statehood —a special census in 1835 showed a total

Arkansas Brags: Humor from the Frontier

Frontier humor was popular throughout the United States in the early nineteenth century, and Arkansas produced its share.

Charles F. M. Noland—the man selected to take the state's new **constitution** to Washington—wrote a series of stories for a national magazine in the form of letters from one "Pete Whetstone" who lived at Devil's Fork on the upper White River. This is the way Pete introduced himself in the first letter in 1837: "Dear Mr. Editor,—Excuse my familiarity, for you must know us chaps on the Devil's Fork don't stand on ceremony . . . I just wish you could come to the Devil's Fork. The way I would show you fun, for I have got the best pack of bear dogs, the closest shooting rifle, the fastest swimming horse, and perhaps, the prettiest sister you every did see."

Probably the best-known Arkansas story in the nineteenth century was "The Big Bear of Arkansas," which appeared in *The Spirit of the Times* sporting magazine in 1841. The author was Thomas Bangs Thorpe, a northerner transplanted to Louisiana, who knew all about the Bear State's reputation for fine hunting and tall tales. In the story, an Arkansan tells a group of strangers on a steamboat all about his home, including a long description of a fantastic bear hunt. This is the way Thorpe's Arkansan introduces his state, after one of the strangers asks where his stories happened: "Happen! happened in Arkansaw: where else could it have happened, but in the creation state, the finishing-up country—a state where the *sile* [soil] runs down to the center of the 'arth, and government gives you a title to every inch of it? Then its airs—just breathe them, and they will make you snort like a horse. It's a state without a fault, it is."

population of 52,240—but most Arkansans did not think of themselves as wealthy. They certainly lacked the cash required for taxes. On the other hand, a state could **charter** banks and in that way create a source of wealth.

At any rate, Arkansas decided to try for statehood. Delegates met in January of 1836 to write a proposed state **constitution** to send to Congress for approval. The issue of slavery, or the influence of slave owners, divided the convention, too.

The southern counties of Arkansas were a part of the cotton belt and had large plantations dependent upon slave labor. The upland counties to the northwest were made up of

4.1. Weapons were usually crafted one at a time by gifted artisans. This one is a rifle made by W. O. Robertson of Pulaski County in 1870. The metal trim is silver, melted from coins. (Courtesy of the Historic Arkansas Museum)

Although slaves were often sold in private business deals between owners, sometimes they were sold at a public slave auction, like this one in Alabama. Buyers closely inspected the slaves offered for sale, then bid for them. (Courtesy of the Arkansas History Commission)

Pottery makers filled an important role in early Arkansas. Vessels of all kinds were required for frontier life. Here is a butter churn made of salt-glazed stoneware, made by J. & N. Bird of Dallas County around 1845. (Courtesy of Henderson State University Museum)

many farmers working small plots with just their family members who held few or no slaves. The document they drew up arranged a compromise on how they would be represented in the proposed General Assembly. The slave counties would have more in the senate, but the free counties would have more in the house.

The delegates picked Charles F. M. Noland of Batesville to take the new **constitution** to Washington. He traveled across the South and then up the Atlantic coast, slowed by winter weather. Meanwhile, William Woodruff had sent a special edition of the *Gazette* contain-

ing the entire state **constitution** by the U.S. Postal Service. The post office beat Noland to Washington, and a congressional committee approved Arkansas statehood on the basis of the newspaper version of the proposed **constitution.**

Ready or not, Arkansas became the twenty-fifth state of the Union on June 15, 1836, with Andrew Jackson signing the act into law. Michigan, delayed by a border dispute with a neighbor state, followed in January of 1837. And in the fall of 1836, Arkansas's three electoral votes helped elect the Democrat Van Buren as president.

THE NEW STATE GOVERNMENT

The most powerful element in Arkansas politics was still that group known as the Family or the **Dynasty**. The Conways, Rectors, Seviers, and Johnsons were all related to each other by birth or marriage. (For example, Ambrose H. Sevier's mother was a Conway, his grandmother was a Rector, and his wife was a Johnson.) In national politics, the Family was associated with the Democratic Party.

Their opponents, with leaders such as Absalom Fowler, Albert Pike, David Walker, and James Woodson Bates, were Whigs in national politics. Although the leaders of both parties came from the wealthy **elite**, those voting for the Democrats tended to be small farmers and the poorer classes. Whig support tended to come from the planters, larger farmers, and town merchants.

The Democrats won most elections for statewide offices and for president. But the Whigs also had their strengths. In the General Assembly elected in 1842, for example, the Whigs won seven of the twenty-one state senate seats and twenty of the sixty-two seats in the house.

By Arkansas law, only white males over twenty-one who had lived in the state at least six months could vote. The voter was not required to be a taxpayer, and there was no system to register voters. Voting was done by voice in public.

On election day, the voter would go to the county seat and announce out loud his

The mouth of the Arkansas River, where it meets the Mississippi River, looked like this in the 1840s to a German artist. A flatboat is in the left foreground. Although flatboats moved downstream with the current, some—like this one—had a sail to help them along. The men at the rear (to the right) are steering with a sweep, a long paddle. (Courtesy of the Chicago Historical Society)

choices to the sheriff or county clerk, who would record the vote. Often a crowd of people, including those running for office, would be present. The crowd listened eagerly to the voting and applauded or booed the voters' choices. For a time in the 1840s, the state used secret paper ballots, but it soon went back to voice voting.

When the voters chose their new state government in 1836, the Family won all the offices. James Sevier Conway became governor and Archibald Yell was sent to the U.S. House of Representatives. (Arkansas's population at first earned it only one member in the U.S. House. The state would have two delegates after the census of 1850 and three after the census of 1860.) Conway was a younger brother of Henry Wharton Conway, the U.S. delegate killed in the 1827 duel.

Archibald Yell was one of the most popular

Bowie Knives to the Death in the House of Representatives

In the first session of the Arkansas General Assembly, the speaker of the house of representatives murdered another legislator on the floor of the house.

It started with a debate in the house on a bill to offer bounties for wolf hides. Major Joseph J. Anthony of Randolph County was bitterly opposed to the Real Estate Bank, which the legislature had created earlier in the session, and he thought he would try to make his point again.

Anthony offered an amendment to the wolf-scalp bill, requiring the president of the Real Estate Bank to sign each bounty certificate. Anthony knew that the president of the Real Estate Bank was John Wilson of Clark County, speaker of the house of representatives.

Wilson, from his chair as presiding officer, demanded to know if Anthony intended a personal slur. As Anthony tried to explain himself, Wilson ordered him to sit down. When Anthony remained standing, Wilson drew his Bowie knife, shouted "Sit down or I'll make you!" and moved toward Anthony.

Anthony drew his Bowie knife, too, and moved to meet Wilson. Wilson seized a chair to use as a shield, and the two fought. Anthony lost his knife and grabbed another chair to defend himself.

Wilson pushed aside Anthony's chair and thrust his knife into Anthony's chest up to the hilt. Anthony died instantly, without a word or a cry. Watching all this were the members of the Arkansas house of representatives, none of whom had even tried to stop the fight.

Wilson wiped the blood from his knife with his thumb and finger and resumed the speaker's seat.

When Wilson was finally brought before a court at the insistence of Anthony's relatives, the jury acquitted him of murder.

One account says that Wilson then treated all the jurors to drinks, and he later led a parade with noisemakers through town to the lodgings of Anthony's relatives "to shout and scream and yell, as in triumph over them and over the law."

James Sevier Conway. (Courtesy of the Arkansas History Commission)

Quilts served the practical purpose of keeping people warm, but their design and execution also offered women a chance for artistic expression. Often, groups of women would come together for a "quilting bee" to join in making a quilt. This quilt was made in Washington County between 1850 and 1860. The design is called "Princess Feather." (Courtesy of the University Museum of the University of Arkansas, Fayetteville)

politicians in Arkansas history. At a very young age, the Tennessean had fought with Andrew Jackson at the Battle of New Orleans. He served again with Jackson in the Florida campaign against the Seminole Indians. Yell's ambition took him to the promising new state of Arkansas, to Fayetteville, where he became a judge. He had a winning common touch that made him a favorite among the people of his new home.

In those days, the state General Assembly, not the direct vote of the people, chose the members of the U.S. Senate. Here, too, the winners were Democrats. They were William S. Fulton, the most recent governor of the ter-ritory, and Ambrose H. Sevier, Conway's cousin and the former delegate from the territory to Congress.

The new state's economy was doing well in the boom years of the late 1830s. In 1837, the state government realized that it had a fifty-thousand-dollar surplus. Some members of the General Assembly wanted to use it to start a state university, but more of them chose to turn the money back to the people in the form of lower taxes.

The government did authorize twenty thousand dollars, and in 1840 another forty thousand dollars, to build a prison on a hill west of Little Rock. (The state capitol building is on the site today.) The federal government began a major building project to create a military **arsenal** at Little Rock. (The **arsenal's** central building is now the MacArthur Museum of Arkansas Military History in MacArthur Park.)

THE STATE BANKS

A serious obstacle to growth in Arkansas was the lack of **capital**, in the form of either cash or credit (through borrowing). Under pressure from planters and businessmen, the legislature decided to establish two state banks. The 1830s were times of great economic optimism all over the country. Almost any hardworking man thought he could get rich if only he could borrow some money to get started. That made it very tempting for banks to grant as many loans as possible. To make matters worse, President Jackson steadfastly opposed a central national bank. He destroyed the Bank of the United States, which had served as a check on unsound expansion of credit.

In Arkansas the Real Estate Bank, primarily for planters and large farmers, and the State Bank, primarily for merchants, opened in 1837. From the very beginning, the banks had problems.

The state gave the banks its formal endorsement and partly financed them through the sale of **bonds.** Still, the government had

Ambrose H. Sevier. (Courtesy of the Arkansas History Commission)

ARCHIBALD YELL
Governor of Arkansas
1840 to 1844

Archibald Yell. (Courtesy of the Arkansas History Commission)

little control over the operation of the banks. Thirty percent of the stockholders in the Real Estate Bank lived in Chicot County. Clearly, the planters were in complete control of its funds.

The Real Estate Bank loaned large sums of money with only land as security for the loans. In one instance, Senator Sevier obtained a $15,000 loan secured by land the bank appraised at $32,000. The tax **assessor** valued the same land at only $13,975. It was not long before the bank ran out of money and had to start borrowing from banks in other states, like New York.

The State Bank fared no better. Two years after it opened, it had debts of two million dollars. Much of that was in loans that had little chance of being repaid.

The state banks issued their own bank notes. The value of this paper money was not supposed to exceed the value of actual gold and silver held by the banks. However, both banks issued far more paper money than their gold and silver reserves would allow. State banks all over the country were doing the same thing. This prompted President Jackson to issue the "**Specie** Circular" which said that the federal government would accept only **specie**—gold and silver—as payment for public lands.

When the **Specie** Circular went into effect, it helped prompt a nation-wide economic disaster, the Panic of 1837. That was the start of a severe economic depression, which rolled westward toward Arkansas. The Panic spelled disaster for the state banks. Borrowers failed to pay their loans, and the banks tried issuing even more paper money to stay ahead. By 1842, both banks were forced to close their doors. Many of those who had run the banks fled Arkansas and moved west to Texas.

The huge debts they left behind, which the state was legally obliged to pay, disrupted state finances for decades to come. In frustration, the state outlawed the existence of banks and proceeded to default on the debts. It was the worst of all possible worlds for a state short of **capital**. There were no state banks, and the state's credit was ruined with all the big banks in the East.

In 1840, in the middle of this unpleasant situation, the popular congressman, Archibald Yell, was elected governor. Despite the dim prospects, Yell chose to look to the future. In his first speech he called for public education, internal improvements, and financial reform.

Putting the governor's program into action, the General Assembly in 1842 passed the "**Common School Law.**" It set aside sixteen sections of land in each township for school revenues. The lands were to be sold and the income used by the local people to build and operate public schools. It was not yet a real public school system, but it was a hope and a promise. Most schools were still private schools, where parents had to pay tuition for their children.

A DEVELOPING STATE

During the early statehood years, the population more than doubled every ten years. New people- poured into the state, mostly from neighboring states such as Tennessee, Mississippi, and Missouri, with others from Alabama, Georgia, and North Carolina. Many of the newcomers were African American families, brought as slaves by their masters to carve out **plantations** in the river bottoms.

It was becoming easier to get to Arkansas. The major overland route was the road from Memphis to Little Rock, completed in 1836 after ten long hard years of work. There was also the old Southwest Trail that slanted from the northeast corner to the southwest corner of the state.

The rivers still carried much of the traffic. On the Arkansas River, steamboats even began to run on regular schedules. In the southwest, Captain Henry Shreve finally cleared the raft of piled-up logs in the Red River by 1838, although the clearing had to be done again later in some places.

The crucial need for **transport** made Arkansans, like the rest of the nation, eager to have railroads. The most discussed route was the Cairo and Fulton, which would run from St. Louis through Jacksonport and Little Rock to Fulton on the Red River. Branch lines would go from Little Rock to Memphis and to Fort Smith.

Late in the 1850s, construction began on the Little Rock-to-Memphis link, but it was hard going. By 1860, only two short segments had been built, from Little Rock east to DeVall's Bluff and from Hopefield (now West Memphis) west to Madison. The state's first locomotive, the *Little Rock*, ran **excursion** trips on the limited rail routes.

Those who left their old homes behind to make a new life on the Arkansas frontier were bold and hardy folk. Many of them were young, single males who could easily cut old ties and take a chance on something new. Part of the violence on the Arkansas frontier was due to the high proportion of young unmarried men in the state.

But a great number of the new settlers were young married couples with very small children. In more settled eastern parts of the U.S. at this time, families were having fewer children, and women were beginning to get involved in life outside of the home. However, in frontier Arkansas, the young women of the 1840s were having more children than those in any other state.

The typical frontier woman married at the age of twenty-two and had a child every two years throughout her child-bearing years, for a total of six to eight children. Infants and children in those days had little protection against diseases like measles and mumps. Complications from even simple illnesses might result in death. Perhaps only four or five of the children born to a family would live to be adults.

THE YEOMAN FARMERS

Most Arkansans were farmers who owned small plots of land, "**yeoman** farmers" in the language of the time. A good-sized farm might have 150 acres, only a third of it in crops, the rest woodlands or pasture. The typical family home was a log cabin. It was often built **dogtrot** style, with two rooms connected by a covered passage open at both ends. Members of large families lived together in very close quarters.

Taking a bath was a major ordeal, not to be endured too often. The water had to be hauled in from the spring or well and heated over the fire. Then chairs or beds or tables had to be moved aside in the crowded room to make space for the washtub. Out back, some distance from the well or creek that provided drinking water, would be a **privy**, the outdoor toilet.

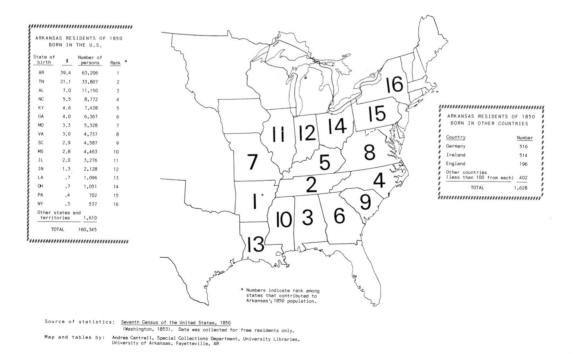

Places of Birth for Arkansas Residents from the 1850 Census of Population. (Andrea Cantrell, University of Arkansas, Fayetteville, Special Collections)

Sometimes a family would simply assume ownership of a likely piece of land. They did not bother to buy it because no one had yet surveyed the land, or there were no nearby land offices in operation to sell property. They often did not have cash or credit to pay for it. People who simply took over land this way were called **squatters**. After a number of years, they might be forced to move to new land. Yet many of these families kept their property for generations without ever having legal title to the land.

For those who had money or credit, buying and selling land could be a source of wealth. A land speculator bought land at the government price, then held on to it to sell later at a higher price.

Arkansas settlers proved to be productive farmers. Arkansas farmers of 1840 raised enough corn to feed everyone in the state for a year plus everyone in a second state of the same size. Arkansas had more cattle and hogs per person than any other southern state, and only Missouri had more horses per person. In 1840, there were four hogs for every person.

Corn and pork—"**hominy** and hogs"—were the basics of the Arkansan's diet. Extra hogs were driven to market to sell, as cowboys would later drive cattle to market. Many families also raised a small crop of cotton or tobacco as a money crop to sell. The money they got was used to buy flour and coffee, nails, and household goods that they could not raise or make themselves.

Family members worked together to make their own clothing. Many families had looms for weaving cloth and spinning wheels for making thread and yarn. These machines were counted among the family's most precious possessions. The pioneers dyed the cloth with colors they made from tree bark, flowers, and berries. Bear oil was still the chief fuel for lighting lamps.

Population Growth in Early Arkansas

The United States census, taken every ten years, shows the rapid population growth in Arkansas. The total population more than doubled every ten years from 1830, in the Territorial period, to 1860, the eve of secession. Note, too, that the black population, almost all slaves, increased at a slightly faster rate than the white population.

	1830	1840	1850	1860
Total Population	30,388	97,574	209,897	435,450
White Population	25,671	77,174	162,189	324,143
Black Population	4,717	20,400	47,708	111,307
Black Population as a percentage of total	15.5	20.9	22.7	25.6

In the same period, the total population of the United States went from about 12,900,000 in 1830 to about 31,500,000 in 1860.

Dr. William H. Hammond graduated from medical school in Louisville, Kentucky, and was the first physician with a degree to practice in Hot Springs. A famous portrait painter named Henry C. Byrd made this picture of the doctor's three-year-old son, John. The little boy refused to sit for the portrait unless his dog, Bounce, was included. Six months after the painting was done, the little boy died. Bounce refused to eat and died just a few days later. (Courtesy of the Historic Arkansas Museum)

THE PLANTERS

Alongside the simple and nearly self-sufficient life of the **yeoman** farmer, the planter class was developing a different life style. Far fewer in number than the **yeoman** farmers, the wealthy planter class was marked by the possession of large amounts of land, the ownership of many slaves, and the production of large amounts of cotton.

Most of the planters lived in the river bottoms. They lived in the Delta of the southeast, the Red River valley of the southwest, and up the Arkansas River Valley as far as Fort Smith. The bottom land was fertile, and the rivers were important for getting the cotton crop to market. Many planters had their own steamboat or flatboat landings, where they received goods and loaded up their cotton for the return journey.

More than 90 percent of Arkansas cotton was grown in ten counties, nine of them in the lowlands and one on the upper Arkansas River. Those same areas had 58 percent of the slaves and only 24 percent of the state's white people.

Unlike **plantations** in the older slave states, such as Virginia and South Carolina, these frontier **plantations** could be crude places. The planter and his family might dream of someday having a big white house with columns in front. For the time being,

The Nobe Dilbeck home, originally built about 1830, was a typical frontier log cabin. (Courtesy of the Faulkner County Historical Society Collection, University of Central Arkansas Archives)

they were likely to be living in a house that began as a log cabin and grew with extra rooms added as the planter's wealth grew. But the planters might also enjoy the luxuries of oysters, champagne, cigars, brandy, silk hose, cashmere, silver, glass, and china.

The planter class tended to dominate the state. About 10 percent of the population owned 70 percent of all the wealth in the state. They held 78 percent of the slaves and 63 percent of the land. It was no surprise that the planters had influence in the state far beyond their numbers.

SLAVERY AND BLACK ARKANSANS

By 1860, 111,115 slaves lived in Arkansas, forming about one-fourth of the population. Slave owners were few in number, and even fewer owned large numbers of slaves. In 1860,

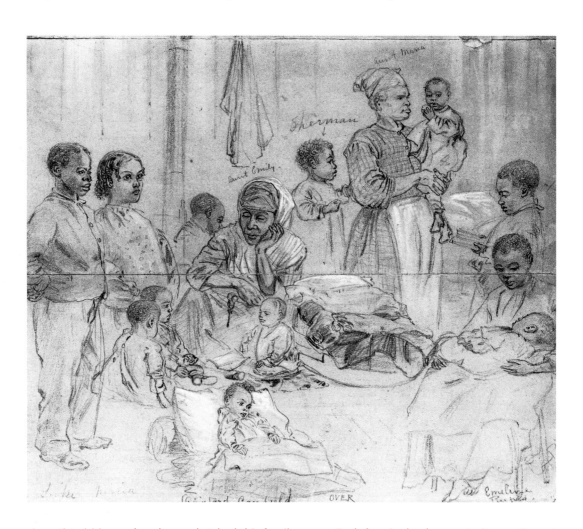

An artist visiting a slave home sketched this family scene. Each face is clearly a portrait, an attempt to show the character and personality of the subject. Although the lettering is too faint to be seen easily, many of the individuals are named. (Courtesy The Historic New Orleans Collections Museum/ Research Center)

only 11,481 white Arkansans, about 3.5 percent of the population, owned slaves. If you assume the average family was about five people, only about 18 percent of the whites were in a slave-owning family. That means 82 percent of the whites, about four out of every five white people, did not have any direct link to slavery.

Among slave owners, more than half of them owned only one to four slaves. Only 1,363 white people owned twenty or more slaves, which placed them in the "planter class." Very large slave holdings were even rarer. Six people owned between two hundred and three hundred slaves, and one man, Elisha Worthington of Chicot County, owned more than five hundred slaves.

About half the slaves were owned in groups of four or less. Often the group was a black family, working side by side in the fields with the white family who owned them. They lived and worked closely with each other. Still, the blacks could never forget that they were the white man's property, to be worked or sold as he saw fit.

Larger groups of slaves, with ten, fifteen, or more to one owner, were almost certainly working on a plantation growing cotton as a cash crop. The plantation boss might have been the owner or a member of the owner's family. The boss may also have been an **overseer,** a white man hired to manage the **plantation.** By 1860 there were about a thousand people in Arkansas who listed their job as **overseer.**

On a well-run **plantation,** the slave labor force was managed to get the most out of each worker. The very old and the very young might have light tasks such as tending the livestock, but most of the slaves, men and women alike, were field hands.

Cotton growing required hard work all year round, each day from "can see to can't see" (from dawn to dusk). Plowing and getting the fields ready began in January. The workers planted the crop in the spring. The field hands spent the long summer growing season "**chopping cotton,**" hoeing up and down the long rows to keep weeds and grasses out of the cotton.

By early fall, the cotton was ready for the first picking. Slaves picked the cotton **bolls** by hand, bending over to reach the scratchy plants that scraped and tore at their hands. They dropped the cotton **bolls** into long sacks slung over their shoulders. The slaves would pick over a single cotton field many times through the fall to be sure they got all the cotton.

The picked cotton went to the gin to have the seeds removed. From there, it went to the **compress** to be pressed into bales. Then there was just barely time left in the year to repair the fences and tools before the cycle started again.

Some slaves had special roles based on their skills. There were slave blacksmiths, brick masons, **wheelwrights,** carpenters, and the like. These workers were valued by their owners and carried a high price. Some slaves might be house servants, cooks, and maids to the planter family, and nurses to their children.

In the towns, slaves were servants, coachmen and stable boys, laborers, and skilled craftsmen. Chester Ashley, a wealthy Little Rock lawyer and real estate investor, had a number of slaves to run his large house. The sons of Anne Warren, his cook, formed a music group that Ashley rented out for parties. They were the most sought-after band in Little Rock at the time.

The slave owner was the total master of his slaves, backed up by local and state customs and laws of the time. Slaves were not allowed to leave their owner's home without

Runaway Negro in Jail.

WAS committed to the Jail of Saline county, as a runaway, on the 8th day of June, 1851, a negro man, who says his name is JOHN, and that he belongs to *Henry Johnson*, of Desha county, Ark. He is aged about 24 or 25 years, straight in stature, quick spoken, looks very fierce out of his eyes, and plays on the fiddle. Had on, when apprehended, white cotton pants, coarse cotton shirt, and black hat. The owner is hereby notified to come forward, prove property, and pay the expenses of committal and advertisement, otherwise the said negro will be dealt with according to law. THOMAS PACK, *Sheriff and Jailor of Saline county.*

Benton, June 21, 1851. 7—26w.

Pay up! Pay up!!

ALL persons indebted to the undersigned, whose notes and accounts are *now due*, are requested to call and *pay up*, by the 1st day of July next. JOHN D. ADAMS.
June 13, 1851. 5—

Thirty Dollars Reward.

LEFT my plantation, in Arkansas county, near Post of Arkansas, on the 26th May (ult.), two Negro Men, viz:
GEORGE, a dark copper-colored man, about 30 years of age, 5 ft. 8 or 10 inches high, forehead rather low, some beard on his chin, stutters considerably and has a habit of winking his eyes when talking. He was recently purchased from Mr. Wm. E. Woodruff, at Little Rock, and has a wife at Dr. Watkins', near that city.

Also, HARRISON, about the same age, as the other, and belongs to Mr. W. R. Perry, of the same county.

The above slaves left in company, and it is supposed will make for Little Rock.

The above reward will be paid for arresting and securing said negroes, so that their owners may get them, or one-half the amount for either of them. Letters will reach me if addressed to Arkansas Post, Ark's. J. FLOYD SMITH.

Arkansas co., June 6, 1851. 4—tf.

These newspaper advertisements of 1851 are typical of many others at the time, showing how frequently blacks tried to escape slavery. Notice in the second advertisement that "George's" purchase separated him from his wife. The pictures were standard illustrations, used in all similar advertisements. (Courtesy of the University of Central Arkansas Archives)

a pass. The whites ran patrols to catch slaves who did not have such a permit. If a slave broke any of the rules or refused to work, he or she would be whipped with a lash.

Although slavery was too strict a system to allow much resistance, some slaves did fight back in many ways. Slave owners often complained that their slaves were lazy or broke tools. This was probably a form of passive resistance. On one **plantation**, a slave refused to submit to the whip and was shot to death by the white **overseer.** Some slaves ran away, and the newspapers were always full of notices in which slave owners sought the return of escaped slaves.

Free African Americans were rare in Arkansas, never reaching more than a few hundred. In many ways their status was unstable. One of the white arguments for slavery was that blacks could not live as free people. This argument assumed that black people were mentally and socially inferior to whites, so that blacks had to depend on their white masters to feed, clothe, and shelter them. The very existence of free blacks was seen as a threat to slavery. In Little Rock, the free black Nathan Warren became famous as a candy maker. Over time, he was able to buy the freedom of his wife, his brother, and some of his children.

As the debate over slavery throughout the country became more intense in the late 1850s, life became even more difficult for free African Americans. Finally, the Arkansas General Assembly passed a law that required all free blacks to leave the state in January of 1860.

Even under these conditions, blacks were still able to maintain home and family life.

Thirty-Nine Lashes "Well Laid On"

The institution of slavery was backed up by a set of state laws, the "slave code." Here are some excerpts from the Arkansas slave code:

No slave shall go from the tenements of his master . . . without a pass, or some letter or token whereby it may appear that he is proceeding by authority from his master, employer or **overseer;** if he does, it shall be lawful for any person to apprehend and carry him before a justice of the peace, to be by his order punished with stripes or not at his discretion. No slave or mulatto whatsoever shall keep or carry a gun, powder, shot, club or other weapon whatsoever, offensive or defensive . . . every such offender shall have and receive . . . any number of lashes not exceeding thirty nine on his or her bare back well laid on for every such offense. Whereas many times slaves run away and lie hid and lurking in swamps woods and other obscure places, killing hogs and committing other injuries . . . any two justices of the peace . . . are empowered and required . . . to direct the sheriff . . . to take such power with him as he shall think fit and necessary for the effectual apprehending of such out lying slave or slaves and go in search of them, and upon their being apprehended commit them to jail . . . for further trial. If any negro or other slave shall at any time consult, advise or conspire to rebel or make insurrection, or shall plot or conspire the murder of any person or persons whatsoever . . . the slave or slaves convicted thereof shall suffer death and be utterly excluded all benefit of clergy.

*For a slave **plantation** to be efficient, everyone had to work in some way. While both men and women worked in the fields, the older women cared for the children in the slave quarters. This is an artist's version of mealtime for the children.* (Courtesy The Historic New Orleans Collection, Museum/Research Center)

Although a slave marriage was not recognized by law, most slaves did marry and raise children. They kept some customs of their African heritage, largely passed down by word of mouth.

For many, religion gave solace. Slaves blended the Christian faith and African traditions in music to produce the sad and lovely songs we know as "spirituals." African traditions also enriched the eating habits of Arkansas. Gumbo, hushpuppies, and fried catfish are just a few of Arkansans' favorite foods that came to us from West Africa.

LIFE IN THE TOWNS

Although most Arkansans were farmers living in rural areas, towns did grow as market and trade centers. Little Rock, the capital, was the biggest town, with 3,727 people by 1860. Other large towns by then were Camden (pop. 2,219), Fort Smith (pop. 1,530), Pine Bluff (pop. 1,396), Van Buren (pop. 969), Fayetteville, (pop. 967), and Arkadelphia (pop. 817).

Every town of any size had a hotel and boarding houses. Merchants offered food, cloth and dyes, kitchen goods, and liquor. Doctors, lawyers, and dentists set up businesses throughout the state. A few women opened hat and dressmaking shops. Other gifted artisans made and sold guns, furniture, and shoes and boots.

People in towns could develop a life of culture with greater ease than rural people could. Reading groups, debate clubs, and history groups formed, such as the Club of Forty and The Lyceum in Little Rock. Speakers traveled from town to town and charged an entrance fee for lectures on a number of subjects. People organized singing clubs, concerts, and dramas to entertain themselves.

Men and women formed civic groups like the Odd Fellows, Daughters of Rebekah, and Masons.

A number of magazines started up, such as *Christian Teacher, Memphis and Arkansas Christian Advocate, Southern Gem,* and *Arkansas Magazine.* Gambling and horse racing, however, were probably the most common, and popular, pastimes. Southwest Arkansas had a race track as early as 1820, but Fort Smith's track was said to be the best.

Local efforts were enriched by traveling artisans and entertainers. Architects, portrait painters, and later, photographers, tended to be **"itinerants,"** traveling from one location

Nathan Warren was a free African American of Little Rock who operated a candy store. His wife was a slave who served as cook for Chester Ashley. Their children had to assume the slave status of their mother. The Warren boys formed a musical group that was the most popular band in town.
(Courtesy of the Arkansas History Commission)

to another. Musicians and comics traveled all over the South, and they visited mainly the river towns in Arkansas. The circus was extremely popular, coming to towns of all sizes on a regular basis.

Holidays offered special times for festive fun. The Fourth of July was perhaps the most important. Parades, speeches, and fireworks marked the event. Christmas, on the other hand, was not such a big holiday. It was of special importance to **plantation** slaves, though, because it brought the only days of rest they were allowed in the year.

RELIGION IN EARLY ARKANSAS

Churches were great civilizing forces on the frontier. As early as 1825, Little Rock had a

This cherrywood corner cupboard was made between 1835 and 1850 in the Hill Creek Community of Conway County. A journeyman made it in payment of his board. He had served an apprenticeship of three years in a workman's guild in England before coming to Arkansas. He carried his tools in a pack on his shoulders. (Courtesy of the Museum of Discovery)

Ann McHenry Reider came to Arkansas in a covered wagon with her parents in 1818. She married Jacob Reider, who was from Switzerland, in 1833, and they bought land in Little Rock. Mr. Reider kept a store at the corner of Main and Markham streets. This portrait of her was painted by Henry C. Byrd. Mrs. Reider lived to be ninety-three and died in 1898. (Courtesy of Mrs. William A. Laing of Hot Springs, Mrs. Reider's great-great-granddaughter)

Baptist meeting house that served as a public gathering spot for all kinds of meetings. Other churches borrowed the meeting space as they started up and worked to raise money for buildings of their own. The Little Flock Baptist Church opened in Crawford County that same year, and Baptist churches began at the towns of White River and Baptist Ford in Washington County in 1830.

Presbyterianism came early to Arkansas, and Little Rock's First Presbyterian Church was organized in 1828. The Christian Church organized in 1832. There were soon many Methodist churches in the northwest. During the 1830s they began meeting at Fayetteville, Elm Springs, War Eagle, and Wager's Mills (Benton County).

Christ Episcopal Church, which first met in the Little Rock home of Chester Ashley, was formed in 1839. This church sponsored special classes in reading and other subjects for slave children a little later in the century. In 1845, a group of slaves under the guidance of slave-pastor Wilson N. Brown formed the First Missionary Baptist Church of Little Rock.

The Roman Catholic church, of course, had been brought to Arkansas with the first French and Spanish settlers, but became a formal diocese in the 1840s. Its school in Little Rock, St. Mary's Academy for Girls, was founded in 1851 by the Sisters of Mercy. It is now the oldest continuing school in Arkansas.

For those living scattered throughout the

Nancy Fletcher O'Kelly McCauley was born May 1, 1788, in Chatham county, North Carolina. She came with her husband, John McCauley, to White County in the 1850s. She died February 14, 1861, in Searcy. This photograph was made between 1856 and 1860, toward the end of her life. (Courtesy of Mr. Francis Hook Jernigan of Little Rock)

countryside, the camp meeting was both a religious and a social event. Once a year, usually in late September, entire rural communities would turn out for ten days to three weeks of preachings. The preacher might be a local man or a visitor from another state.

Some camp grounds were used over and over and had a building to house the pulpit and rows of "mourners' benches." Many came to stay for the whole meeting, living in wooden "log tents," brush arbor lean-tos, or the backs of their wagons.

The camp meetings bound people together in shared moral teachings. But besides hymn singing, preaching, and praying, camp meetings gave young farm men and women rare chances for meeting and courting. The events also drew merchants selling their wares, including liquor at times, and politicians. The camp meeting also put all the people on an equal footing as sinners and converts. Despite wealth, gender, color, or age, all were free to express their fears and hopes and feelings.

WAR WITH MEXICO

The year Arkansas gained statehood, 1836, was also the year of the Texas Revolution. Arkansans had watched events to their southwest with interest. Many American settlers in Texas had moved through Arkansas to get there, and quite a few Texas leaders had Arkansas connections.

Stephen Austin had been one of the land

speculators who backed the city of Little Rock as Arkansas Territory's capital city. Davy Crockett was honored with a dinner in Little Rock on his way to Texas. Jim Bowie's famous Bowie knife was fashioned by James Black of the town of Washington. (Crockett and Bowie both were to die at the Alamo.)

When Texas staged its revolt against Mexico in 1836, it quickly applied for American statehood. But the admission of Texas raised the issue of whether or not to expand slavery. U.S. leaders, including President Andrew Jackson, were not yet ready to face that question. So Texas waited, as the Republic of Texas.

By the mid-1840s, the urge of Americans to expand the size of their country—they called it "**Manifest Destiny**"—became all powerful. Congress voted to annex Texas in 1845. Arkansas was no longer the state farthest west in the Union.

From the standpoint of Mexico, which had never given up its rights to Texas, the United States had just annexed a state of Mexico. Talk of war became common. Americans also had their eyes on Mexican lands in California and New Mexico.

An exchange of shots along the Rio Grande brought war in the spring of 1846. President James K. Polk asked Arkansas to provide a regiment of mounted infantry to fight in Mexico. He also asked for soldiers from Arkansas to relieve regular U.S. Army troops on the Indian frontier.

Arkansans quickly volunteered. By this time, Archibald Yell was back in Congress, and Thomas Drew, a Lawrence County planter who had come from Tennessee, was governor. Yell came home from Washington, D.C., to enlist as a private. State volunteer units in those days could elect their own officers, and to no one's surprise Yell was elected colonel. Solon Borland, a newspaper editor known for

Timeless Advice on Elections

When Davy Crockett visited Arkansas on his way to Texas and the Alamo, Little Rock citizens honored him with a banquet. In his speech after dinner, the former Tennessee Congressman offered some general advice on running for office.

When the day of election approaches, visit your constituents far and wide. Treat liberally, and drink freely. . . . Do all you can to appear to advantage in the eyes of the women. That's easily done—you have but to kiss and slobber their children, wipe their noses, and pat them on the head; this cannot fail to please their mothers. . . . Get up on all occasions, and sometimes on no occasion at all, and make long-winded speeches . . . talk of your devotion to your country, your modesty and disinterestedness, or any such fanciful subject. Rail against taxes of all kinds, office holders, and bad harvest weather; and wind up with a flourish about the heroes who fought and bled for our liberties in the times that tried men's souls.

James R. Masterson, *Arkansas Folklore* . . . (Reprint, Little Rock: Rose Publishing Co., 1974), pp. 23–24.

"The Fine Arkansas Gentleman"

Albert Pike was a politician, editor, farmer, soldier, and writer. He was most proud of his extensive writings about the Masonic Order, but his most popular work was a lilting ditty he wrote in 1852 about "the fine Arkansas gentleman." The unnamed subject is almost certainly Elias Rector, who lived near the border with the Indian country. The first verses go like this:

> Now all good fellows, listen, and a story I will tell
> Of a mighty clever gentleman who lives extremely well
> In the western part of Arkansas, close to the Indian line,
> Where he gets drunk once a week on whiskey, and
>   immediately sobers himself completely on the
>   very best of wine;
> A fine Arkansas gentleman,
> Close to the Choctaw line!
>
> The fine Arkansas gentleman has a mighty fine estate
> Of five or six thousand or more acres of land, that
>   will be worth a great deal some day or other
>   if he don't kill himself too soon, and will only
>   condescend to wait;
> And four or five dozen negroes that would rather work
>   than not;
> And such quantities of horses, and cattle, and pigs,
>   and other poultry that he never pretends to know how
>   many he has got;
> This fine Arkansas gentleman,
> Close to the Choctaw line!
>
> This fine Arkansas gentleman has built a splendid house
> On the edge of a big prairie, extremely well populated
>   with deer, and hares, and grouse;
> And when he wants to feast his friends he has nothing
>   more to do
> Than to leave the pot-lid off, and the decently behaved birds
>   fly straight into the pot, knowing he'll shoot them
>   if they don't; and he has a splendid stew,
> This fine Arkansas gentleman,
> Close to the Choctaw line!

Albert Pike. (Courtesy of the Arkansas History Commission)

his frequent duels and author of the state's first medical treatise, became a major.

Yell and Borland were Democrats. Albert Pike, a Whig, served as a captain and later had many bad things to say about both Yell's and Borland's lack of military skill.

In fact, the Arkansas troops, like most volunteers in the Mexican War, were strong on spirit and weak on training. Some newspaper reporters called them "The Mounted Devils of Arkansas."

The Arkansas soldiers' major battle was at Buena Vista, deep in northern Mexico, on February 22 and 23, 1847. Under Mexican attack, the Arkansans began to break ranks and some men ran away. Trying to rally the men, Colonel Archibald Yell was killed when a Mexican lance pierced his head. Meanwhile, Major Solon Borland had been captured. He escaped and joined General Winfield Scott's successful assault on Mexico City.

The war secured Texas for the United States, claimed the life of one of Arkansas's favorite sons, and made Solon Borland a hero. Borland became the next U.S. senator from Arkansas; William K. Sebastian, a lawyer from Helena, took the other Senate seat. John S. Roane of Van Buren, another war hero (he

The Arkansas memorial in Mexico honoring those who died in the Battle of Buena Vista. (Courtesy of the Arkansas History Commission)

This painting shows the U.S. Army post at Fort Smith about 1855. (Courtesy of the University of Arkansas, Fayetteville, Special Collections)

had taken over command when Yell was killed), became governor.

As soon as the war with Mexico was over, Arkansans heard great news from California. Gold had been found and the gold rush was on. The first groups of Arkansas "forty-niners," 128 men in 50 wagons, left Fort Smith for the gold fields in April of 1849.

Arkansas was the starting point for one of the major trails to California. This southern route led from Fort Smith, Van Buren, or Fayetteville through Santa Fe and on to the gold fields. Thousands of men, many of them Arkansans, made the long journey to California. A few got rich, but most failed to find wealth.

THE UNION TREMBLES

The 1850s were boom years for Arkansas. Coming out of its frontier era, the state was growing swiftly in population and wealth. The cotton trade was prosperous, and railroad construction had begun at last.

Elias Nelson Conway, the governor from 1852–1860, did much to put the state on a sound fiscal footing. Conway was yet another brother of the slain congressman, Henry, and former governor, James. He managed to obtain an accurate account of the Real Estate Bank's assets and put the bank into **receivership.**

The Prosperous 1850s

The decade of the 1850s, the last ten years before the Civil War, was a very prosperous period for Arkansans, most of whom were farmers. Statistics from the United States census show large increases in almost every farm measurement.

	1850	1860
Number of farms	17,785	39,004
Acres in farms	2,598,214	9,573,706
Improved farm acres	781,530	1,983,313
Average acreage per farm	146	245
Average value of farms	$860	$2,350
Total value of farm livestock	$6,647,969	$22,096,977
Average livestock value per farm	$374	$567
Bales of cotton	65,344	367,393
Bushels of corn	8,893,939	17,823,588
Pounds of tobacco	218,936	989,980
Pounds of rice	63,179	16,831

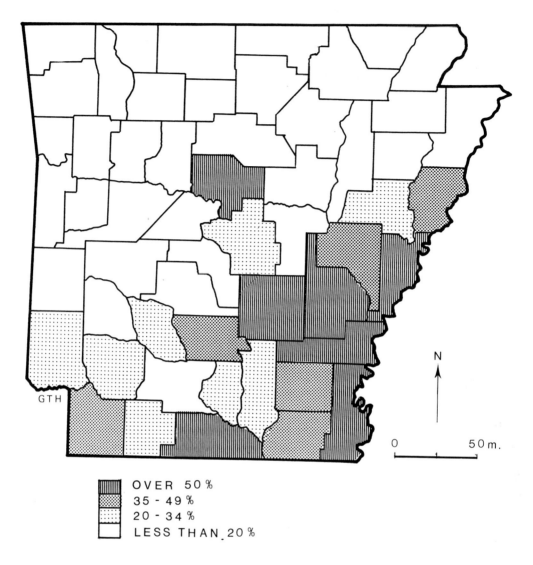

OVER 50 %
35 - 49 %
20 - 34 %
LESS THAN 20 %

By 1860, on the eve of the debate over secession, Arkansas's African American population was concentrated in the southern and eastern counties. The shaded areas indicate the percentage for each county. (Courtesy of Gerald T. Hanson, UALR)

Economic growth increased the state's tax base by one hundred million dollars. Conway left more than three hundred thousand dollars in gold and silver in the state treasury and vetoed a bill to reduce taxes that the General Assembly had passed.

But looming over all was the growing quarrel between the North and South, between free and slave states. Starting with a dispute over the status of slavery in the new lands obtained from Mexico, the fight grew harsher and more intense throughout the decade. Border states such as Arkansas, as much western as southern, were being pushed closer to the point where they would have to choose sides.

Many Arkansans, particularly those in the

northwestern counties where there were very few slaves, were confused. They did not wish to cut off ties to the Union they had so proudly joined less than twenty-five years before. But the planters worked hard to create a **"Southern consciousness."** They made people feel they were not loyal if they bought goods from northern states or sent their young people east to school.

There were old divisions between northwest and southeast and between small farmer and planter in the state. Hard feelings grew stronger as people were swept up in the issues and emotions of the time. Arkansas would have to face the fateful election of 1860 and the need to choose whether to stay with the Union or secede.

*The federal government built a military **arsenal** in Arkansas at Little Rock during the early years of statehood. The main buildings are shown here at a later date. The property now belongs to the city of Little Rock and is known as MacArthur Park. The building to the left is now the MacArthur Museum of Arkansas Military History.* (Courtesy of the MacArthur Museum of Arkansas Military History)

VOCABULARY

arsenal (AHR-suh-nuhl) storage or repair place for firearms or other weapons.

assessor (uh-SES-er) one who determines the value of land or other property.

bolls (BOHLZ) the fruit of cotton plants that is picked and spun into cotton thread.

bonds (BAHNDZ) interest-bearing certificates of public or private indebtedness; a method of borrowing money.

capital money available for investment, construction, or expansion of business.

charter (CHAHR-ter) a guarantee of privilege granted by the power of a state or county.

chopping cotton hoeing rows of cotton to keep down weeds.

Common School Law setting aside of public lands for sale to raise cash to build schools.

compress (KAHM-prehs) a device that pressed loose cotton into bales.

constitution (KAHN-stih-TOO-shun) fundamental laws of a state or nation.

dogtrot popular pioneer style of home consisting of two square cabins connected by a breezeway.

dynasty (DIE-nuhss-tee) another name for the "Family," the Democratic power elite of territorial and early statehood days in Arkansas; in general, the term means a group of rulers related by birth or marriage.

elite a small, wealthy (or otherwise gifted), and powerful group of individuals.

excursion (ehks-KER-zhun) a short trip or voyage, usually for pleasure.

Forty-Niners gold hunters who traveled to California in the Gold Rush of 1849.

free state a state of the U.S. in which slavery was illegal.

hominy (HAH-mih-nee) hulled corn with the germ removed, from which grits are made.

itinerants (i-TIHN-er-uhnts) workers who travel, offering their services in one place and then moving on to the next.

Manifest Destiny the belief that Americans had a right to expand westward all the way to the Pacific coast.

overseer boss of a group of slaves, usually a white man.

plantation a very large farm devoted to production of one chief crop, such as cotton or sugar, associated with a slave labor force; a farm with at least a thousand acres and twenty slaves was considered a plantation.

privy (PRIH-vee) outdoor toilet or "outhouse."

receivership placing a bankrupt institution into the hands of new management, often appointed by a court.

slave state a state of the U.S. in which slavery was legal.

southern consciousness the belief that the southern way of life was distinct from and incompatible with the northern, Yankee way of life.

specie (SPEE-shee) hard currency, namely gold or silver, as opposed to paper money.

squatters (SKWAH-terz) residents on land who do not hold legal title to the land.

transport means of moving from one place to another.

wheelwright (HWEEL-rite) one who makes wheels.

yeoman (YOH-muhn) independent farmer; small farmer; family farmer.

STUDY QUESTIONS

1. What were the arguments for and against Arkansas becoming a state?

2. How was national politics involved in the decision to make Arkansas a state?

3. What was the compromise over representation in the new state constitution?

4. Describe the dramatic incident in the first session of the Arkansas legislature that left one representative dead.

5. Explain the similarities and differences between Democrats and Whigs.

6. Who were James Sevier Conway, Ambrose Sevier, and Archibald Yell?

7. Where did the new settlers in Arkansas come from?

8. Describe the differences between a "yeoman farmer" and a "planter."

9. Describe life under slavery for African Americans.

10. Tell about the role of Arkansans in the Mexican War.

5 Secession and Civil War

1860–1865

What to Look for in Chapter 5

This chapter covers only five years, from 1860 to 1865, but those are the years of secession and the Civil War.

As the argument over slavery and other aspects of the national union intensified, Arkansans were divided over the seriousness of the threat. But after the Republican Abraham Lincoln was elected president in 1860, some thought his election alone was reason to secede, while others suggested waiting for some act against the South. Arkansas first voted not to secede. Then the national government fired on a fort in South Carolina, and Lincoln called for soldiers to attack the South. In a second vote, Arkansas approved secession with only one dissenting vote.

The major battles in Arkansas were at Pea Ridge, Prairie Grove, and along the route of the Union's Red River Campaign. By the summer of 1863, the Union army controlled much of the state. The Confederate government fled to Washington in southwest Arkansas. Large parts of the state had no government at all, and were devastated by roving bandits.

After the Emancipation Proclamation of 1863, slaves were freed wherever the Union army advanced, including Arkansas.

THE UNION BREAKS APART

After more than a decade of national debate over slavery and other issues that tended to separate North and South, Arkansans were deeply divided and badly confused as they approached the fateful year 1860. Southern "fire-eaters" were talking about leaving the Union if those wishing to abolish slavery succeeded in electing a president of their choice in 1860. To secede might mean war, but many welcomed what they thought would be a brief war and a clear victory for southern arms.

In Arkansas the times were very unstable. In part this was due to the state's long-standing division between slave and nonslave areas. There had also been some recent political changes. The Whig Party had broken apart over the slavery question and vanished, leaving Arkansas Whigs without a home. Also, the Democratic "Family," strong for so long in Arkansas politics, was weaker than it had been in years.

A newcomer to Arkansas, Thomas C.

Thomas Hindman. (Courtesy of the Chicago Historical Society)

Hindman, challenged the Family's control of the state. Hindman was born in Tennessee, grew up in Mississippi, and moved to Helena in the 1850s. At first he was an ally of the Family. He broke away from them in the late 1850s, probably over **patronage** disputes. In the governor's campaign of 1860, he backed Henry Rector against the Family's Richard H. Johnson. Rector won.

Meanwhile, all eyes focused on the presidential race. In the spring of 1860, the Democratic Party split and nominated two candidates for president. Stephen A. Douglas of Illinois was the candidate of the regular Democrats. They still voiced a moderate position on the slavery issue. John C. Breckinridge

of Kentucky was the man for the states' rights Democrats. They maintained that the time had come for the southern states to insist on their rights, especially against the growing strength of the Republican Party.

The Republican Party faced the election with sure hopes of victory. The Republican Party had been formed in the 1850s out of several political factions in the northern states. The Republican Party stood for some policies that southerners had opposed, such as federal aid to railroads and a **homestead** law to give free land to settlers.

The Republican Party was also against extending slavery into the western lands. However, most members of the Republican

Governor Henry M. Rector. (Courtesy of the University of Arkansas, Fayetteville, Special Collections)

Party did not support **abolition,** the principle of immediately ending slavery in the southern states. The distinction between the two positions was neither very clear nor very important to many white southerners.

The Republican candidate for president was Abraham Lincoln of Illinois. Very little was known about him at the time. Many people assumed he would be a tool of the more radical elements of his party, who tended to favor **abolition.** The important thing in 1860 was that the Republicans were convinced that Lincoln could be elected on the vote of northern states alone. This was because the northern states had a larger population than the southern states. Lincoln did not intend to campaign in the South and was not even on the ballot in the southern states.

To further confuse matters, a group of former Whigs put up John Bell of Tennessee for president. His platform asked only that everyone follow the Constitution and maintain the Union.

In Arkansas the race appeared to go along strict party lines, or at least along what was left of the old party lines. Hindman, along with the leaders of the Family, viewed Breckinridge as the true Democratic candidate. The old Whigs thought of Bell as a revival of their party. The vote in Arkansas was Breckinridge, 28,783 votes; Bell, 20,094; and Douglas, 5,227. There were no votes cast for Lincoln in the state.

Lincoln won the national election. He got more popular votes than any of the other three men, and he carried 18 free states to win a clear victory with 180 votes in the **electoral college.** Lincoln did not get any southern votes. Breckinridge carried Arkansas and 10 other slave states, but he had only 72 electoral votes. In fact, the North had elected a president.

THE MOVEMENT FOR SECESSION

Now the question facing the slave states was this. Did the election of Lincoln in itself mean that the South would have to **secede** from, or leave, the Union? Some said it did. Others said the South should wait until the new president really did something against the wishes of the South. Few argued about the right to **secede.** The Southern doctrine of states' rights had long been held as a means to justify secession.

Most Arkansans at first took the wait-and-see stance. Some, including Johnson and Hindman, urged prompt action. When Governor Rector spoke to the General Assembly soon after the election, he took a fairly moderate tone. However, he did warn Arkansans that they might soon have to choose between "the Union without slavery, or slavery without the Union."

South Carolina was the first to make that choice. It seceded late in December of 1860. Mississippi, Florida, and Alabama joined it early in January of 1861.

Still Arkansas was reluctant to act. Demands for quick action from southern and eastern counties were matched by pleas for caution and patience from northern and western counties. The General Assembly's answer, put forward on January 15, 1861, was to call for a vote of the people. On February 18, there would be a statewide election. The people would vote on whether or not to hold a secession convention, and at the same time they would select delegates to the convention.

Meanwhile Georgia, Louisiana, and Texas also left the Union. The seven states that had **seceded** so far met in Montgomery, Alabama, early in February. They formed a government, the Confederate States of America, and elected a president, Jefferson Davis of Mississippi.

coming
eir own
sembled
S. Army
ler, Cap-
prevent
...ay with
...eave the

7,412 to
...s seces-
...e mostly
...nted to
17,927
further
...eration-

ists" or "**Conditionalists**") got a total of 23,626 votes.

The convention met on March 4, the same day Lincoln was sworn in as president. The moderates were in control by a slim margin. Judge David Walker of Fayetteville, a Unionist, was chosen to preside. After two weeks of debate, the group turned down the chance to **secede** by a vote of thirty-nine to thirty-five.

They also called for a new vote of the people to be held directly on the question of secession, to be held in August. That vote never took place.

In the harbor at Charleston, South Carolina, Fort Sumter stood as a symbol of national authority. South Carolina demanded its

Judge David Walker.
(Courtesy of the UALR Archives and Special Collections)

Fort Smith sits quietly above the river, shortly after Confederates occupied it early in the Civil War. The picture is from the London Illustrated News *of May 25, 1861. (Courtesy of the University of Arkansas, Fayetteville, Special Collections)*

surrender. Lincoln refused to give it up. When a U.S. Navy ship tried to supply the fort with food, the South Carolinians fired upon it. It was the first shot of the Civil War.

Lincoln declared that an **"insurrection"** was taking place and asked for seventy-five thousand volunteer soldiers. They came, and more besides. The North would fight to preserve the Union.

In Arkansas Governor Rector refused Lincoln's request for volunteers. He said, "The people of this commonwealth are freemen, not slaves, and will defend to the last extrem-

ity their honor, lives, and property against Northern **mendacity** and **usurpation."**

The issue in Arkansas and the other slave states in the Union was now clear. If it is war, which side are you on? As Virginia, Tennessee, and North Carolina acted to **secede,** the Arkansas convention met once again.

David Walker, now on the side of the Confederacy himself, called the group back into session at the state house on May 6, 1861. After a few hours of talk, all but five men voted to **secede.** Walker called for a second ballot to make the vote **unanimous.**

Only one man, Isaac Murphy of Madison County, refused to change his vote to stay with the Union. The other members were angry at him. But Mrs. Frederick Trapnall of Little Rock threw him a bouquet of flowers from the upstairs gallery to honor the courage he showed in sticking with his beliefs.

How long and how difficult a path Arkansas had chosen would only be revealed in the brutal years to come.

PREPARING FOR WAR

In those first heady days, young men in Arkansas, like young men all over the country, scrambled to get into the action. They feared the war would be over before they could get their share of the glory and thrills. It was common to hear southerners talk about "one big battle" that would whip the Yankees once and for all. The first volunteers signed up for three months, because that was as long as it was supposed to take.

In almost all Arkansas towns, military companies formed, chose their officers, and picked fancy names. Arkansas had the Hempstead Hornets, the Tyronza Rebels, the Polk County Invincibles, the Camden Knights, the Montgomery Hunters, and the Muddy Bayou Heroes. Some units had uniforms, boasting dressy militia costumes. Some just showed up in their everyday homespun. The men brought their own weapons, a mixture of rifles, muskets, shotguns, and Bowie knives.

The women created bright flags, made uniforms, and urged the men on. If a young man was too slow to sign up, the women sent him a petticoat, a symbol that he was not a real man.

Before it was all over, about sixty thousand Arkansas men would serve, at one time or another, in the Confederate armies. That was more than one-third of the adult white male population of Arkansas in 1860.

Some joined army units from other states, but most served in Arkansas units. The state raised thirty-six **infantry** regiments, fifteen **cavalry** regiments, and thirteen **artillery batteries.** Most of these (for example, twenty-six of the **infantry** regiments) served outside the state.

The First Arkansas Infantry Regiment formed and moved out in time to be at the first battle of Bull Run (or Manassas) in Virginia in July. They were not actually in combat that day, however. The regiment did see action at Shiloh, Tennessee, in April 1862, losing thirty men in the bloody fighting

The Third Arkansas **Infantry** Regiment joined the Army of Northern Virginia before the Seven Days' Battle in July 1862. They stayed there through the surrender at Appomattox in April 1865. When Company H of the Third Arkansas stacked its rifles at Appomattox, only seven men were left.

As the war dragged on, the enthusiasm for volunteering lessened. The Confederacy started drafting soldiers in the spring of 1862. Every healthy white male from the age of eighteen to thirty-five was required to serve. The draft law did exempt some, such as managers of plantations with more than twenty slaves. The draft served to encourage volunteering, because men who volunteered got to choose their units. A Confederate **infantry** private, when he was paid at all, received eleven dollars a month.

Sixteen Arkansans reached the rank of general in the Confederate army. The best known was Patrick Cleburne, said to be the best division commander in the Army of Tennessee. This was the Confederacy's main army in the Western Theater. Born in Ireland but living in Helena, General Cleburne led a brigade at Shiloh. Later, he was promoted to command a division.

General Cleburne offered a novel plan in 1863. He suggested that the Confederacy ought to arm slaves as soldiers, giving freedom to any African Americans who would fight for the South.

Cleburne's troops repelled General William T. Sherman for an entire day at Chattanooga's Missionary Ridge. He was killed in December 1864 at Franklin, Tennessee. This was a battle that cost the Confederacy the lives of five of its generals in one day.

In keeping with the pre-war social and political factions in the state, 8,289 white Arkansans served in the Union army. That was more than any other Confederate state

A Guide to Some Civil War Terms

Many Civil War battles have two names, one favored by the Union forces and the other used by Confederate forces. For instance, the first and second Battles of Manassas (the name of a town) are also known as the first and second Battles of Bull Run (a creek). In Arkansas, the Battle of Pea Ridge is sometimes referred to as the Battle of Elkhorn Tavern, named after a nearby building. Other examples are Antietam (a creek) and Sharpsburg (a town), Shiloh (a church building) and Pittsburgh Landing (a town).

The name of the entire war has also been a subject for debate. The Civil War is the most common expression. But the national government, in its official history of the war, used the term the War of the Rebellion. Southerners have used several names, ranging from the War Between the States to the War for States Rights to the War to End Yankee Arrogance.

During the war, people came to be familiar with the "theaters," or major regions, of war. The Eastern Theater was the area east of the Appalachian Mountains, and most of the battles were fought in Virginia. The Western Theater was the area between the Appalachians and the Mississippi River. Arkansas, along with Louisiana and Texas, was in the Trans-Mississippi Theater, the area west of the Mississippi River.

Civil War military units varied a great deal in their size. Roughly, an **infantry** company was fifty or a hundred men. A unit of the same size in the **cavalry** was called a company or a troop, and a unit of the same size in the **artillery** was called a **battery.** Officers at this level were lieutenants and captains.

Several companies together made up a regiment, which was supposed to be about a thousand men but in the Civil War was usually much less. Officers at the regimental level, or field-grade officers, were majors, lieutenant colonels, and colonels.

Several **infantry** regiments, along with supporting **cavalry** and **artillery** units, could be organized into a brigade. A general officer (brigadier general) commanded at this level.

Finally, both sides organized brigades into corps (pronounced "cores") and corps into armies, commanded by major generals and lieutenant generals. Neither side had one single overall military commander of all its armies until the very last of the war. Then, Ulysses S. Grant of the Union and Robert E. Lee of the Confederacy were given those positions.

General Patrick Cleburne of Helena, Army of the Confederate States of America. (Courtesy of the Chicago Historical Society)

except Tennessee. One of these, First Sergeant William Ellis of the Third Wisconsin Cavalry, was the first Arkansan to win the Medal of Honor. In a skirmish at Dardanelle, he held his position even after being wounded three times.

More than 5,500 African American Arkansans also joined the Union forces, in **infantry**, **cavalry**, and **artillery** units. The army put the former slaves into all-black units with white officers. The black soldiers were proud members of regiments such as the U.S. First Arkansas, African Descent.

THE FIRST FIGHTING

In the spring of 1861, the "Arkansas army" gathered under the command of Governor Rector and a board of officers. In haste and confusion, the state was trying to provide weapons and supplies and get the army organized. No one was very sure about what to do first, but there were plenty of rumors. The Yankees were going to invade, or the slaves were going to revolt, or something equally exciting was going to happen.

As it turned out, Missouri would set the stage for the first major battle for Arkansas. The people of Missouri were seriously divided over the war. Unionists managed to stay in control of Missouri, but there were enough Confederate supporters to create their own civil war within the state. The future of Missouri was important. It could be a major addition to either side.

The pro-southern forces in Missouri called for help, and Arkansas and the Confederacy answered. In the late summer of 1861, three groups gathered to invade Missouri: the

Letters to Home from Arkansas Soldiers in Virginia

Most of the soldiers from Arkansas were ordinary men who believed in what they were doing and did the best job they could. The conditions of their lives in camp were hard, and they missed their families. Here are letters home from two of the four Butler brothers of Tulip, Arkansas (Dallas County), to their sister Emma Butler. The Butler boys were with the Confederate army in Virginia.

Lewis Butler wrote Emma three weeks after the first Battle of Bull Run (Manassas):

Camp Alleghany, Va.
August 12, 1861

Last night was Sunday night, a night always commemorated by you all by singing the sacred melodies which have been hymned in our house since childhood. Billy Paisley, Dunkan Durham, Mr. Jones and myself gathered around one of our camp fires and made the camp ring with some of the same good old songs which we have learned to love for their very age, and which I doubt not you were singing in that same hour. I remembered you all then, and imagination showed me the lighted parlor, and my ear caught the sound of my mother's voice as she sang the treble to some of those time honored songs, and my heart ran out in sighs that I might be permitted once again to be with you all at home, dear home. . . .
It is now growing late at night, it has been raining hard upon our tents for hours and many a sick soldier is now suffering and moaning as the rain borne on the wind beat upon the thin covering above him and sends the damp to his weakened and languishing frame. . . .

Tomorrow we leave here to go in the neighborhood of our enemies, and in a short time we expect to meet and conquer them. How pleasant it would be to be with you all this Summer enjoying the luxuries of the season, but we willingly yield up this when a more important work calls us away, and if we can be instrumental in speedily establishing our government in peace and prosperity we shall be content.

George Butler's letter to Emma was written just after the terrible series of battles called the Wilderness, Spotsylvania, and Cold Harbor. General U. S. Grant's Army of the Potomac was battering General Robert E. Lee's Army of Northern Virginia:

near Richmond
June 9, 1864

We have been fighting in Va. more or less every day for one entire month, and still the fighting continues. Cannon are now booming in the distance. Bro. Henry is still safe. He had one horse killed under him. You just ought to be thankful to God that none of your brothers have been killed in so many battles. I have heard (indirectly) from brother Charlie. He is certainly in Ft. Delaware [Yankee prison in Maryland], and is well. . . .

Our soldiers have fought well since the commencement of these fights. Gen. Lee, by the blessing of God, has not been driven from any position he has taken. . . . Our loss has been very small in comparison with that of the enemy. They have lost four or five times as many men as we have. Thousands of them were left unburied on the field of battle. The inhumanity of Gen. Grant to his own men, well, wounded, and killed is beyond question. Our men are in good spirits and never more confident of success.

Elizabeth Paisley Huckaby and Ethel C. Simpson, eds., *Tulip Evermore: Emma Butler and William Paisley: Their Lives in Letters, 1857–1887* (Fayetteville: University of Arkansas Press, 1985), pp. 26, 43.

Arkansas army under General N. B. Pearce, a Confederate force under the former Texas Ranger General Ben McCulloch, and the Missouri soldiers under General Sterling Price. In the total force there were about 12,000 men, 2,200 of them Arkansans.

These were still amateur armies, poorly equipped, poorly trained, and poorly organized. The three generals disliked each other and could not agree on a battle plan. They stumbled toward a place called Wilson's Creek in southwest Missouri near Springfield, 40 miles north of the Arkansas border. Near there was a small Union army, about 5,400 men led by General Nathaniel Lyon.

They met at the Battle of Wilson's Creek on August 10, 1861. All morning the two armies fought each other, more than 17,000 men on a field just a half-mile wide. Some broke and ran, but most stayed and fought.

They were learning their new trade the hard way.

The Arkansas troops had with them some of the cannon from the Little Rock arsenal. Though they did not know it, in command of an **artillery battery** on the other side was Captain James Totten, formerly of the Little Rock Arsenal.

The total **casualties**—the number of men killed, wounded, or missing—were about 1,300 on the northern side and about 1,200 on the southern side. It was one of the bloodiest days of the war in view of the number of soldiers involved.

Wilson's Creek was also an early example of an indecisive battle. In one sense, the Confederates won. The Union army left, leaving the Confederates in control of the field. But the Confederates were too weak and disorganized to follow up on their victory. The

The color guard for one of Arkansas's African American Union army units, with (on the left) *its fife-and-drum corps.* (Courtesy of the Arkansas Historical Commission)

three parts of the southern army went their separate ways, and the Arkansas soldiers headed back to their home state. Missouri was still controlled by Unionists.

BATTLE OF PEA RIDGE

Early in 1862, events in Missouri again called Arkansans back into action. Federal forces led by General Samuel R. Curtis pushed General Sterling Price's Missouri Confederates out of the state into northwest Arkansas. Curtis followed them, moving into Arkansas.

Price's Missourians rallied with General Ben McCulloch's Confederate army in the Boston Mountains. They were about seventy miles south of the Missouri border. Price and McCulloch, as usual, quarreled with each other about what to do next.

At that point, the Confederacy sent a new general to take command in Arkansas. He was General Earl Van Dorn, a West Point graduate with a good record in the Indian wars and the Mexican War. His orders were to invade Missouri, but first he had to deal with the threat to Arkansas.

Under Van Dorn's command, Price and

The artist caught the early stages of the Battle of Pea Ridge, as the Confederates (on the right) charge toward the Union defensive position. During the Civil War, artists on the battlefield made quick sketches which others turned into finished drawings, like this one. The method allowed newspapers and magazines to give their readers news pictures quickly.
(Courtesy of the University of Central Arkansas Archives)

At the Battle of Pea Ridge, General Frantz Sigel (center) *led one division of the Union army. A native of Germany and a graduate of the German military academy, he came to the United States as part of the great wave of German immigrants in the 1840s. A resident of Missouri, he helped encourage German immigrants in that divided state to remain loyal to the Union.* (Courtesy of the Chicago Historical Society)

McCulloch began to work together. They chose to attack Curtis, who had only about 10,500 soldiers. The Confederate forces in northwest Arkansas had about 15,000 men on hand to fight. Within this group was one of the war's most unusual units, the Confederate Indian brigade. Arkansas's Albert Pike was now General Pike, Confederate commissioner to the Indians in Oklahoma. He had convinced some of the Indians to fight with the South, and now he led two regiments of Cherokees.

Van Dorn ordered his army northward toward the Federal army. They marched for days in cold and wet snow. Some loyal Unionists from Fayetteville rode north to warn

Curtis that the Confederates were coming. Curtis placed his outnumbered troops in a defensive position to meet the attack.

The Union army was just inside the Arkansas border, on the main road to Missouri. It was called the Telegraph Road or the Stagecoach Road. The road ran past the Elkhorn Tavern stage stop, through a long low hill called Pea Ridge. Curtis had his army lined up facing south along Little Sugar Creek, with the ridge behind them. The Confederate army moved into place in front of them, so close they could see each other's campfires.

Van Dorn had a daring plan. The night of March 6 he ordered the soldiers to leave their campfires burning to fool the enemy. Then he moved his army out on a night march, around Curtis's forces, to come up behind the Union army and attack from the north. But during the night the Confederate army split apart. When morning came on March 7, Van Dorn and Price were north of Curtis with about half the army, and McCulloch and Pike were about two miles away to the west with the other half.

The battle of Pea Ridge (or Elkhorn Tavern) opened in the middle of the morning. Van Dorn attacked Curtis from the north, and McCulloch attacked from the west. The attack in the west collapsed when McCulloch was killed. Meanwhile, to General Pike's horror, the Confederate Indians scalped eight of the Federals and murdered others after they were wounded. On the other part of the battlefield, Van Dorn and Price's troops fought hard all day, but could not break the Federal lines.

Both armies slept that night around Elkhorn Tavern. The next morning the Federals attacked and forced the Confederates to retreat. The Union army lost 1,384 men, counting all those killed, wounded, and missing. The Confederates lost nearly 2,000 men. The Federal army still controlled the road to Missouri and the Confederate army in Arkansas was in disarray.

Pea Ridge was the largest battle fought west of the Mississippi River. The Federal victory there meant that the Confederacy had to give up any hope of winning Missouri. Now Arkansas was open to Federal attack.

Things were not going well for the Confederacy elsewhere in the Mississippi River valley that spring of 1862. The Union army captured Forts Henry and Donelson in February to open the Kentucky and Tennessee rivers to attack. The Federals defeated a Confederate army at Shiloh in April. Then they captured New Orleans in April and Memphis in June. Only Vicksburg held out as a major Confederate stronghold on the Mississippi River.

WAR IN ARKANSAS

General Curtis led his army from Pea Ridge across north Arkansas to Batesville. From there, in the summer of 1862, he moved south to Helena. The Union soldiers stripped the land bare of food, horses, and firewood as

A second and later view of the Battle of Pea Ridge, from the New York Illustrated News *of March 29, 1862, shows the Confederate army abandoning the battlefield, toward the left.* (Courtesy of the University of Arkansas, Fayetteville, Special Collections)

Elkhorn Tavern—here as it looked some years after the Civil War—saw some of the hardest fighting of the Battle of Pea Ridge. (Photo by John Bledsoe, Courtesy of the University of Arkansas at Fayetteville Special Collections)

they went. At Cache River, near Cotton Plant, a small battle took place on July 7. The Federals easily defeated a small force of Confederate **cavalry** that tried to block the road to Helena.

Governor Rector was convinced that the Confederacy had abandoned Arkansas. He was so upset that he threatened to recommend that Arkansas **secede** from the Confederacy to become a free-standing state. The Confederacy sent Thomas C. Hindman, now a general, to take control of events in Arkansas.

Hindman was deadly serious and took a "total war" approach that shocked even the

most loyal Confederates in Arkansas. He took money, weapons, medical supplies, and men wherever he could find them. He encouraged the cruel, uncontrolled **guerilla** fighters in the mountains.

Hindman put the state under **martial law**, placing army officers, instead of elected public officials, in charge of affairs. He shot alleged deserters without a trial. He brought in all the cotton he could find so that it could be burned instead of letting it fall into the hands of the enemy.

Hindman strengthened Arkansas for the Confederacy, but his methods lost him the

Campaigning in Arkansas

For most soldiers with the Confederate forces in Arkansas, the war was a lot of waiting broken by small skirmishes and raids.

This is part of a letter from William Wakefield Garner of Quitman, who was a lieutenant in a "Home Guard" mounted **infantry** company. His company served mostly in central Arkansas, but in 1863 it was part of a raid into Union-occupied Missouri. The letter was written after the raiders were back in Arkansas.

> Greene County, Ark.
> 30 miles East Powhatan
> May 6th, 1863
>
> The enemy followed us from Cape Girardeau [Missouri] to St. Francis River, over 100 miles. We fought them every day for 7 days. When we could make a stand they would not attack us, but made their attack while [we were] on march. They surprised us once by **calvary** [*sic*] raid, run into our lines while we stopped to cook. . . . If I should always feel as I did then I will never suffer from fear. We killed many a Blue Coat and think got but 5 killed. . . .
>
> We took a decided stand at Bloomfield, stayed on the battlefield 24 hours: lay on our arms all night without fire. Suffice to say we made a speedy and successful retreat: but the trip or raid I look on as a complete failure, done but little less than rob and steal from friend and foe alike. In some instances took the last horse, bushel of corn, lb. of bacon from women and their husbands in our army. Took all the horses on the way. Took mares from young colts. I think the Federals do not do worse than we have done. . . .
>
> I have stood this trip very well. I had sore eyes a few days very badly caused for want of sleep and exposure. I did without sleep, only what I got on my horse for 60 hours. We did without anything to eat except some corn burnt on the cob and 2 small slices of bacon. . . . We bake bread on a board and broil our meat and think we are doing well. . . .

"Documents: . . . Letters of an Arkansas Confederate Soldier," *Arkansas Historical Quarterly*, II (March 1943), pp. 69–70.

support of the Arkansas people. Albert Pike was a very vocal critic of Hindman, and he was arrested for his efforts.

The Union renewed the attack on Arkansas, again from the northwest, with a small army led by General James G. Blunt. Hindman responded by marching across the Boston Mountains to meet the Federal troops at Prairie Grove, southwest of Fayetteville, on December 7, 1862. Each side had about 10,000 men, but the Confederates had the advantage of fighting from a defensive position on top of a hill.

The battle was very intense and losses were very heavy considering the number of troops involved. The Federals lost 1,251 men killed, wounded, and missing. The Confederates suffered the loss of well over 1,300

These people are modern-day Arkansans who remember the Civil War by recreating the clothing, equipment, and weapons of the time. A Civil War artillery piece and crew must have looked very much like this. They are at Prairie Grove Battlefield State Park for "Civil War Days." (Courtesy of Robyn Horn, Arkansas Dept. of Parks and Tourism)

men, and maybe many more who were never counted. Once again, as at Pea Ridge, the Federals won a hard fought victory. Hindman's army retreated all the way to Little Rock. Union soldiers pursued his troops, raiding Van Buren and destroying supplies.

On January 10–11, 1863, a force of 33,000 Union troops routed a defending force of 4,500 Confederate troops at Arkansas Post. This opened the way to Little Rock. In July 1863, in an effort to divert Union pressure on Vicksburg, a Confederate force tried to retake Helena. They failed and suffered heavy losses.

The attack on Helena came the same day that Vicksburg fell, July 4.

The capital city at Little Rock was now exposed to capture. The Confederate government of Arkansas fled the city and moved to Washington in the southwest part of the state. Meeting little resistance, General Frederick Steele led Federal troops into the city in September of 1863. Fort Smith fell to a Union army coming out of Indian Territory the same month, and the entire Arkansas valley was in Union hands.

The Civil War in Arkansas and Elsewhere

This is a chronology (a list in the order they happened) of the major battles and other events of the Civil War. Those events that happened in Arkansas or that directly involved Arkansas are listed in boldface.

1860

November	Lincoln elected president
December	South Carolina secedes

1861

January	Mississippi, Florida, Alabama, Georgia, Louisiana secede
February	Texas secedes
March	Lincoln inaugurated president
April	Fort Sumter surrenders; Lincoln calls for troops
May	Virginia, **Arkansas**, Tennessee, North Carolina secede
July	Battle of First Manassas
August	**Battle of Wilson's Creek**

1862

February	Battle of Forts Henry and Donelson
March	**Battle of Pea Ridge**
	Monitor and the *Merrimac* (the *C.S.S. Virginia*) sea battle
April	Battle of Shiloh
	Battle of New Orleans
May–July	**Union forces capture Batesville, Helena**
June	Battle of Memphis
March–July	Peninsular Campaign, including Seven Days' Battle
August	Battle of Second Manassas
September	Battle of Antietam
October	Battle of Perryville
December	**Battle of Prairie Grove**
	Battle of Fredericksburg

1863

January	Emancipation Proclamation
	Union forces capture Arkansas Post
May	Battle of Chancellorsville
July	Battle of Gettysburg
	Battle of Vicksburg
	Battle of Helena
September	**Union forces capture Fort Smith**
	Union forces capture Little Rock
	Battle of Chickamauga
November	Battle of Chattanooga

1864

April	Red River Campaign
	Battles of Poison Spring, Marks' Mill, Jenkins' Ferry
May–June	Grant in Virginia: Battles of Wilderness, Spotsylvania, Cold Harbor, siege of Petersburg
September	Atlanta falls to the Union
November	Lincoln re-elected president
November–December	Sherman's "March to the Sea" through Georgia
December	Battles of Franklin and Nashville

1865

January–March	Sherman's march through the Carolinas
April	Lee surrenders at Appomattox
	Assassination of Lincoln
	Confederate eastern and western armies surrender
June	Confederate Trans-Mississippi armies surrender

STEELE'S SOUTHERN CAMPAIGN

There would be one more Civil War campaign in Arkansas. In the spring of 1864, the Union army planned the Red River Campaign. The goal was to take Shreveport, Louisiana, a center of the cotton trade and headquarters of the Confederate forces west of the Mississippi River. The main Federal army advanced northward from Alexandria toward Shreveport. General Steele, in Arkansas, was ordered to meet the approaching Federal troops at Shreveport.

With little in the way to stop him, Steele moved south from Little Rock with a small army of five thousand men. They took over Camden, a trade center and manufacturing town. Meanwhile, the major Union advance in the Red River valley had been turned back at Mansfield, leaving the Confederates free to focus on Steele. At Camden, Steele was short of supplies.

He sent seven hundred men, including the five hundred men of the First Kansas Colored Infantry, to find food for his soldiers. A Confederate force of Arkansas, Texas, and Indian troops met them at Poison Spring. The Confederates almost wiped out the Union force, and they were accused of shooting wounded black soldiers.

Steele now had to depend on supplies

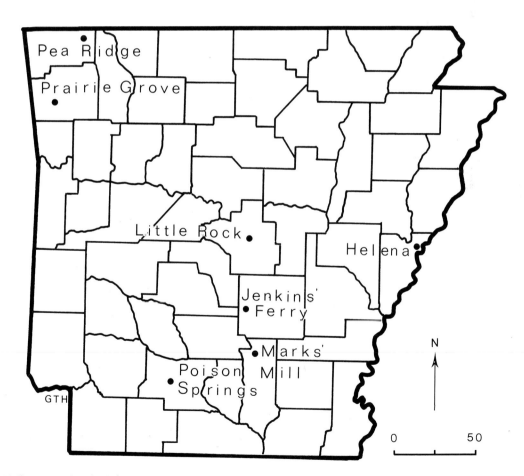

Civil War Action in Arkansas. (Courtesy of Gerald T. Hanson, UALR)

from Pine Bluff, but at the Battle of Marks' Mill the Confederates captured his supply train. That meant Steele had to leave Camden and return to Little Rock. On the way, Steele's men slowed down trying to cross the Saline River at Jenkins' Ferry. A force of ten thousand Confederates attacked them there, but the Federals managed to fight them off and escaped to Little Rock.

That was the last of the organized fighting in Arkansas. In the same spring of 1864, General U. S. Grant in Virginia and General William T. Sherman in Tennessee began to move south against the remaining Confederate armies. These were the final campaigns of the war.

LIFE IN WARTIME

The impact of the war was very different on the North than on the South. In the North, where there was more industry, the war demands on factories of all kinds increased production and fed a growing economy. The northern states emerged from the conflict with a streamlined and efficient industrial complex ready to compete on a world scale.

In the South, however, there was little industry to begin with. What commerce there was came to a halt with the first firing of guns. The few supplies the South could provide to its armies came from captured Federal goods or straight from people's homes.

David O. Dodd The "Boy Hero" of Arkansas

David O. Dodd was seventeen years old in 1863. He had spent the early war years traveling with his father, who had business dealings in several southern states. They eventually came back to Camden, which was in Confederate hands. Dodd decided, late in 1863, to visit friends in Little Rock, then occupied by Union troops under the command of General Frederick Steele.

As Dodd was leaving Little Rock to return to Camden, a Union patrol stopped him, searched his clothes, and discovered a paper with mysterious markings. The marks turned out to be Morse code, which Dodd had learned when he worked in a telegraph office. The code could be interpreted as a list of the numbers and locations of Union forces in Little Rock.

Dodd was arrested and charged with spying, specifically with carrying military information for the Confederate forces in Camden. A court martial—a Union army court—found him guilty and sentenced him to death by hanging.

Although many Little Rock residents pleaded with General Steele for mercy on the grounds of Dodd's age, Steele said Dodd had been found guilty and would have to pay the penalty. One version of the story says that Steele did offer Dodd his freedom if he would name the person who gave him the military information, but Dodd refused to tell.

Dodd was executed on January 8, 1864.

Thus Arkansas acquired a Civil War martyr. David O. Dodd became the "boy hero" of the Confederacy, although many "boys" of seventeen were serving in the armies on both sides. A monument to Dodd stands near Little Rock's MacArthur Park.

An unidentified African American Arkansan in Union army uniform. The portrait photographer may have posed the man's head behind a painting of a uniform. (Courtesy of the Arkansas History Commission)

The women of Arkansas took on the kind of work that was being done by entire factories in the North. They carded, spun, wove, and dyed cloth at heroic levels of production. They turned out uniforms, blankets, and bandages for an entire army. There were some sewing machines at that time, but most of the work was done by hand.

Keeping the armies supplied with boots was another matter. The few shoe factories that did exist were faced with a shortage of leather, and Arkansas soldiers sometimes fought despite bare and bleeding feet.

With the men off to war, the women maintained their typical roles while also taking over the men's jobs. They managed businesses and farms, harvested the crops, and, in some areas, tried to manage the black slaves. Some slaves stayed to serve their owners, while many others ran away.

Women also smuggled food and medicine to the soldiers, sometimes hiding them under their clothes. They cared for the sick and wounded, buried the dead, and tried to raise their children.

Women also had to defend their homes and fields. Both Union and Confederate armies on the march had need of food, and they took it where they could find it, even if the citizens were starving. The women in many northern counties drew together from the country into villages where they could find greater safety in numbers. Wives of Union and Confederate soldiers sounded the alarm for one another when strangers approached. If the strangers were Confederate, a Confederate wife went out to plead with them to leave them alone. If the troops were Union, the wife of a Union soldier would do the same.

Almost as soon as the war began, south-erners suffered a severe shortage of salt and coffee. Salt was needed to preserve meat, and the armies were lost without it. Civilians in Arkansas opened salt works long since shut down as obsolete. In the northern counties a family retrieved what salt they could from the floor of their smokehouse. To replace coffee, people tried all kinds of substitutes, such as acorn coffee.

Food was in short supply too. Efforts were made to convert cotton plantations to fields of grain to feed those at home and the armies. Even when food was grown, the breakdown of transportation often kept it from getting to where it was needed.

The worst thing that could happen to a soldier was to fall ill. A trip to an army hospital during the Civil War was very often followed by a trip to an early grave. Many more soldiers died of disease than died in battle. The extreme shortage of food greatly increased the men's chances of getting sick.

In Arkansas, there was added danger because of the shortage of medicines. **Morphine** was used to kill pain. Without it, a man might have to have his arm or leg sawed off while fully awake. Another very important medicine in the South was **quinine,** or Peruvian bark. This was needed to fight the fevers of malaria so common to the region. **Quinine** had to be brought in from South America, and supplies were used up very quickly.

Measles, mumps, and **dysentery** from bad water supplies, and smallpox, malaria, and flu were greater enemies than the Yankees. Caring for the wounded and burying the dead were tasks that women of local areas in which battles were fought helped the armies perform. After the battle of Prairie Grove, for instance, the entire city of Fayetteville became one big hospital.

GOVERNMENT IN WARTIME

The new Confederate state constitution, written in 1861, called for an election for governor in 1862. Henry Rector claimed that he should complete the four-year term he began in 1860, but the state Supreme Court ordered a new election. Rector ran for governor again. Because Rector was widely blamed for Arkansas's slow progress in getting ready for war, he was beaten with ease by Harris Flanagin of Arkadelphia. A former Whig, Flanagin was a colonel with the Second Arkansas Mounted Rifle Regiment. He was serving with the Confederate Army of Tennessee.

Less than a year after his election, Flanagin led the Confederate state government out of Little Rock to the town of Washington in southwest Arkansas. He moved the capital to avoid capture by the Federals when Little Rock fell in September of 1863. For the rest of the war, the Confederate state government was run from Washington.

Meanwhile, late in 1863, President Lincoln issued a Proclamation of Amnesty and Reconstruction, a preview of his "soft" Reconstruction plan to come. Lincoln asked for a promise of future loyalty to the Union from a group of voters in a state equal to 10 percent of the people who voted in 1860. Then those voters could elect a Unionist state government.

Governor Isaac Murphy.
(Courtesy of the University of Arkansas, Fayetteville, Special Collections)

This was done in Arkansas early in 1864. In an election with only twelve thousand voters, Isaac Murphy was elected Union governor of Arkansas. He was the man who had refused to change his vote at the secession convention in 1861.

In fact, Confederate Governor Flanagin controlled little beyond south Arkansas. Union Governor Murphy controlled little beyond those areas occupied by the Union army. Among the Union cities were Little Rock, Pine Bluff, Helena, Fort Smith, and DeVall's Bluff (the end of the railroad link to Memphis).

Most of Arkansas was a no-man's land, at the mercy of ruthless **guerilla** fighters, deserters, and outlaws. They were known as **"jayhawkers"** or **"bushwhackers."** Some of these claimed to belong to one of the armies, but most were just plain outlaws. The lack of law and order also drew other bandits from Texas, Missouri, and Kansas. Among the outlaws who got their start in wartime Arkansas were the James brothers, the Younger brothers, and the Dalton gang. They kept up their reign of terror long after the war was over.

Many times, the **bushwhacker** raids were made by neighbor upon neighbor. In the mountain counties of north Arkansas, many

Simon Sager was an early settler in the Siloam Springs area, a German immigrant for whom Sager Creek was named. He and his brother Christian gained renown as cabinetmakers. They made this bureau with mirror of yellow pine sometime before the Civil War. During 1864, when bands of outlaws roamed the Arkansas hills, the Sagers' shop was robbed, and Simon was murdered by the robbers. (Courtesy of the Siloam Springs Museum)

places were split in their loyalties: some families were loyal to the Union side and some families supported the Confederacy. Great bitterness and hatred arose between some of these families. Many Union supporters were forced to flee to the North or to Texas, leaving their Arkansas homes behind. Others kept up family feuds for many years.

Nearly every family north of the Arkansas River had a **bushwhacker** story to tell. In one case, Nancy Morton Staples of Washington County watched while her father's feet were burned by robbers who wanted their money. She threw water on the hot shovels the bushwhackers were using to burn her father. One stuck a pistol in her face, and she was beaten until she was black and blue. But when the men tried to put hot coals on her father's body, she was ready again and threw water on the fire, putting it out. Only when the **bushwhackers** choked her mother and threatened to hang her father did the family reveal where their money was hidden.

One man described this life in a letter to his soldier son. "I tell you," he wrote in 1864, "this country has gone up . . . both sides emulate each other in robbing, killing, and destroying. Whatever you do, my son, do not come home; your safest place is in the regular army."

One place where things seemed to work out was the city of Fayetteville. The stresses of the war at first turned the "pleasant and genial little town . . . into a hamlet of suspicion." The advances and retreats of armies from both Pea Ridge and Prairie Grove, however, had an effect. The town changed hands so often that "the citizens of different views [grew] extremely tolerant of each other—neither party knew how long the other might be in the **ascendancy;** and though the warmth of former friendship was neither felt nor expressed, the bitterness of past **enmity** was, if not forgotten, at least restrained."

THE END OF SLAVERY

Arkansas African Americans were at the center of the war from its start to its finish. As the war began, slave owners hoped their slaves would remain loyal but feared revolt. Some slaves did stay through the troubled times, but many ran away.

Sometimes a young southern soldier volunteered not only himself for service in the Confederate army but also his servants. A number of African American slaves made the trek from Arkansas to northern Virginia with their masters to tend the horses and cook meals. No doubt they did heavy labor for the army when the need arose. They faced danger, illness, and hardship.

During wartime, the food shortages on the home front that sometimes neared the starvation level were doubly hard on the slaves. Black families, although they had grown the crops and tended the livestock, always received second best. They got what was left over after the master's white family had eaten their fill. Black families had always kept small gardens around their cabins and filled out their diet with small game the men would hunt. But during wartime, guns and bullets for hunting were not to be had.

With the movement of the Union armies into Arkansas, slaves in the state began to have their first taste of freedom. This began as Union soldiers took control of parts of Arkansas, starting with General Curtis's march from Pea Ridge to Batesville and then to Helena. African American men, women, and children swarmed to the army camps for safety. The Union army called them "**contraband,**" the term for the property of an enemy.

At the Union army camps, African Americans lived a harsh life. The Union troops had trouble enough keeping themselves supplied so deep in Confederate lands. Finding food, clothing, and shelter for growing numbers of freed slaves was beyond their scope. Many African American people, often the small children, sickened and died in the Union army camps.

For some Arkansas slaves, the war meant a forced exile. To keep their slaves of greatest value from running away or being taken by the enemy, some planters sent their young male slaves to Texas. Entire African American communities were broken up, and countless families were torn apart in this way. The years after the war were lonely, painful years of searching for lost family members, most of whom were not found again.

Moses Mitchell, born near Arkansas Post, was moved to Texas and sold at age twelve. "When they took us to Texas they left my mother and baby sister here in Arkansas . . . I never saw her [my mother] again and when I came back to Arkansas, they said she had been dead twenty-eight years. Never did hear of my father again."

Many of the African American people who lived as freedmen in Arkansas after the war were not natives of Arkansas at all. They were ex-slaves who had been moved here from Mississippi, Tennessee, and Alabama as Union troops moved into those states.

The federal government answered the crisis

The Emancipation Proclamation: "Then, Thenceforward, and Forever Free"

When the Civil War began, President Abraham Lincoln made preserving the Union the major goal of the United States. Making the end of slavery a goal was difficult. Several slave states (Missouri, Kentucky, West Virginia, Delaware, and Maryland) were still a part of the United States. Lincoln feared that some of them might join the Confederacy if the Union announced that slavery was ended everywhere. As the war continued, however, more and more northern people wanted the emancipation, or freeing of, the slaves to be a clear goal of the Union.

Lincoln first issued a preliminary Emancipation Proclamation after the battle of Antietam in September 1862. Then he issued the permanent Emancipation Proclamation on January 1, 1863. The Emancipation Proclamation did not free all the slaves immediately. It freed the slaves in those southern states that were fighting against the Union. But that meant the end of slavery was now a goal of the Union. If the Union won the war, slaves would be, in the words of the proclamation, "then, thenceforward, and forever free."

As the Union armies advanced, Union commanders began treating the slaves as free. In Arkansas, the Union army housed and fed former slaves, accepted them as soldiers, and in some cases helped them get farm land.

Federal officials in Texas declared slavery ended in that state as of June 19, 1865. Blacks in Texas made "Juneteenth" a regular holiday celebration, an idea that spread to other states.

The official end of slavery everywhere in the United States came after the war with the Thirteenth Amendment to the Constitution, approved by the states in December 1865. It says "Neither slavery nor involuntary servitude . . . shall exist within the United States. . . ."

"Blissville" was a home for black refugees during and immediately after the Civil War. (Courtesy of the University of Central Arkansas Archives)

This was the scene in Little Rock when Arkansas black soldiers in the Union army were "mustered out"—returned to civilian life—in May of 1866. (Courtesy of the University of Central Arkansas Archives)

of displaced African American people by forming the **Freedmen's Bureau.** Funded and run by the government, the Bureau relied heavily on volunteers from religious groups. Quakers and members of the American Missionary Association, in particular, helped to staff these programs. They started schools in eastern Arkansas counties. They opened refugee camps, called "home farms," near Pine Bluff, DeVall's Bluff, Little Rock, and Helena.

THE END OF THE WAR

The long and tragic war finally groaned to an end in the spring of 1865. Cut off by Grant's forces, Lee surrendered at Appomattox Courthouse in April of 1865. Just days later, President Lincoln was assassinated. The battered remnants of the Army of Tennessee, in which so many Arkansans had served, surrendered a few days later. Then, in June, the Confederate forces in the Trans-Mississippi Theater gave up. It was over. More than six hundred thousand men of both sides were dead. Another four hundred thousand were wounded, many of them missing arms or legs.

The war settled at least two important issues. The United States of America was one nation that could not be divided, and slavery would not exist in this nation. But Arkansas and the rest of the country paid a terrible price. Nothing in the history of America compares to the sufferings of the Civil War. It remains a central fact of the American experience. Its causes and its **consequences** haunt us nearly a hundred and fifty years after the last battle was fought.

VOCABULARY

abolition (AB-uh-LISH-shun) the immediate and total end to slavery.

artillery batteries heavy guns and cannon and the soldiers who operate them.

ascendancy (uh-SEND-un-see) on the rise; moving up.

bushwhackers (BUSH-hwak-erz) guerilla fighters and outlaws who terrorized civilians during and after the Civil War.

casualties (KAZH-oo-ehl-teez) those killed, wounded, or missing after a battle.

cavalry soldiers mounted on horseback.

Conditionalists (kuhn-DISH-shun-uh-lists) those in the South who wanted to secede from the Union only under certain conditions, namely, on the condition that President Lincoln took actions harmful to the South.

consequences something that happens as a direct result of certain actions; the outcome of an act.

contraband the Union army term for slaves from the Confederacy who fled from their homes into the Union army camps to find freedom.

Cooperationists those in the South who were willing to wait and see what Lincoln might do as president rather than secede merely on the basis of his election.

dysentery (DISS-uhn-tair-ee) a disease characterized by severe cramps and diarrhea resulting in dehydration and sometimes death. It is usually caused by bacterial infection from unclean water or food.

electoral college (ee-LEK-toh-ruhl KAH-lej) group representing all states which casts the final vote in presidential elections, based upon the majority vote in each state. A candidate may win only 51 percent of the popular votes in a state but win all the state's electoral votes. The number of electoral votes assigned each state is based upon population; the electoral vote of each state is equal to the number of its members of the House of Representatives plus its two senators.

enmity (EHN-mih-tee) hostility; the state of being enemies.

Freedmen's Bureau an agency set up by the U.S. government to provide food, clothing, shelter, and education to black Americans after they were freed from slavery.

guerilla (guh-RILL-uh) individuals and independent bands taking part in irregular warfare, or special forces engaged in harassment and sabotage.

Homestead Law (HOHM-sted law) to encourage western settlement, the U.S. Congress in 1862 passed a law granting 160 acres free to any man and family who would occupy and cultivate the land.

infantry (IN-fun-tree) foot soldiers carrying rifles; the largest group in an army.

insurrection (IN-sir-EK-shun) revolt, uprising.

Jayhawkers outlaws who terrorized civilians during and after the Civil War; so-called because they were believed to have come from Kansas, the Jayhawk state.

martial law (MARSH-uhl law) military rule which may take over the civil government in times of crisis or war.

mendacity (men-DASS-ih-tee) lying, dishonesty.

morphine (MORE-feen) a powerful narcotic derived from opium used to deaden pain.

patronage (PAT-ruh-nej) the power to make appointments to government jobs based on grounds other than merit.

quinine (KWI-nine) a drug derived from cinchona ("Peruvian") bark used to treat the symptoms of malaria.

secede (seh-SEED) to withdraw from an organization or a government.

unanimous (yoo-NAN-ih-muss) in total; 100 percent agreement.

usurpation (yoo-sur-PAY-shun) taking by force a position of power that does not belong to one.

STUDY QUESTIONS

1. Describe the political situation in Arkansas before the election of Abraham Lincoln.

2. Explain the first reaction in Arkansas to the secession crisis, then explain how and why opinion changed.

3. Tell how many Arkansans served in the Confederate and the Union armies.

4. What was the importance of the battles of Pea Ridge and Prairie Grove?

5. Who were Gen. Earl Van Dorn, Gen. Thomas Hindman, and Gen. Patrick Cleburne?

6. Describe the battles of the Red River Campaign.

7. Describe the Union and Confederate governments in Arkansas after 1863.

8. What was life for ordinary citizens like in Arkansas during the Civil War?

9. Tell the story of David Dodd.

6

Reconstruction and the New South

1865–1900

What to Look for in Chapter 6

These were difficult years for Arkansas, from 1865 to 1900. Right after the Civil War, from 1865 to 1868, the Arkansas government was in the hands of the same people who had run the government before the war. They acted as if nothing had changed, continuing to discriminate against the former slaves. By 1868, Congress began "Radical Reconstruction," with state governments dominated by Republicans, African Americans, and former Whigs. The controversial Arkansas Reconstruction government did enact many positive measures, such as the first public school system.

The traditional leadership of Arkansas reasserted itself by 1874. They wrote a new constitution limiting the power of state government, and reduced the taxes that had supported the new services.

Too poor to develop industry, the state continued to be mostly agricultural. Black Arkansans, without the money to buy land, became workers on white men's land, the beginning of sharecropping. The brightest spot in the economy was the beginning of railroads.

By the end of the century, small farmers, white and black, tried to make the state government pay more attention to their needs. Their movement failed, but the threat of African Americans active in politics brought segregation and political discrimination.

THE LAST YEARS OF THE NINETEENTH CENTURY

As the war ended in 1865, Arkansans faced the problems of settling back into daily life and rebuilding. The wounds of war, physical and mental, would last for a long time. The violence of the war years would also linger for a while.

The economic structure, suffering more from disruption than ruin, would have to be rebuilt. Above all, there was the new role of the African Americans, now legally free but socially and financially deprived.

From 1868 to 1874, Arkansas endured **Reconstruction**. This was the effort of the Republican Party and the U.S. government to

The Arkansas River froze over at Little Rock–North Little Rock in 1876. (Courtesy of the Arkansas History Commission)

bring rapid change to the South. Then the state, under the slogan the "New South," tried to bring itself more slowly into the modern age. The years 1865–1900 were a bridge from the well-known and comfortable past into the unknown and sometimes frightening world of the future.

THE BEGINNING OF RECONSTRUCTION

When Abraham Lincoln was killed in April 1865 just as the war was ending, his vice president, Andrew Johnson, became president of the United States. A Tennessean who had opposed secession, Johnson shared Lincoln's basic ideas about **Reconstruction.** He too believed in a "soft" plan that asked mainly for a promise of future loyalty from southern voters. The aim was to get the southern states back in the Union as quickly as possible.

Under this plan Isaac Murphy served as governor in Arkansas. The General Assembly, however, was composed mostly of Democrats and ex-Confederates. Isaac Murphy upheld the principles of civil rights, but the state senate and house refused to honor the rights of African Americans. They were kept from voting, serving on juries, going to school with whites, and marrying outside their race.

By a vote of seventy-two to two, the General Assembly refused to accept the Fourteenth Amendment to the U.S. Constitution. This amendment made African Americans citizens of the United States and prevented states from denying the rights of any citizen. Congress considered acceptance of the amendment a sign that a state was ready to rejoin the Union.

Actions like rejecting the Fourteenth Amendment in the former Confederate states forced the U.S. Congress to take a tougher stand on **Reconstruction.** After the congressional elections of 1866, most members of

Congress favored harsh treatment of the South. Congress's new stand became known as "**Radical Reconstruction.**" The Radicals' motives were mixed but included a desire to punish the South for the war. They also wished to continue the power of the Republican Party and to protect the newly freed African Americans.

The control of **Reconstruction** passed from President Johnson to the Republican Congress. (Congress, angered by Johnson's moderate approach to **Reconstruction**, impeached Johnson, or charged him with improper conduct of his office, but he was not convicted.) Congress passed several **Reconstruction** Acts, the first in the spring of 1867, that laid down the rules for new state governments in the South.

Under the **Radical Reconstruction** Plan, officers of the U.S. Army would register the voters in each of the Confederate states. All adult black males could vote. White males could vote if they took the **"iron-clad oath"**: the voter must swear that he would be loyal to the Union in the future *and* had been loyal in the past.

The intent was to deprive men who had been state officials before the war and had then supported the Confederacy of the right to vote and hold office. In Arkansas probably about 20 percent of the possible white voters were not able to pass this test.

By 1868 Arkansas had a new state constitution and a new state government, with Radical Republicans in control. The new governor was Powell Clayton. Born in Pennsylvania, he had moved west to Kansas in the 1850s and had come to Arkansas in 1863 with the Union Army. He became a general and a well-known cavalry commander. He bought a cotton plantation near Pine Bluff, married a local woman, and decided to stay in Arkansas.

In June 1868, Congress approved Arkansas's actions and allowed its elected members into

Congress. The **Radical Reconstruction** period in Arkansas had begun.

It is hard to make sense out of these years in Arkansas. Times were confused, and many people were bitter about the war and **Reconstruction.** Also, white southerners would later create an image of **Reconstruction** as all bad. It would be seen as a time when the southern states were unfairly and badly ruled. Those in power were made out to be a combination of African Americans, "**scalawags**" (or native southerners who were regarded as traitors to their state), and "**carpetbaggers**" (or northerners who came to the South to get rich). **Scalawag** was an old southern term meaning a low-down rascal. A **carpetbagger** was a Yankee who was so poor that he could put all he owned in a suitcase made of carpet fabric.

But the situation in Arkansas and the other southern states was much more complex than that. Although the Republicans did promote black voting with vigor, many African Americans did not vote, and most of the people who held major offices were white. The **scalawags** included as leaders many Arkansans who had been Whigs before the war. They tended to share the Republicans' economic ideas.

Most of the native-born white Arkansans who voted Republican in this period appear to have been ordinary men. Perhaps they hoped the Republicans would do more for them than the pre-war Democrats had done. Arkansas, of course, had a long history of factions opposed to the Democratic Party. During the secession debate and the war, many Arkansans expressed a strong Unionist bent.

Some of the **carpetbaggers** may have been out to make themselves rich. But many first saw Arkansas during service with the Union army, liked the state and its people, and chose to make a new home there. People had been moving into the state from all over the country for decades before the war began. Some of these new people brought with them much-needed cash. Many northerners, like the teachers in Freedmen's Bureau schools, came purely to help the African Americans.

THE REPUBLICAN GOVERNMENT

The first job of the new Republican government was to bring law and order to the state. Brutal assaults and murder were still common, continuing in the wake of violent wartime conditions. Also, Arkansans opposed to African American rights formed a terrorist group called the **Ku Klux Klan**, based on a similar movement in Tennessee. Hiding behind masks and robes, Klansmen tried to frighten African Americans and sometimes murdered them. The names of members were kept secret, but they seemed to have the support of many of the state's pre-war leaders.

Powell Clayton, the state's new governer, had strong powers under the constitution of 1868 and tended to approach problems like the military man he was. He was determined to stop the violence. He called out the militia and declared martial law in a number of counties. The violence was brought under control, but many whites deeply resented Clayton's methods.

As order was being restored, the Republicans set out to enact their plans for the state. Economic progress and public education were

Henderson School in Fayetteville, about 1865. (Courtesy of the University of Central Arkansas Archives)

When a railroad completed part of its line, it called for a ceremony and a celebration. This one is on the Iron Mountain Railroad, probably in the late 1860s. (Courtesy of the University of Arkansas, Fayetteville, Special Collections)

two major goals. In many ways, the Republicans hoped to bring to Arkansas the kind of active state government that was common in the northern states.

A real education system was a crucial need. In the 1860s, about 30 percent of the whites and 95 percent of the blacks were unable to read and write. The Republicans began the first statewide public school system. It featured trained leaders, a standard curriculum, and requirements that teachers had to meet to get a license. It was, however, a **segregated** system with separate schools for black and white children.

The new school system got off to a fine start. In 1869, there were 632 school buildings in the state. Just two years later there were 1,289. The number of students increased from 67,412 in 1869 to 107,863 in 1871. Of those, about 88,500 were white and about 19,000 were black. The number of teachers almost doubled.

The new government also started the state's first public college, the Arkansas Industrial University. Later, this would become the University of Arkansas.

Economic progress focused first and foremost on railroad building. To aid private railroad companies, the state borrowed money by selling bonds and gave the money to railroad companies. Almost ten million dollars was raised this way. During the **Reconstruction** period, more than six hundred miles of track were built. The most useful project was building the Memphis to Little Rock railroad.

The state was still too poor, though, for many of the railroads to make a profit. Also, some of the state bond money was wasted on unsound projects. That would cause trouble later on.

The **Reconstruction** government also offered new state programs. It opened the School for the Deaf and moved the School for the Blind from Arkadelphia to Little Rock. It also formed a Bureau of Immigration and State Lands to recruit people to move to Arkansas. The state also funded levee building and swamp drainage to make more farmland.

All of these programs cost a great deal of money, far more than the state had spent before the Civil War. Even though the Republicans raised taxes, the cost of government and the state bonds meant that the state was

The University of Arkansas

One of the legacies of **Reconstruction** is the University of Arkansas. As part of the effort to create an educational system, the Republican legislature in Arkansas authorized the creation of the Arkansas Industrial University, with a Normal (teacher training) Department, in 1871. That was Arkansas's first state-supported college, which was later renamed the University of Arkansas in 1899.

The legislature asked communities to bid for the location of the college by offering local financial support. In Little Rock the voters turned down both city and county bond issues for the university. Batesville and Independence County offered $69,000, but Fayetteville and Washington County offered $150,000 in bond issues and gifts. The legislators on the committee to review possible sites reported back that Fayetteville had every requirement for the university, although they had some questions about its remote location. To get to Fayetteville the committee went by train from Little Rock to the end of the line in Morrilton, by steamboat from there to Van Buren, and by stagecoach from there to Fayetteville. To return, the committee took a stage to the railhead in southwest Missouri, then traveled by train through St. Louis and back to Little Rock.

The exact site ended up being the 160-acre McIlroy farm, then about a mile northwest of Fayetteville. Classes started in January 1872. None of the first students were high school graduates, because Arkansas then had no public high schools. The first year of work was the "preparatory program" to get the students ready for college-level work. This practice continued well into the twentieth century.

The first real commencement ceremony was held in 1876 for eight graduates, three of whom had been preparatory students in the first class. Total enrollment in the 1870s was usually 250 or 300 students, about two-thirds of whom were preparatory students and one-third college students. The Main Building, modeled on the Main Building at the University of Illinois, was also completed in the 1870s.

Under the terms of the national Morrill Act, passed during the Civil War and later applied to the former Confederate states, the university became a land-grant institution. That meant that the national government gave the state federal land—150,000 acres for Arkansas—to sell, and the state was directed to use the proceeds to support a university. In return the university was to include the teaching of agricultural and mechanical skills in its curriculum.

building a large debt. There were also some corrupt leaders among the Republicans who achieved personal gain from their connections with state government.

AFRICAN AMERICANS IN THE RECONSTRUCTION PERIOD

Meanwhile, ex-slaves were intent on building new lives in freedom. As early as 1865, a group of African American leaders convened in Little Rock to define the goals of their people. Their wishes were simple. They wanted to own land on which to farm, and they wanted good schools for their children. They wanted legal protection so they could go about their lives in peace.

By and large, they were not keen on revenge or on getting even with the former slave owners. They only wished to be equal citizens. William H. Grey, a Helena grocer, put it this way: "Our future is sure—God has marked it out with his own finger; here we lived, suffered, fought, bled, and many have died. We will not leave the graves of our fathers, but here we will rear our children; here we will educate them to a higher destiny; here, where we have been degraded, will we be exalted—*Americans in America, one and indivisible.*"

The newly freed African Americans had nothing and had to work themselves up from the very bottom of society. Farming was their major skill, but most of the good farmland was still owned by whites. In the 1870s, perhaps only one in twenty black farmers owned

A family near Pine Bluff and their collard patch, about 1897. (Courtesy of the University of Central Arkansas Archives)

land. African Americans heard rumors that the U.S. government was going to give every black family forty acres and a mule. But the truth was that even the Radical Republican Congress would not think of taking land from whites to give to blacks.

The white landowners, on the other hand, were concerned about getting a stable supply of labor for their fields. The sharecropping system came out of this plight. A white landowner would allow a group of black families to farm part of his land in return for a share of the crop. The landowner would provide land, a house, and perhaps mules and tools.

The landowner would also allow the sharecropper to buy food and clothing at his store on credit. The debt was to be paid when the crop came in. The sharecropper and his family would provide the labor. To make sure he got paid, the landowner held a mortgage, or crop lien, on the sharecropper's harvest.

It was a bad system. The sharecropper could not get ahead. Each year his crop would just barely pay off his debt to the landowner; sometimes he could not pay off his debt, and he would owe even more the next year. The system also helped keep cotton as the main crop, since people thought it was the easiest crop to sell. Most blacks, and later many whites, would be trapped in the sharecropping system for decades to come.

Some African Americans did, however, manage to get ahead by moving to town. There they had the chance to create good careers as barbers, bakers, plasterers, brickmasons, blacksmiths, and carpenters. Little Rock's African American population increased from 23 percent (3,500 in number) in 1860 to 43 percent (13,708) in 1870.

For some, mostly women, careers as teachers offered another way to make a solid living. Charlotte Stephens, a former slave who had gone to Oberlin College in Ohio, was Little Rock's first African American teacher. She worked in the city's schools for seventy years, from 1869 to 1939.

African American women also found work as laundresses, cooks, and maids. Stephens later called them "homespun heroines who kept their own homes neat, made their children's clothes, cooked and washed for them and sent them to school, while working from daylight to dark in a white woman's kitchen."

Republican **Reconstruction** meant that many African Americans could hold public office. Blacks never did hold office in equal proportion to their numbers in the state, however, though many served in the state legislature. During the **Reconstruction** period there were also many African American local officials, including 160 justices of the peace and 95 constables, and sheriffs, county clerks, assessors, and militia officers.

William A. Rector served as Little Rock city collector and as city marshal for six years. Mifflin W. Gibbs of Little Rock was the first African American municipal judge in the United States and later served as the United States consul to Madagascar.

THE END OF RECONSTRUCTION

The Republicans tried to do a great deal very quickly. What they were doing may well have been against the will of most of the state's people. Most of the whites who had been kept from voting got the vote back in 1872 when Congress passed a general Amnesty Act.

As the state sank more and more deeply into debt, many began to worry about the cost of the **Reconstruction** programs. The state's revenues declined as cotton, still the chief crop, fell in price from twenty-five cents

Charlotte Stephens. (Courtesy of the Arkansas History Commission)

Mifflin W. Gibbs. (Courtesy of the University of Central Arkansas Archives)

a pound in 1868 to eleven cents a pound in 1874.

The Republicans also had troubles within their own party. It began to split into two separate groups or factions. Democrats (or **Conservatives** as they called themselves) made the most of these problems. They were able to play one Republican faction against the other.

Although some friction began to appear within the Republican Party as early as 1869, Powell Clayton remained in control. Even after he was named U.S. senator in 1871, he ran the party from Washington. By 1872, another Republican leader, Joseph Brooks, was forming an opposing group in the party.

An Iowa-born Methodist preacher, Brooks arrived in Arkansas after the war and hoped to become governor in 1872. He was willing to seek support from Democrats to help him defeat the Clayton group. The Democrats had by now begun to increase their power in the legislature.

The election for governor in 1872 was the final split in the Republican Party. Clayton's "Regular Republicans" chose Elisha Baxter, an Arkansas Unionist. The opposing Republicans got behind Brooks. The Clayton-Baxter group was called the "**Minstrels**" because one of their number had appeared in **minstrel** shows. (**Minstrel** shows featured white entertainers made up in "black face" to resemble black men. The troupes traveled from town to town, often on steamboats.) The Brooks group was called the **"Brindletails"** because someone said Brooks's loud voice sounded like the bellow of a brindle bull.

It was a close and confusing election. In some areas, there were two polling places and some voters cast their ballots at both places. The Brooks people believed that their man had won by 1,500 votes out of 80,000 votes cast. But the election officials were Clayton men. They threw out the entire returns from four counties (which had no doubt voted for Brooks) and claimed that Baxter had officially won by 3,000 votes.

While Brooks appealed his case to the courts, Baxter took office as governor and tried to strengthen his support by courting the Democrats. He named some Democrats to office and gave the lucrative state printing contract to the Democrats' newspaper, the *Arkansas Gazette*. These actions in turn upset his backer, Powell Clayton, who began to think that maybe Joseph Brooks should be declared governor after all.

At that point, in April of 1874, a Pulaski County circuit court declared that Brooks was the legal governor. Brooks then marched on the state house with a band of armed men and threw Baxter out. The last act of **Reconstruction** in Arkansas, the **Brooks-Baxter War,** had begun.

Baxter moved a few blocks down the street to the Anthony House, a well-known Little Rock hotel. He began to gather armed supporters. At the state house, Brooks put up a **barricade** on the grounds and assembled his armed force. The "armies" would grow to about two thousand on each side. Each man claimed he was the legal governor and asked others to choose sides. (The Little Rock postmaster solved his problem by holding mail addressed to the governor of Arkansas at the post office.)

While this was not really a full-scale war, there were a few bloody **skirmishes**. These took place in Little Rock, in Pine Bluff, and along the Arkansas River. Perhaps as many as two hundred people were killed during the month or so that the **Brooks-Baxter War** raged. U.S. Army troops from the Little Rock Arsenal, stationed along Main Street between the two armed camps in Little Rock, helped prevent a major clash.

Lee County Sheriff W. H. Furbush, who was African American, expressed the feelings of most Arkansas voters in his telegram to President Ulysses S. Grant: "We do not care . . . who is governor; all we want is peace. The people will obey. Answer."

The question was now in the hands of President Grant. Brooks had won the support of Clayton, but Baxter had the support of many of the best legal minds in Arkansas. These included some Democratic-**Conservative** leaders, such as future governor Augustus Hill Garland. President Grant, and later a Congressional review team, ruled in favor of Baxter.

The **Brooks-Baxter War** was over, and with it ended **Reconstruction** in Arkansas. The real winners were the Democratic-**Conservatives**. They liked to call themselves the "Redeemers" who had freed the state from the Radical Republicans. They had Baxter in their debt. They controlled the legislature, which soon called for a constitutional convention. That took place during the summer of 1874.

The new state constitution was a direct response to the burdens of **Radical Reconstruction**. It retained some of the features of the **Reconstruction** constitution of 1868, such as support for public schools. But the new document made it very hard to raise

An artist captured this scene in front of the State House in Little Rock as volunteers chose up sides in the Brooks-Baxter War. (Courtesy of the University of Central Arkansas Archives)

taxes. In addition, it cut the power of the governor by changing his term from four years to two years. It also took away much of his power to appoint people to office. Major state offices, such as secretary of state, attorney general, treasurer, auditor, and land commissioner would be elected, not appointed.

This constitution of 1874 is still the basic law that governs the state. It has been amended often, and thoughtful attempts have been made to replace it entirely.

The new constitution called for a prompt election for a new governor. The **Redeemers** offered the job to Baxter, but he declined. Their second choice was Augustus Hill Garland. He was a former Whig, now a Democrat, who had served in the Congress of the Confederate States of America.

Garland was also a man of learning, an expert on constitutional law, and a kind man. He went on to enjoy a long and distinguished career as a U.S. senator and as attorney general of the United States under President Grover Cleveland.

THE DEMOCRATS IN POWER

From 1874 into the 1880s, the Democratic Party was firmly in control of the state with no major threats to its power. The leaders of the party were a close-knit group of planters and businessmen, many of whom were former Confederates. They allowed African American voting, since they were certain that they could control that vote with their economic power over the sharecroppers. A small Republican Party remained, but it was too weak to elect people to statewide office.

The Democratic leaders were very concerned with cutting the cost of state government. The state debt, almost eighteen million dollars in 1877, had to be addressed. The state had to pay a large amount of interest each year on the debt. Some wanted simply to cancel the debt. They argued that the state had not gotten its money's worth. They said that they should not be made to pay for the actions of the Reconstruction Republicans.

Others pointed out that canceling the debt would destroy the state's credit rating. That would make it almost certain that the state could never borrow money again.

In the end, the debt was cancelled. In 1877 the state Supreme Court declared part of the debt invalid. In 1885 the legislature proposed, and the voters approved, a constitutional amendment that wiped out most of the rest of it. Therefore, the people who had lent money to Arkansas by buying state bonds, mostly eastern banks and businessmen, lost their money. Of course, they refused to invest in Arkansas for many years to come.

The Democrats also kept taxes very low. That in turn meant that such state-funded programs as did exist were cut back or dropped. And, despite the Democrats having made much of Republican corruption during **Reconstruction**, three of their state treasurers in a row had to resign because of scandals.

In addition, the **Redeemers** wanted to keep the costs of running the state prison as low as they could. To help the prison pay for itself, they leased the inmates out to work for private business and industry. The practice had been going on since the 1840s. This, too, caused a string of scandals, since the inmates were overworked, poorly fed, and ill housed. Many of them died while working on lease. Conditions were so bad in the mines at Coal Hill that the prisoners leased to the mines went on strike. Still, there were no changes in the system.

The Democrats' low taxes also hurt education in Arkansas. The public school system dating from the **Reconstruction** era was still

Students at the one-room Clover Bend School in Lawrence County, about 1890. (Courtesy of the University of Central Arkansas Archives)

in place, but it suffered badly from a lack of funding. The school term was short, sometimes only a few weeks long. Rural schools closed down so children could help with the spring planting and the fall harvest. There was no law that required children to attend school. Books and other supplies were hard to get. Few teachers had gone past the eighth grade themselves. By 1900, about one-half of the children in Arkansas were going to school. The literacy rate had improved, but still nearly 20 percent of the people could not read and write.

THE NEW SOUTH

Although Arkansas was and would remain dependent on agriculture, the Democratic-

Conservative leaders of the state wanted to promote industry. All over the South, people were talking about a "New South" that would have its own factories. Arkansas, though, lacked much of what was needed for such progress. It lacked money to invest, a skilled labor force, people wealthy enough to buy goods that such plants might produce, and good transportation.

The move to develop industry went forward very slowly. In 1900, the U.S. Census counted 4,794 "manufacturing establishments" in the state, made up generally of small units with five or six people in their work force. Only about 26,500 Arkansans, or 2 percent of the total, were listed as wage earners in industry.

The state did see some success in railroad building. The state no longer offered bond money to railroad companies, but it did promise few or no taxes and little regulation. The U.S. government aided the building program by giving the railroads huge grants of public lands along their routes.

By 1900, Arkansas had more than three thousand miles of track. Large areas in the Ozarks and Ouachitas were still out of reach. But railroads covered much of eastern, central, and southern Arkansas. They also opened routes to Arkansas's neighbors and the rest of the nation. There were four lines crisscrossing the state. The Rock Island Line went from Memphis into Oklahoma. The Missouri Pacific went from Memphis to Fort Smith. The St. Louis Southwestern, or "Cotton Belt," crossed the southern part of the state through Pine Bluff and Texarkana and on to Texas. The Frisco went from Memphis up the Delta and into Missouri.

The railroads had almost the power of life and death for Arkansas towns. A town bypassed by the railroad might vanish, while new towns sprang up along the routes. Most areas were served by only one railroad, so the people in those places had to pay any price the railroad wanted to charge to move their goods. Almost all of the railroad mileage in Arkansas was owned by five large companies based in the North.

The railroads, eager to sell their land grants, joined the state in trying to attract

On a small farm, everyone did a share of the chores. Lawrence County, 1890. (Courtesy of the University of Central Arkansas Archives)

Steamboats continued to be dangerous. The Golden City *exploded and burned at Memphis in 1882.* (Courtesy of the University of Arkansas, Fayetteville, Special Collections)

new settlers. Glowing notices raved about Arkansas as a fertile garden. In 1875, the railroads brought in news writers from the North and West to tour the state as the "New Arkansas Travelers." To promote itself as a place to settle, Arkansas sponsored an award-winning state building at the 1876 Philadelphia Centennial Exhibition.

Some effort was made to attract settlers from Europe. There were quite a few Germans in Arkansas, and more moved to Little Rock, Fort Smith, and Stuttgart. A Polish group settled at Marche, near Little Rock. A group of

Italians tried Delta farming in Chicot County. Some of them then moved to found Tontitown north of Fayetteville. In spite of these efforts, by 1900 just a little over 1 percent of Arkansas's people were foreign-born.

THE BEGINNING OF THE FARMERS' REVOLT

At the end of the 1800s, more than 90 percent of the people lived and worked on farms. The "New South" concept urged planting diverse crops, but almost all Arkansas farmers, large and small, still grew cotton as their "money crop." By 1880, Arkansas was growing more cotton than it had before the Civil War. The welfare, sometimes even the survival, of Arkansas farmers was tied up in that one crop. But the price kept going down.

Cotton was eleven cents a pound in 1874, and the price declined to five cents a pound by the mid-1890s. At that price, it cost more to produce cotton than the farmer would get paid for the harvested crop. Few farmers knew it, but they were the victims of a worldwide market glut. Egypt and India were growing cotton too. The more cotton the world's farmers produced, the lower the price went.

The farmers also had other troubles. The U.S. government kept the supply of money tight, which meant that loans were hard to get. Moreover, the farmers had to move their crops to market by the railroads, which charged high rates. The middlemen, or those who processed and sold the crops, all took a share of the profit. They often made more than the farmers.

Under these conditions, more and more small farmers, white and black, went broke. They had to give up their land to the banker or merchant and become sharecroppers.

These stark conditions moved the farmers to organize in hopes of solving their problems. They were not sure what the basic

Selected Census Data for Arkansas 1870 to 1900

	1870	1880	1890	1900
Total population	484,471	802,252	1,128,211	1,311,564
White population	362,115	591,531	818,752	944,580
Black population	122,169	210,666	309,117	366,856
Number of farms	49,424	94,433	124,760	178,694
Average acres per farm	153.7	127.7	119.4	93.1
Cotton bales produced	247,968	608,256	619,494	709,880
Bushels of corn produced	13,382,145	24,156,417	33,982,318	44,144,098
Manufacturing establishments	1,079	1,202	2,073	4,794
Wage earners	3,206	4,557	14,143	26,501

Notes:

The figures for white and black population for each year will not add up to the exact figure for total population. The difference is the small number of other races in the population.

The U.S. Census, in counting the number of farms, tended to count a sharecropper's assigned land as a farm. Therefore, the number of farms given here does not represent the number of landowners.

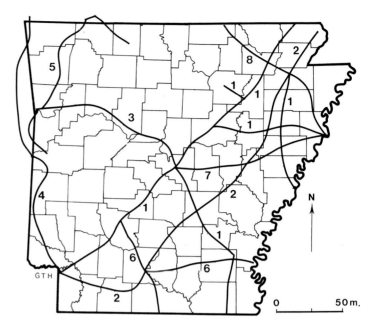

Arkansas's Major Railroads, 1900.)

1. *St. Louis & Iron Mountain*
2. *Texas, St. Louis & Arkansas*
3. *Little Rock & Fort Smith*
4. *Kansas City, Texas, Gulf*
5. *St. Louis & San Francisco*
6. *St. Louis, Mississippi & Southern*
7. *Memphis, Little Rock*
8. *Missouri & North Arkansas*

"On a Slow Train through Arkansas"

By the late nineteenth century, joke books were using Arkansas to represent everything backward and hillbilly. All kinds of jokes, some of them very old, were presented as if they happened in Arkansas. One of the most popular of these joke books was *On a Slow Train through Arkansas,* compiled and published by Thomas W. Jackson of Chicago. The first edition appeared in 1903, and it stayed in print for the next 30 years.

It was down in the state of Arkansas I rode on the slowest train I ever saw. It stopped at every house. When it came to a double house it stopped twice. They made so many stops I said, "Conductor, what have we stopped for now?" He said, "There are some cattle on the track." We ran a little ways further and stopped again. I said, "What is the matter now?" He said, "We have caught up with those cattle again. . . ." A lady said, "Conductor, can't this train make any better time than this?" He said, "If you ain't satisfied with this train, you can get off and walk." She said she would, only her folks didn't expect her til the train got there. A lady handed the conductor two tickets, one whole ticket and a half ticket. He said, "Who is the half ticket for?" She said, "My boy." He said, "He's not a boy; he's a man. Under twelve, half fare, over twelve full fare." She said, "He was under twelve when we started. . . ." One of the passengers tried to commit suicide. He ran ahead for half a mile, laid [*sic*] down on the track, but he starved to death before the train got there. . . .

This sort of thing helped create an image of Arkansas in the minds of many Americans.

James R. Masterson, *Arkansas Folklore . . .* (Reprint, Little Rock: Rose Publishing Co., 1974), pp. 276–77.

causes of their problems were. They did know some of the blame belonged with the bankers, the middlemen, the railroads, and the politicians. The farmers' protest movement spread all over the country, with Arkansans playing a key role.

The first effort to organize produced the **Patrons of Husbandry**, or **Grangers**. The organization began in the 1870s as self-help improvement clubs for rural men and women. The **Grangers** pushed for better homes, growing more varied types of crops, and more. The master of the Arkansas state **Grange** was John T. Jones of Helena. He was chosen Master of the National **Grange** in 1875, and Mrs. Jones was elected "Ceres," the top national office for women.

As times grew tougher, some farmers began to think about political action as a way to solve their problems. In 1880, some Arkansas farmers worked for the small **Greenback Party.** This group called for the U.S. government to print paper money in order to make money easier to obtain. The **Greenbackers** did not have much success, though.

THE FARMERS IN POLITICS

The next stage in the farmers' protest was the founding of the **Agricultural Wheel** in 1882. Their rallying song began, "Come all ye sunburnt sons of toil, Arise from thine oppression." They were aware that the problems of farmers were the same no matter what race a farmer happened to be. White Wheelers urged blacks to form similar groups. The Wheel wanted fairer taxes, easier credit, better public schools, regulation of the railroads, and a

To publicize the state, Arkansas sponsored exhibits at several world fairs and expositions. This one, emphasizing the variety of the state's agricultural produce, was at St. Louis in 1894. (Courtesy of the Arkansas History Commission)

political process more open to the common man.

In Arkansas, as in many southern states, the major question was whether the farmers should work within the Democratic Party or form a new party. The leaders of the Democratic Party did not seem to show very much concern about the farmers' demands. But to challenge the Democratic Party was to challenge its image as the "Redeemer of the South" and the white man's party.

The farmers were so desperate that many of them did break with the Democratic Party. In 1888, white and black members of the **Agricultural Wheel**, joined by the Republicans, formed a new party, the **Union Labor Party.** They supported Charles M. Norwood of Prescott, a one-legged Confederate veteran, for governor. The Democrats offered a party regular, James P. Eagle of Lonoke, a Baptist minister and also a Confederate veteran.

The farmers worked hard for Norwood in the stiffest challenge to the Democratic Party since the end of **Reconstruction.** Many be-

Life on a Small Farm

John Quincy Wolf grew up in the 1870s and 1880s in the "Leatherwoods" near Calico Rock. His parents died when he was twelve years old, and he and his sister went to live with an uncle and aunt, Mr. and Mrs. William T. Swann. (The Swanns, childless themselves, raised at least thirteen orphans, children of their relatives and neighbors.)

In his autobiography, Wolf described growing up on Uncle Will's nearly self-sufficient eighty-acre farm.

> Unlike almost all the other houses in the Leatherwoods, which were one-room cabins, the Swann home had two good-sized rooms and porch in the front the entire width of the house. There were no windows in either room, but each had two doors and a fireplace. The kitchen and the smoke-house were twenty-five feet removed from the cabin. Three hundred yards away a fine cold spring poured out of a limestone cave. . . . We were a hundred miles from a railroad, and the so-called roads through the hills were very bad. Reaching our cabin by buggy was out of the question, and by wagon, difficult. Mail came to the post office a few miles away once a week, on Saturdays. . . . We got up at 4 A.M., and in the warm months we planted, plowed, hoed, chopped cotton, picked cotton. In the winter we cut wood, made fires, cleaned out fence corners, cleared land, shucked corn, fed the horses, often nubbined [fed] stunted ears of corn to some thirty head of cattle, and gave corn to the hogs. We went to bed not long after dark. . . .
>
> We never had to look for entertainment. If we were not eating or working or pampering the animals or teasing them, we might be trying to follow a bee-line or playing games with the large green glade-lizards—very handsome creatures—that sunned themselves on sandrocks all over the hills. Hunting bee-trees was an interesting pastime, and sometimes we were rewarded with rich finds. . . .

John Quincy Wolf, *Life in the Leatherwoods* (1974; reprint, Fayeteville: University of Arkansas Press, 2000).

A farm family in Lawrence County about 1890 is doing the wash in the backyard. Clothes are washed in hot water in the iron kettle, then rinsed in the wooden tub behind it.
(Courtesy of the University of Central Arkansas Archives)

lieved that a truly fair election would have given the office to Norwood. However, the Democratic election officials declared Eagle the winner with 56 percent of the vote.

That was the peak of the farmers' protest in Arkansas. Still, the movement went on into the next decade. Its support went to the **Populist Party** in 1892 and to William Jennings Bryan as the Democratic candidate for president in 1896. They did not have any real success. In Arkansas, the Democrats did pass some laws that appeared to regulate railroads and limit the power of big business. The measures were more an effort to take the heat out of the farmers' protest than real reforms.

THE BEGINNING OF JIM CROW

In fact, the major effect of the farmers' protest in Arkansas and in other southern states was

The members of the Enola Farmers' Union assembled for a formal photograph in 1900. (Courtesy of the University of Central Arkansas Archives)

to remove African Americans from voting and, therefore, from any political power. The farmers' protest movement had threatened to divide the white vote, which in turn meant that black voters might hold the balance of power.

The Democratic leaders played upon that fear and also urged the common people to take out their frustrations on African Americans. The state legislature in the early 1890s passed a series of measures that served to keep African Americans from being involved in politics.

One act put control of the voting process fully in the hands of the Democratic Party, with no role for other parties or groups. A second law made it still harder for those who could not read or write to vote. This law required that only the precinct election judge could help such a person mark his ballot.

The toughest measure required a one-dollar poll tax for voting at a time when many Arkansans did not see twenty-five dollars cash in a year. The law further required that the poll tax be paid well in advance of an election.

Also, the Democratic Party proclaimed that its primary elections, which selected the party nominees, were for whites only. Since the primary was the only real election in a one-party state like Arkansas, the whites-only primary finished the process of ousting blacks from politics. Some African Americans would keep on voting, but none held any high office after the 1890s.

The voting laws also hurt many poor whites. From 1890 to 1900, the usual voter turnout in Arkansas elections declined by 30 percent.

Besides severe limits on being active in politics, there was social **segregation**, which capped off the "**Jim Crow**" system. (The name comes from a leading role in **minstrel** song-and-dance shows.) In all aspects of public and private life, blacks and whites were kept apart.

White-owned businesses and public places either did not serve African Americans or had a special entrance or a separate section for them. On public transport, including railroads and streetcars, blacks could ride only in their own cars or in the back of the cars. State laws, such as Arkansas's Separate Coach Law of 1891, combined with social custom to enforce separation.

The U.S. government went along with these customs of racial discrimination. Federal buildings in the South, such as courthouses and post offices, were fully **segregated**. In the 1896 ***Plessy vs. Ferguson*** case, the U.S. Supreme Court endorsed the practice, using the phrase "separate but equal." The case applied to railroads, but the practice of **segregation** was soon applied to all other aspects of life. In no place was this more true than in public schools.

Legal and public sanction of an inferior role for blacks unleashed pent-up anger among white Arkansans. This sometimes expressed itself in violence against African Americans. This violence sometimes turned into **lynching**. **Lynching** meant a mob torturing or killing a black person without a trial for a presumed crime. In 1892 alone, mobs killed twenty African Americans in Arkansas.

The Polk family gathers in front of the main house on their prosperous farm at Muddy Fork, about 1900. (Courtesy of the Arkansas History Commission)

Although the railroads were taking more and more of the traffic, steamboats continued to flourish into the twentieth century. Here the Kate Adams *comes into Helena in 1903.* (Courtesy of the University of Central Arkansas Archives)

AFRICAN AMERICAN SELF-HELP IN A DUAL SOCIETY

African Americans spoke out against the rising tide of racism, but they could not prevent it. Black leaders shifted to seeking the well-being of African Americans within the two-part social system. M. M. Murray of Lafayette County sized up the challenge to blacks by saying, "The salvation of our race lies entirely with us." It was the concept expressed elsewhere by leaders like Booker T. Washington. Many blacks hoped that the American ideals of hard work and self-reliance would work for them as well as for white people.

Most Arkansas African Americans were still farmers, and most of those were sharecroppers. To own land was their major goal. By 1900, about 25 percent of African American farmers in Arkansas had achieved that dream. Among the more successful was Scott Bond, who started out as a sharecropper near Forrest City. He saved enough money to buy land and in time owned twenty-one farms with about twelve thousand acres of land, five cotton gins, and a large general store.

Black businesses began to flourish. At the end of the nineteenth century, African American people had developed their own banks, insurance companies, hospitals, and old people's homes. By 1900, the state had 680 African American preachers, 400 teachers, 91 physicians, 27 lawyers, and 101 others in professions.

Some of these were real success stories. Wiley Jones of Pine Bluff started as a barber. He bought real estate, built Pine Bluff's first streetcar line, and ran a fifty-acre park and racetrack south of the city. His park was the site of the yearly Colored State Fair, which featured music and art as well as farm produce and livestock.

In the black communities, the central hub was the church, which was more than a religious institution. The church was the social center of African American life and often the center for politics, too. Preachers were seen as leaders in the black community, and they were often seen by whites as spokesmen for the race. When in the coming years African Americans would need a place to organize and produce leaders, the church structure would be there for them.

Black Arkansans kept their faith in education as a road to a better future. Although black schools were in all ways kept below the standards of white schools, they still stood as symbols of hope.

To train teachers, the state in 1875 created the Branch Normal College in Pine Bluff. (This later became Arkansas AM&N College and is now the University of Arkansas at Pine Bluff.) J. C. Corbin, an African American man who had been superintendent of public instruction for the entire state during **Reconstruction**, headed the new college.

There were also private and church sponsored colleges, such as Philander Smith, started in 1877 by the Methodists. Arkansas

Wiley Jones began as a barber and became quite wealthy. Here he holds his race horse, "Executor," near his Pine Bluff racetrack. (Courtesy of the University of Central Arkansas Archives)

The Sisters of the Holy Family at Pine Bluff, 1900.
(Courtesy of the Arkansas History Commission)

Baptist College was begun in 1884 to prepare preachers. Shorter College opened in North Little Rock in 1887 as an African Methodist Episcopal school. Southland Institute at Helena, which had been founded by Quakers in 1863 as a home for African American orphans, also became a college.

Other key social features of the African American community were the secret fraternal societies. Besides recreation, the clubs also offered business services, such as insurance, that African Americans could not get elsewhere. One of the first of these organizations was the Sisters Union Society, founded by thirty-eight African American women of Pulaski County in 1877. It was a self-help group designed to improve "elocution, composition, and debate and for enlarging our fund of general intelligence." The Mosaic Templars of America started in Arkansas. Formed by John E. Bush and Chester W.

Keatts of Little Rock in 1883, it had chapters in twenty-six states.

THE CHANGING ROLE OF WOMEN

These were changing times for women, too. At least some of the legal problems women had suffered under for years were removed. The constitution of 1874 at last honored a woman's right to own property in her own name. In the remote rural areas, however, life was still very hard. Rural women, by and large, lived out days of harsh, routine drudgery with only the company of their many children. In a rural setting, the poorly paid schoolteacher might be the only woman for miles around with any money of her own.

The growing cities in Arkansas offered new freedom to many women. There was greater wealth in the cities. This greater wealth, the smaller number of children an urban woman was likely to bear, and the increased convenience of town services spawned a new upper middle-class of city women. These women had the time, the chance, and the skills to work to improve their own status and that of their towns.

By the 1880s, women were forming clubs to channel their efforts. Some groups were for the cultural uplifting of their members, focusing on the study of art, music, or books. Other clubs had civic reform goals, such as better schools. In 1897, forty-eight clubs joined into the Arkansas Federation of Women's Clubs. Mrs. William C. Ratliffe of Little Rock was its first president.

Much of this reform urge focused on the **temperance** movement, the effort to reduce or outlaw the use of alcohol. Alcohol abuse was a serious problem for many men, women, families, and society at large. The efforts of women's groups helped to enact a series of laws from 1881 to 1897 that tightened local control over alcohol. By 1900, forty-two of Arkansas's seventy-five counties had fully banned the sale of liquor.

This black fraternal group at Helena in 1880 includes A. H. Miller, a state representative, and J. T. White, a state senator. (Courtesy of the Arkansas History Commission)

ARKANSAS APPROACHES THE END OF THE CENTURY

In these final years of the nineteenth century, rapid progress was being made all over America in spreading culture and making life more convenient. The number of newspapers and magazines in Arkansas tripled from 56 in 1870 to 257 in 1900. Arkansas writers included poets Albert Pike and Fay Hempstead, novelists Alice French (who wrote under the name Octave Thanet) and Ruth M. Stuart, essayist U. M. Rose, and humorist Opie Read. While many of these writers featured the best of Arkansas to the rest of the nation, others made fun of the state. Joke books about Arkansas, often some variation of *On a Slow Train through Arkansas*, were popular all over the country.

Much of the frontier violence that marred the post–Civil War period was gone. Judge Isaac Parker, called "The Hanging Judge," sat on the U.S. Federal District Court bench in Fort Smith. His rule reached into Indian Territory in Oklahoma. Until Parker's court cleaned up the area, outlaws could live outside the state in the Indian Territory. From there, they could raid towns in western Arkansas. Serving 21 years as a judge, until 1896, Parker convicted some 9,500 men and sentenced 88 outlaws to death by hanging.

Arkansas slowly became more urban. By

In this 1890 photograph, Alice French, who wrote as Octave Thanet, poses in the Black River country, the scene of many of her Arkansas stories. (Courtesy of the University of Central Arkansas Archives)

Judge Parker. (Courtesy of the University of Arkansas, Fayetteville, Special Collections)

Bass Reeves was one of the deputy U.S. Marshals serving Judge Isaac Parker's court, with the job of tracking down badmen in the Indian Country of Oklahoma and bringing them to Fort Smith for Judge Parker's justice. (Courtesy of the University of Central Arkansas Archives)

the late 1800s, there were 15 places in the state with a population of more than 2,500. That was the U.S. Census Bureau's definition of "urban." Those places had 8.5 percent of the state's population in 1900. Only three cities had populations greater than 10,000 people: Pine Bluff, 11,496; Fort Smith, 11,587; and Little Rock, 38,307.

The technical advances that were making life easier for Americans showed up most strikingly in cities. Little Rock's first street car came in 1876. Ice plants opened in Little Rock, Batesville, and other towns around 1877. Electric street lamps came in 1888. In 1892, Little Rock started a full-time professional fire department. Little Rock, Fort Smith, and a few other cities had opera houses.

When the United States entered the Spanish-American War in 1896, Arkansans were once again ready to serve under the Stars and Stripes. The state produced two regiments of volunteers, which got only as far as training bases in Alabama and Georgia before the war ended. The war produced a surge of national patriotism that made many believe the hatreds of Civil War and **Reconstruction** had now gone.

But Arkansas faced the new century with severe handicaps. The **Reconstruction** period and the threat of change in general had prompted a conservative reaction. The restrictive new state constitution and its reins on taxation and the executive branch coupled with the **Jim Crow** backlash against African American citizens hampered progress. The result was a state government that did not respond to the wishes of the people.

That reaction also furthered the system of racial **segregation.** The unfairness, hardship, and sheer awkwardness of keeping a dual society would soak up huge amounts of human and **fiscal** resources. Both of these were always in short supply in Arkansas.

Judge Parker on Justice

In the 1890s, Ada Patterson, a famous woman reporter on the *St. Louis Republic,* came to Fort Smith to interview Judge Isaac Parker. She was expecting the "Hanging Judge" to be mean and cruel. Here is part of her report:

> He is the gentlest of men, this alleged sternest of judges. He is courtly of manner and kind of voice and face, the man who has passed the death sentence on more criminals than has any other judge in the land. . . . He spoke his personal views of crime and law enforcement. . . . "I have been accused of leading juries. I tell you a jury should be led! They have a right to expect it; if they are guided they will render justice, which is the great pillar of society. . . . People have said that I am a cruel, heartless and bloodthirsty man, but no one has pointed a specific case of undue severity. . . . I have ever had the single aim of justice in view. No judge who is influenced by any other consideration is fit for the bench. 'Do equal and exact justice' has been my motto, and I have often said to grand juries, 'Permit no innocent man to be punished; let no guilty man escape.'"

Glenn Shirley, *Law West of Fort Smith* (Lincoln: University of Nebraska Press, 1968), p. 203.

VOCABULARY

Agricultural Wheel national farmers' political organization.

barricade (BAIR-ick-aid) physical obstacle thrown up as a defense against attack; to keep people from crossing a boundary.

Brindletails (BRINN-dull-taylz) followers of Joseph Brooks in the gubernatorial campaign of 1872 and subsequent Brooks-Baxter War.

Brooks-Baxter War armed conflict following the election of 1872 when the results were deemed unfair.

carpetbaggers northerners who moved south after the Civil War, presumably to get rich.

Conservatives (kun-SIR-vuh-tivz) name adopted by the Democrats to distinguish themselves from the "radical" Republicans during and after Reconstruction.

fiscal (FISS-kull) relating to money; financial matters.

Grangers (GRAYNJ-erz) another name for the Patrons of Husbandry; each chapter is known as a "grange." (The word is an old-fashioned word for granary or barn.)

Greenback Party political party formed among farmers to support increased paper money supply.

iron-clad oath sworn loyalty to the United States both prior to the war and following the war; effectively excluded all ex-Confederates from voting during Reconstruction.

Jim Crow the name given to the system of laws and social practices which intimidated, disenfranchised, and oppressed black citizens in America for ninety years.

Ku Klux Klan (KOO KLUKS KLAN) secret terrorist group organized to harass and harm black citizens to obstruct their participation in society.

lynching (LINCH-ing) acts of mob violence against black people; most often associated with illegal hangings.

Minstrels (MINN-strulls) followers of Elisha Baxter in the gubernatorial election of 1872 and subsequent Brooks-Baxter Wars; a blackface song-and-dance show.

Patrons of Husbandry (PAY-trunz uhv HUZ-bun-dree) farmers' self-help improvement organization. (Husbandry is the raising of crops and animals.)

Plessy vs. Ferguson the U.S. Supreme Court Decision in 1896 that accepted the principle of "separate but equal," the legal foundation for all the laws and practices of segregation.

Populist Party a political party formed by joining many farmers' and working men's organizations together nationwide to fight big business on behalf of the common man.

Radical Reconstruction harsh measures imposed by the U.S. Congress upon the South following Lincoln and Johnson's unsuccessful "soft" presidential approach.

Reconstruction the United States government's plans to rebuild the South following the Civil War.

Redeemers (ree-DEE-merz) name taken by the Democrats who came to power following the Brooks-Baxter War and who ended Reconstruction.

Scalawags (SKAL-ih-WAGZ) native southerners who supported the Reconstruction governments.

segregation (seg-ruh-GAY-shun) the deliberate and forced separation of one group of people from another (blacks from whites) resulting in unfair and unfavorable discrimination against black citizens.

skirmish small, armed battle.

temperance (TEM-per-uns) the restriction or abolition of the use of alcohol.

Union Labor Party a political party formed by joining the Agricultural Wheel with Republicans.

STUDY QUESTIONS

1. How did the first state government right after the Civil War discriminate against African Americans?

2. How did the Radical Reconstruction government get into power and stay in power?

3. Describe both the good and bad things about the Radical Reconstruction government.

4. Describe the circumstances of the newly freed slaves right after the Civil War. What were their goals?

5. What were some of the things that brought an end to the Radical Reconstruction government?

6. What were the major features of the state constitution of 1874, after Reconstruction?

7. What were some of Arkansas's difficulties in developing industry?

8. What were the effects of railroads on the state?

9. When the farmers "revolted," and entered politics, what were their major goals? How far did they succeed?

10. Describe the social and political discrimination enacted against African Americans by the end of the century.

7

Arkansas in the Progressive Era

1900–1920

What to Look for in Chapter 7

As the new century began, in the years 1900 to 1920, it seemed to Arkansans and other Americans that things were changing rapidly. Small businessmen and small farmers especially felt pressed by the growth of big business on one side, and by the needs of the poor and landless on the other. It was also clear that there needed to be many changes in society.

Thus was born the Progressive Movement, an attempt to adjust society to modern needs. Government became more active in areas such as prison reform, public health, and more and better schools. The new automobile meant roads were a major need. The prohibition of alcoholic beverages became an important and controversial issue.

During this time two new industries developed, lumbering and mining. In agriculture, cotton was still the major crop, but rice and fruit began to be grown.

The period ended with Arkansans participating in another war, the Great War of 1914–1918, or World War I as it was later called.

And racial tensions were always just below the surface, sometimes breaking into the open, as in the Elaine race riot.

THE PROGRESSIVE SPIRIT

Arkansans and other Americans greeted the new century with a sense that life was starting to change rapidly. Arkansas shared in those changes, but it still retained its unique traits in many ways.

The wild, open lands of the American frontier were gone, as the last of the good farmland in the public domain came into the hands of private owners. In Arkansas many of the frontier ways of life began to fade. Americans moved to the cities in huge numbers.

In the American North and Far West, waves of immigrants from Europe and from the Orient brought labor, the richness of foreign cultures, and often conflict. Few such immigrants touched Arkansas, where black and white remained the major ethnic groups.

Great factories and new industry shaped

The leisurely pace and certain values of the nineteenth century gave way to times of rapid progress and abrupt changes in the twentieth. At the turn of the century, in 1900, this happy crowd of young people went fishing at Gold Lake near Conway. (Courtesy of the University of Central Arkansas Archives, the Faulkner County Historical Society Collection)

the economy and lifestyles of Americans. Arkansas also saw its first major industries, chiefly in timber and mining. America by the early 1900s produced the tools and technology that would change people's lives. Automobiles and airplanes, electric lights and motion pictures all had an impact. Science and medicine had perhaps the greatest impact, bringing major improvements in health care.

The urge to adjust America's institutions to match the modern way of life revived in a new form, the **Progressive movement.** The first of the great reform movements, the farmers' Populist movement of the late nineteenth century, had lost its force. Daunted by their lack of real success and lulled by an increase in prices for their crops, the farmers were quiet. Now the urban middle class saw a need

for changes, a widespread feeling that was called **"Progressive."**

Some of the **Progressive** reforms were carried out by private action. People worked through churches or other groups to deal with a wide range of problems, such as drinking, **illiteracy,** and poor health care. More people seemed to have a little more money and a little more extra time to give to civic work by the beginning of the twentieth century. The results across the nation and in Arkansas were impressive.

Many of the problems, though, seemed too large for anything but government action. These problems included the vast power of huge businesses, the low wages and bad working conditions in the factories, and the growing need for good schools. Many **Progressives** believed that state governments could best

William Jennings Bryan, a compelling orator from Nebraska and Populist champion, was a hero to farmers everywhere. When Bryan lost his bid for the presidency in 1896, the farmers' revolt lost much of its steam. Bryan appears here (seated, center) *in 1910 with local leaders in Fayetteville.* (From *Fayetteville, A Pictorial History* by Kent Brown, The Donning Company/Publishers, courtesy of the University of Arkansas, Fayetteville, Special Collections)

An Ozark mountaineer, about 1900. (Courtesy of the University of Central Arkansas Archives)

meet the needs of the people. Some also called for a more active U.S. government.

THE RISE OF JEFF DAVIS

Many of Arkansas's rural farm people felt that they were being left out of the new progress and that no one in power cared about them. The city-dwellers were "rich folks" to the common farmer. The farmers had been given some hope by the Populist movement. The anger they felt at being left out of the new social structure found an outlet in Jeff Davis, a man of awesome force and energy.

Although Davis was a lawyer raised in the city, he had a gift for reaching the small farmers and hill-country folks. They were his **"wool hat boys,"** as opposed to the silk-hat crowd in the cities. Davis dominated Arkansas politics for ten years by posing as the champion of the poor whites against the rich.

Although Davis's speeches expressed ideas from both the older Populist movement and the new **Progressive** movement, he was not really a reformer. His main goal was to get and to keep public office, and his actual achievements were few. He was close to being a **demagogue**, a person who gains power by stirring up the fears and biases of the public. Davis showed a mean and bitter streak of racism. He made it clear that he was the white man's man, determined to keep blacks "in their place."

Arkansas was not the only state to produce such a leader during these times. James K. Vardaman in Mississippi, Tom Watson in Georgia, and Cole Blease in South Carolina were all products of the same mixture of poverty, racism, and fear.

Davis was born in 1862 near Rocky Comfort in Sevier County. When he was eleven, his family moved to Russellville. His father was a lawyer, editor, real estate dealer, and state legislator. Young Jeff went to the University of Arkansas and Vanderbilt Law School. He was not related to Jefferson Davis, the former president of the Confederate States of America, but he did not mind if the voters thought he was. To keep them from missing the point, he dressed in suits of Confederate gray.

Davis began his public career in 1898 as the state's attorney general, winning when his opponent died during the race. Davis dug up the state **anti-trust law**, passed years before during the farmers' revolt but never enforced. In the language of the time, a trust was a **monopoly**. That was a company that controlled everything in its area of business, with no competition.

Knowing that the common people blamed many of their troubles on the trusts, Davis read the law to mean that no trust could do business in Arkansas. He filed a law suit against the insurance companies, which the people seemed to dislike most.

Jeff Davis was a three-term Arkansas governor and a U.S. senator. His vicious attacks on business, African Americans, news editors, and city dwellers made him wildly popular with poor, rural people. He is thought to have coined the term "red-neck." (Courtesy of the University of Arkansas, Fayetteville, Jeff Davis Papers, Special Collections)

Jeff Davis Talks to His People

In the days when political campaigning was a major form of entertainment, part of Jeff Davis's appeal to the rural white farmer was his speaking style. He made sure the people knew he understood their resentment against big corporations, rich people, city dwellers, and newspaper editors. And he said things like these selections from different speeches:

I have got a little eight year old boy at home. I have been thinking of making a preacher out of him. Some want me to make a lawyer out of him . . . but when he gets grown and I find he hasn't got any sense at all I am going to make an editor out of him; then there will be one more squirrel-head in Arkansas. Most newspaper editors can live on sawdust and wind and make the wind themselves.

Some men want a woman to sing "Amazing Grace How Sweet the Sound," and know how to tune a piano, but I want one that knows how to tune a hot stove and bake big, hot biscuits with pimples on them.

During the sitting of the last Legislature you couldn't even get the Holy Bible through the Legislature until you got the O. K. of [the] railroad attorneys, who kept a paid lobby hanging around the Legislature.

I am a Hard Shell Baptist in religion; I believe in foot-washing, saving your seed potatoes, and paying your honest debts.

Old Armour and Cudahy [meat processors] never raised a sow and pigs in their lives. Yet the prices of meat are so high that I can hardly buy breakfast bacon in Little Rock enough to support my family. I just buy one little slice, hang it up by a long string, and let each one of my kids jump up and grease their mouths and go on to bed.

I had rather eat turnip greens, hog jowls and cornbread with you fellows out here around the wagon than go into the hotel and eat with the high-collared crowd.

When I licked that gang in Little Rock during the last campaign they went around on the streets with faces as long as a saddle blanket. The barbers in Little Rock would actually charge them forty cents each for a shave, their faces were so long.

The papers say that no one will vote for me except the fellows that wear patched britches and one gallus [suspender] and live up the forks of the creek, and don't pay anything except their poll tax. . . . I want to tell you that there is no great reformation that ever originated on this earth that did not come from the ranks of the humble and lowly of the land. Jesus Christ, when He went out and started the greatest reformation that ever blessed mankind, went to the humble and the lowly.

If you red-necks or hill-billies ever come to Little Rock you be sure and come to see me. . . . If I am not at home tell my wife who you are; tell her you are my friend and that you belong to the sun-burned sons of toil. Tell her to give you some hog jowl and turnip greens. She may be busy making soap, but that will be all right; you will be properly cared for, and it will save you a hotel bill.

The fight is on; it is between the trusts and the corporations and the people. If I win this race I have got to win it from 525 insurance agents . . . . every railroad, every bank, two-thirds of the lawyers and most of the big politicians; but if I can get the plain people of the country to help me, God bless you, we will clean things up. Do you mean it? Are you in earnest? If so, help me; as I say, all that I am, all that I ever expect to be, I commit into your hands and your keeping, knowing that if I deserve your confidence I will receive it. If I do not merit it, you will withhold it.

Jeff Davis, Governor and United States Senator, His Life and Speeches, L. S. Dunaway, ed. (Little Rock: Democratic Printing and Lithographing Co., 1913), pp. 40, 31, 37, 38, 39, 33, 43, 42.

Davis had found his role. The insurance companies proved their power by canceling all their policies in Arkansas. The city merchants were shocked, fearful that Davis would drive all business out of the state. And the **wool hat boys** loved it. The more Davis was attacked by the "high-collared crowd" and the "squirrel-headed editors," the more the common people liked him.

In 1900, Davis became the Democratic candidate for governor. Since Reconstruction, control of the Democratic Party had been in the hands of the planter and business class. Their control of the party had allowed them to select the Democratic nominees, who in turn always won the elections. That group would never have chosen Davis, but the choice was no longer in their hands alone.

Thanks to the Populist movement, there was now a primary system. The voters now picked the party's candidates. Davis carried seventy-four of the seventy-five counties in the Democratic primary. In the general election, Davis won by two to one over Harmon Remmel, a fine man who had the misfortune to be a Yankee, a Republican, and an insurance agent.

DAVIS AS GOVERNOR

Davis was to serve three terms as governor from 1901 to 1907. He was able to achieve very little. He always stirred up conflict and could not work with the General Assembly.

At one point, the legislators learned that Davis wanted to **veto,** or cancel, some of their new laws. To get around the **veto,** they saved up all the bills until after the session was over, without turning them over to Davis to sign. They thought the bills would become law in this way, since Davis would surely not take the time to sign all the bills at once. But Davis

vetoed every one of their bills. Then he carted the work of their entire session in a wheelbarrow to the secretary of state's office and dumped the bills on the floor.

The one area in which Davis made some headway was with the state's disgraceful prison system. For years the state had leased or rented the convicts to businesses, such as railroads and coal mines. Some of the business owners worked the inmates like slaves, whipping them and keeping them in poor living quarters with little food.

By leasing the convicts out, the state had no direct control over their lives. In some years, the annual death rate among convicts was 25 percent. Six out of every one hundred inmates were children under the age of sixteen, some as young as nine years of age. Two out of every three convicts were African American. Many of them were serving lengthy terms for "crimes" such as moving during the summer, selling cotton after dark, or buying whiskey.

People knew that the system was awful, but the convict-lease system earned the state twenty-five-thousand dollars a year. No public official had the courage to raise taxes to pay for a better system.

A report on conditions at the Coal Hill mines released in 1887 caused such a large public scandal that the state was forced to adopt a penal farm system. The state prison west of downtown Little Rock was torn down in 1899 to make room for a new state capitol. Then the state bought the 11,000 acre Cummins farm, in Lincoln County southeast of Pine Bluff. Later the state added a second prison farm by buying the nearby Tucker plantation.

The state thus began to take control of the lives of the inmates, but the prison system still leased out some of them. Davis, although he did not like paying the cost of the Cummins farm, raised his voice against the horrors of the convict-lease system. He also started a reform school for boys so that children in trouble with the law did not have to serve in prison with grown men.

Davis pardoned hundreds of African American convicts and worked to reform a prison system whose inmates were mostly black. At the same time, he became more and more racist in his speeches and his actions. In the 1904 campaign, for example, he said: "I stand for the Caucasian race in government, and I say that [Negro] dominion will never prevail in this beautiful Southland of ours, as long as shotguns and rifles lie around loose, and we are able to pull the trigger."

He took the lead in making the vote in the Democratic primary for whites only. This removed what little remained of black partici-pation in voting. When President Theodore Roosevelt came to Arkansas in 1905, Davis used his formal speech of welcome to defend lynching. Roosevelt, who had shocked southern whites by having Booker T. Washington to lunch, ignored his prepared remarks and condemned such lawlessness.

In 1906, Davis was elected to the U.S. Senate, but his methods did not work as well in Washington. His colleagues refused to treat the "**Tribune** of the Haybinders" with respect, and Davis spent most of his time at home with his family in Little Rock. He won a second term in 1912 by the smallest margin of his career. Dismayed and out of his element, Davis died of a fatal heart attack at his home in Little Rock on New Year's Day, 1913. His funeral was the largest Little Rock had ever seen.

Scipio Jones, Jeff Davis, and Prison Reform

An incident involving Scipio Africanus Jones and Jeff Davis illustrates how complicated race relations in Arkansas were.

Jones was an African American, a Little Rock attorney, and a powerful voice for the black community for many years. Davis, at the time of this incident, had just entered politics as state attorney general and was beginning to be interested in prison reform.

Jones pointed out to Davis the impossible situation of prisoners, most of them African American, who were supposed to work off their fines on the county prison farm. "How much," Jones asked, "shall county convicts . . . be allowed upon their fine and costs for each day that they labor?" Up until that time, convicts had been credited fifty cents per day's labor against the fine that they were charged. But on Sundays, no labor could be performed, so they were charged an extra fifty cents for their room and board. And if it rained or if they could not work because of illness or injury, they were charged another fifty cents. A person could stay a prisoner on the county farm for many years working off a fine of fifty dollars.

Davis agreed with the point. But when he explained it to white audiences, he started by saying, "Scipio A. Jones, a [Negro] lawyer in Little Rock, an insignificant personage, submitted to me and to my office a very important question." Then Davis changed the system so that it paid seventy-five cents a day whether convicts worked or not.

Charles Hillman Brough.
(Courtesy of the University of Arkansas, Fayetteville, Special Collections)

THE ARKANSAS PROGRESSIVES

A **Progressive movement** did come to Arkansas after Davis, mostly in the persons of George W. Donaghey and Charles H. Brough.

Born in Louisiana in 1856, George Washington Donaghey struck out for Texas on his own at the age of fifteen. After working as a cowboy and a farmer, he moved to Conway, Arkansas. He started as a carpenter and became a major builder. He was named to the state capitol building commission, and that sparked his interest in government. He became governor in 1909, serving until 1913.

Donaghey lost his bid for a third term to Joseph T. Robinson, a well-liked member of Congress from Arkansas. But Senator Jeff Davis died just three days before Robinson was to take office, and the legislature promptly chose Robinson to be senator. Because of the timing, Robinson was briefly both senator and governor. In fact, in a space of just two weeks he was a congressman, governor, and senator. He moved to the Senate, where he began a long and full career.

George W. Hays, a lawyer and county judge from Camden with little taste for reform, served two terms as governor from 1913 to 1917. Next came Charles Hillman Brough (pronounced Bruff), a professor at the University of Arkansas.

Brough was born in Mississippi in 1876 and had lived with his family in Utah. In 1898, he earned a doctoral degree in history, economics, and law from Johns Hopkins University in Maryland. Brough came to the University of Arkansas in 1903 to teach law, economics, sociology, and history. He also became well known as a speaker for Progressive Democratic candidates. He ran for governor in 1916, on a reform platform. Elected then and re-elected to a second term, he served until 1921.

Nationwide, the reform movement was in full swing. Nearly half of the American states had some form of reform government during this time. In Washington, Republican Teddy Roosevelt, U.S. president from 1901 to 1909, and Democrat Woodrow Wilson, U.S. president from 1913 to 1921, showed how government action could improve the lives of people.

Growing Up in the Country

Bethel May Stockburger Jones, born in 1903, grew up in Washington County on farms near West Fork and Winslow. Years later, this is how she remembered her childhood:

Mama had us three girls and house to keep and laundry to do. Laundry? What a job that was! She'd haul her big black iron kettle down to the cave-spring. Rubbin' clothes on a washboard and punchin' 'em with a stick is a far cry from washing machines today. Next day she kept a fire going all day to heat the little sad irons. . . . One of my jobs was churnin' the sour milk into butter. When I first started doin' this chore, I'd stand on a box 'cause I was too short to reach the dasher otherwise. I'd pump that dasher up and down for about thirty minutes, but o' course, it seemed a lot longer than it was when I wanted to be out playin'. . . .

Papa's work day was almost as full as Mama's. There was wood to chop, or things to fix, or fields to work. Papa'd be growin' corn or winter wheat or oats to feed to stock, nothin' to sell or help make a living. . . .

Our house was up on one hill and we had to go down through town and up to the schoolhouse on the other side. On cold wintery days we wrapped up in everything we had, but we still got so cold it was pitiful. We always wore long underwear. . . .

When we first started school I couldn't separate multiplication and division; those two words just didn't make any sense to me. . . . I loved English, we'd diagram sentences and I was pretty good at it. I could not remember geography, though, and I couldn't remember dates. Another special time was Christmas—goin' to the Christmas tree. People didn't have Christmas trees at home, they'd put the tree up at the church. The young people gathered to decorate the tree, then waited for everyone else to come for the program. We could hardly wait in the crowded church for the program to be over and Santa Claus to come.

Behold, Our Works Were Good: A Handbook of Arkansas Women's History, Elizabeth Jacoway, ed. (Little Rock: Arkansas Women's History Institute, in association with August House, 1988), pp. 63–75.

J. C. Corbin edited The Colored Citizen *in Cincinnati during the Civil War, then moved to Little Rock in 1871. He was elected state superintendent of public instruction during Reconstruction, and it was he who oversaw the beginning of the University of Arkansas system. When the Redeemers regained control, he was removed from statewide office, but was appointed as the first principal of Branch Normal College in Pine Bluff (now UAPB). This picture was taken around 1900.*
(Courtesy of the University of Central Arkansas Archives)

Progressives believed that businessmen, like Donaghey, and scholars, like Brough, could bring special skills to government. Arkansas began to make real progress in providing schools, roads, health, prison reform, and many state services. Donaghey, Robinson, and Brough were responsible for many of the reforms discussed in the rest of this chapter.

IMPROVEMENTS IN EDUCATION

The Arkansas superintendent of public instruction said in 1904 that "in the cause of education we stand at the bottom, or dangerously near, no matter how the states are grouped or classified in respect to the length of school terms, the amount expended per pupil, average daily attendance, in salaries paid, and in providing the means of training teachers."

Fewer than half of the school-age children went to school in 1900. For those who did attend school, the needs of the farm still set the schedule. The school term ran from July through September and took a break for harvest time. It resumed for the three winter months (if the local school had a stove for warmth). Arkansas teachers were paid $34.46

Four young women are baptized in a river near Mountain Home in 1915 as the rest of the church congregation looks on. (Courtesy of the Keller-Butcher Photo Collection, University of Central Arkansas Archives)

per month, compared to $59.80 in other states.

The state began to address some of these problems. New laws required all children between seven and fifteen years of age to attend school and called for standard textbooks in the grade schools. The number of high schools more than doubled between 1909 and 1919.

Through the efforts of the Arkansas Farmers' Union, four technical high schools opened in 1909 at Russellville, Jonesboro,

Magnolia, and Monticello. They taught farming and textile making. (All of these schools eventually became four-year colleges.) In 1911, the state formed a State Board of Education and offered aid to high schools. By 1920, over half of school-age children were going to school.

Since 1899, when the legislature dropped funding for "normal" schools, teacher training had been left to summer institutes. In 1907, the state opened the State Normal School at Conway to prepare teachers. (It later became the University of Central Arkansas.) The state teachers formed their own group during this period and had 1,500 members by 1915.

A rural state with poor roads had to have many school districts since people could not travel far to get to schools. But the number of districts in Arkansas was extremely large. In spite of some efforts toward merger, there were 5,143 school districts in 1912. Some of them had as few as 40 students in the entire district. In Washington County alone, there were 161 school districts. About half the school buildings in the state were one-room buildings, trying to serve all grades.

The state school systems were still racially segregated and far from equal. The state spent about twice as much on white schools as it did on black schools. There were very few black high schools in the state.

The efforts in education did begin to show results. A new State Literacy Council kept track of the number of people who could not read or write. About 20 percent of the people could not read or write in 1900. By 1920, the figure was down to about 9.4 percent.

One of life's great pleasures was a holiday to celebrate, and none was more important than the Fourth of July. Here, a group of youngsters are in a parade at Mountain Home in 1915. Note the decorations on the carriage, the ribbons in the girls' hair—and the bare feet. (Courtesy of the University of Central Arkansas Archives)

Work at home was more important than work in school for children at certain times of the year. Here, two boys in Baxter County help their father butcher a hog in the autumn. (Courtesy of the Keller-Butcher Photo Collection, University of Central Arkansas Archives)

ARKANSAS TAKES TO THE ROAD

The coming of the automobile in the early years of the century brought the start of a road system. In 1903, there were only fifty cars in the state, but their owners formed the Arkansas Good Roads Association. They started to lobby for new laws to promote road building.

The legislature answered in 1909 with a law that allowed local improvement districts to levy local taxes to pay for roads. That

replaced the old system under which the county could require able-bodied males to work a certain number of days per year building roads.

In 1913, the State Department of Lands, Highways, and Improvements was begun, funded by a ten-dollar tax on motor vehicles. By 1914, there were 4,800 cars in Arkansas, and the state required drivers to have a license. W. H. "Coin" Harvey, who had moved to Monte Ne after a national career in money reform, founded the Ozark Trails Association in 1913. The Association marked roads clearly and painted white rings around trees along roadsides. They also published a guidebook. The state began a system of numbered highways in 1917.

Roads were further fostered by the Federal Road Act of 1916, through which the U.S. government paid half the cost of road building. By 1921, Arkansas had about seven thousand miles of roads. Along with the road system came a large debt that would cause trouble later on. Still, even an "improved" road was most often a gravel road. Less than two hundred miles of the state's highways were all-weather, hard-surfaced roads.

A HEALTHIER STATE

Nothing improved life in Arkansas more than new knowledge and action on how to prevent and cure diseases. Progress in science inspired private groups and government workers to control many of the diseases that had given Arkansas its reputation as an unhealthy place to live.

Malaria, for example, had weakened Arkansans through the years. Then medical research discovered that malaria was caused by a germ carried by a certain kind of mosquito. That knowledge meant malaria could

Students and their teacher at the Brady School near Little Rock, in July of 1909. Students of all ages attend the one-room school house. They're going to school in July so that they will be out of school in the fall, to help with the harvest. The school was built by Frederick Kanis, one of the area's citizens of German descent. (Courtesy of the UALR Archives and Special Collections)

The development of roads in Arkansas took many years. Well into the modern era, much rural travel continued to be by horse (or, in this case, burro) drawn carts and wagons. The caption on this photo is "overland mail." (Courtesy of the University of Arkansas, Fayetteville, Special Collections, from the H. L. Miller Collection as copied by Robert O. Seat, 1982)

be controlled. Draining swamps both destroyed the breeding areas for mosquitoes and put more land into farming. Spraying areas of standing water could also prevent breeding. Devices as simple as window screens could keep out mosquitoes and other insects.

The progress of medical research also led to the end of **hookworm** and **pellagra.** Although little had been known about them, both are the kinds of chronic illnesses that make the victim tired all the time. People began to suspect that the image of the "lazy South" might have been based on the effects of these common diseases.

Hookworm came from animal wastes by way of bare feet. It is a parasite that lives in the host's intestines and drains nutrition from the body, leaving the victim weak. Controlling it was as simple as cleaning up the barnyard and wearing shoes. **Pellagra**, a deficiency of niacin that results in chronic fatigue and a skin disease, was caused by poor diet, such as the standard "hogs and hominy." It could be controlled by learning better eating habits with more varied foods. Additional vitamins could also limit its effects. Private groups, such as the Rockefeller Foundation, were very helpful in the attack on this disease.

The state joined the nationwide public health movement by forming the state Board of Health in 1913. The next year a Bureau of Vital Statistics opened to record births, deaths, and marriages. Other laws authorized a system to license doctors of all types, dentists, nurses, midwives, and embalmers.

The state built a tuberculosis hospital at Booneville. Arkansas also passed the nation's first law that required all children to have a smallpox shot. Before that practice became common, the state had nearly ten thousand cases of smallpox a year, many of them fatal. At the local level, towns began to build pure water systems and sewer systems. That in turn meant that some Arkansans began to have the modern blessing of indoor plumbing.

Mainly because of the civic involvement of women, private groups, such as the Red Cross, the Arkansas Tuberculosis Association, and the Arkansas Society for Crippled Children, began to promote better health education and care. The Arkansas Federation of Women's Clubs began to sponsor "healthy baby" contests to promote and reward concern about health in the home.

A MORE ACTIVE STATE GOVERNMENT

The Progressive goals called for more active oversight of abuses in the world of business. Under Brough, for example, Arkansas formed a Corporation Commission. It had the power to control the prices charged by electric power and gas companies. The Railroad Commission that already existed was given more power over railroad business practices. The state also made it against the law to employ children under sixteen in most kinds of work.

Governor Donaghey brought an end to the shameful convict-lease system with a single act. He studied the records of all the state prison inmates, learning that many were serving long terms for minor crimes. Some were even still in prison after their terms were done. In December of 1912, he pardoned and released 360 men from prison.

What's a State without a Flag and Flower?

Arkansas got an official state flower in 1901 and a state flag in 1913.

The designation of a state flower came after a fierce battle between the passion flower and the apple blossom. Each had its supporters: the Arkansas Federation of Women's Clubs wanted the passion flower and the Floral Emblem Society wanted the apple blossom. The 1901 legislature, heavily lobbied by both sides, picked the apple blossom.

The state flag originated when the Pine Bluff chapter of the Daughters of the American Revolution wanted to present a state flag to the newly commissioned U.S. Navy battleship *Arkansas*. They discovered that there was not a state flag.

So the DAR sponsored a state-wide contest to design a flag. The winner, picked from sixty-five entries by a committee headed by Arkansas Secretary of State Earle W. Hodges, was Miss Willie K. Hocker of Wabbaseka. The state legislature made it official in 1913.

The design, reminiscent of the Confederate battle flag, has a white diamond bordered by a starred blue band on a field of bright red. The committee added the word Arkansas in the diamond.

Those 360 men made up about half the total male prison population in Arkansas at the time. Donaghey's actions reduced the value of a convict lease and focused the public eye on the prison system. The next year, the General Assembly ended the convict-lease system altogether.

Now all convicts had to be kept on the prison farms and could no longer be abused by private leaseholders. The state was better off without the convict-lease system, but the prison farms would become almost as bad.

Progressives also thought the state government should respond more to the will of the people. The formation of the primary system had been a step in this direction. Arkansas also put into effect the **initiative**, which allows voters to write their own laws or

Selected Census Data for Arkansas 1900 to 1920

	1900	1910	1920
Total population	1,311,564	1,574,449	1,752,204
White population	944,580	1,131,026	1,279,757
Black population	366,856	442,891	472,220
Total urban population	111,733	202,681	290,497
Population of Little Rock	38,307	45,941	65,142
Percent urban population	8.5	12.9	16.6
Number of farms	178,694	214,678	232,604
Average acres per farm	93.1	81.1	75
Cotton bales produced	709,880	776,879	869,350
Bushels of corn produced	44,144,098	37,609,544	34,226,935
Bushels of rice produced	(See below)	1,282,830	6,797,126
Manufacturing Establishments	4,794	2,925	3,123
Wage earners	26,501	44,982	49,954

Notes:

The figures for the white and black population for each year will not add up to the exact figure for the total population. The difference is the small number of other races in the population.

Rice production was measured in pounds before 1910; Arkansas's rice production in 1900 was 8,630 pounds.

The U.S. Census, in counting the number of farms, tended to count a sharecropper's assigned land as a farm. Therefore, the number of farms given here does not represent the number of landowners.

People made progress against disease and ignorance, but nature could still overcome. A terrible tornado hit Brinkley and the surrounding area in the spring of 1909. This photo has two arrows, #1 pointing to "where Mr. J. L. Starrett was killed" and #2 to "where Mrs. Philips was killed." Some of the survivors survey the damage. (Courtesy of the University of Central Arkansas Archives)

Automobiles and railroads were not the only new means of transportation in the growing state. Trolleys like this one at Sulphur Rock gained popularity in towns and cities of every size. In the background is John Huddleston's Hotel. The year was 1911. (Courtesy of the University of Central Arkansas Archives)

amendments. They also adopted the **referendum,** which allows the General Assembly to refer a law to a vote of the people.

The **Progressive** movement gave new life to the effort to allow women to vote. After the all-male legislature failed in 1911 and 1913 to approve voting for women, the Arkansas Woman **Suffrage** Association formed to press hard for such a measure. National leaders, such as Carrie Chapman Catt, president of the National American Woman **Suffrage** Association, came to the state. Local leaders included women like Bernie Babcock, whose 1900 reform novel *The Daughter of a Republican* sold a hundred thousand copies. Dr. Ida Jo Brooks, a professor at the University of Arkansas Medical School, was involved. Rosa Marinoni of Fayetteville, who would become Arkansas's poet laureate in 1953, was also a leader in the **suffrage** movement.

The woman's **suffrage** movement sponsored rallies and parades with women, children, and a few men dressed all in white marching to show support for the movement. At last, in 1917, the General Assembly allowed women to vote in the crucial primary election. Two years later, in 1919, Arkansas passed the Nineteenth Amendment to the Constitution, which allowed women to vote in all elections. Arkansas was the twelfth state in the nation, and the second in the South, to ratify the amendment.

Bernie Babcock was a writer, a leader of the women's rights movement, and the founder of the Arkansas Museum of Science and History, now the Museum of Discovery. (Courtesy of the University of Arkansas, Fayetteville, Special Collections)

The "petticoat government" at Winslow, in 1925. Seated at the table in the center is Maud Duncan, the mayor. She was also the city's only pharmacist and the editor and publisher of the town's newspaper. The city council includes Lydas Cole, Florence Marley, Audie Crider, Bee Chervery, Daisy Miller, Etta Black, Martha Winn, Virginia C. Dunlap, and Stella Winn. (Courtesy of the UALR Archives and Special Collections)

Shortly after the passage of the Nineteenth Amendment, the town of Winslow, in Washington County, won national fame by choosing an all-woman town government. The town government worked so well that all the women were elected to a second term.

The campaign to end the making and sale of alcohol also revived with some success. Active in this movement were many groups, such as the Women's Christian Temperance Union and the Anti-Saloon League. One of the temperance movement's famous figures, Carry Nation, moved to Eureka Springs. "Hatchet Carry" pursued the cause by breaking up bars and taverns with a hand axe.

By 1913, a state local-option law required a yes vote of all adult white males before a liquor license could be issued in a town. That law almost dried up the state by 1915, when the General Assembly passed a total prohibition law. The U.S. law, the Eighteenth Amendment banning the production and sale of alcoholic beverages, was passed later, in 1919.

Arkansas also gained a new state capitol building during these years. The state had outgrown the 1836 building on Markham Street in Little Rock, and work started in 1899 on a new one. The site was a low hill in western Little Rock where the old state prison had

A thoroughly modern Little Rock of 1910 boasts its spanking new State Capitol Building. This view is looking west along Capitol Avenue. Note the trolley tracks on the street. (Courtesy of the University of Central Arkansas Archives)

been. Governor Jeff Davis had delayed work on the building for a while, claiming that rich people were getting richer by building it.

But Governor Donaghey pushed to complete the work. The new building, very much like the U.S. Capitol in Washington, D.C., was complete enough in 1911 for the General Assembly to meet there. By 1914, other state agencies moved in.

LUMBERING AND MINING

Timber companies that had "cut and run" from the northern states during the 1880s and 1890s turned their eyes to Arkansas's vast

acres of untouched timber around 1900. Two-thirds of the state was still forest land, much of it highly valued pine woods. Growing quickly, the timber industry employed more than thirty-six thousand workers by 1909. This was about three-fourths of all the state's non-farm wage earners.

The virgin Ouachita Mountains area held the greatest appeal for the timber companies. Bigelow Brothers and Walker Company was a Chicago-based firm that had just shut down in Michigan and Wisconsin. They moved into the area along the Fourche LaFave River in 1904.

Using the name Fourche River Lumber Company, they built Arkansas's first large, modern two-band sawmill (a mill that cuts a log with two saw blades at once). The town of Bigelow grew up at the mill site. At least a dozen more big mills in the Ouachitas were to follow.

The logging industry had no trouble finding workers to fell the trees and run the sawmills. Farmers in the Ouachitas were tilling land that could barely produce enough to feed a family, let alone provide a cash crop for sale. The wage offered by the lumber companies, although low by national standards, was more money than most of the workers had ever seen before.

A logging job often came with room and board, sometimes in portable towns. When the company cleared out a section of forest, it laid new railroad tracks into the next section of timber. There it took apart its houses, churches, stores, and schools, and loaded them onto railroad cars. These were moved down the line to be rebuilt, making a new town.

What Do You Do with an Old State House?

As the state legislature prepared in 1911 to move into the new state capitol in western Little Rock, the future of the old capitol was the subject of debate. Some people suggested that the state's financial needs were so great that the building should be sold, torn down, and the valuable downtown land used for something else.

Fortunately a number of groups, especially women's civic and patriotic societies, intervened to save the historic building, which dated back to the granting of statehood for Arkansas. With the Arkansas Federation of Women's Clubs leading the campaign, the legislature was persuaded to keep the building.

Under the name War Memorial Building, through the 1920s and 1930s it housed the law and medical departments of the University of Arkansas and a variety of state offices. Several patriotic and historical societies also kept offices there, such as the Arkansas Pioneers Association, the Daughters of the American Revolution, the United Daughters of the Confederacy, and the Daughters of 1812.

By the late 1940s, the building had fallen on hard times again. Its major tenant, the medical school, had moved to better facilities, and thirty-five years of varied use had badly worn the building.

Once again, the civic and patriotic groups rallied to convince the legislature to restore the building and dedicate it to historical use. Under the name "the Old State House" and operated by the Arkansas Commemorative Commission, it served as a museum and as home to the Arkansas History Commission, which preserves the archives, or historical records, of the state.

When the History Commission moved in the 1970s to new quarters on the state capitol grounds, the Old State House expanded its museum facilities. Today, as part of the Arkansas Department of Heritage, it is a popular attraction for Arkansans, tourists, and thousands of students on field trips.

The U.S. Forest Service became active during the days of heavy logging in the Ouachita Mountains. Here, a firefighter demonstrates his equipment, packed in by horseback, in 1910. (Courtesy of the University of Central Arkansas Archives)

A good-sized mill town had a boarding hotel for single men and a store where families did their shopping. The towns offered baseball teams, motion pictures, races, picnics, and other ways to entertain the workers. The companies employed black and white workers, but the mill town living areas were segregated. Often, the white workers' houses were painted and the black workers' were not.

Not all of the mills were run by northern concerns. James Thomas Rosborough of Texarkana owned the Bowie Lumber Company. This was the training ground for his son Thomas Whitaker Rosborough, who became owner of the giant Caddo River Lumber Company. The Bemis family of Prescott, which was related to Rosborough, owned the Ozan Lumber Company. The Dierks Lumber and Coal Company was the largest and longest-lived of its kind in the state.

The mills produced mostly plain lumber, as well as some barrel staves and railroad crossties. Some related firms also opened, such as furniture-making plants in Fort Smith and Little Rock. In 1909, at the peak time of the timber industry in Arkansas, the state was the fourth largest producer of lumber in the nation.

The "cut out and get out" techniques of the time soon used up the forests. Logging began to fade as a major industry, to be revived later by other, newer methods.

One source of jobs was in the mining industry, chiefly coal mining in Sebastian, Johnson, and Franklin counties in western Arkansas. The high-quality coal produced in Arkansas was used to power railroad engines.

A key mineral resource in Arkansas was **bauxite**, the raw ore for aluminum. **Bauxite** is found in only a few places in the United States, and the deposits in Arkansas are the nation's largest. The Aluminum Company of America (Alcoa), based in Pennsylvania, began large scale **bauxite** mining in Saline and Pulaski counties during the early 1900s.

The **bauxite** ore was mined in Arkansas and then shipped elsewhere to be made into metal. **Manganese**, which was used to strengthen steel, was mined around Cushman in Independence County. Zinc and lead were also produced in small, remote areas of the Ozarks, such as the mining town of Rush on the Buffalo River.

Some of the workers in the new timber and mining industries tried to form labor unions, uniting in groups to bargain with the owner or manager about wages and working conditions. Neither Arkansas nor the United States as a whole was very friendly to labor unions at the time. The Brotherhood of Timber Workers tried to recruit blacks and whites in the lumber industry in Arkansas, Texas, and Louisiana, but owners broke the union. There were always more people needing jobs and willing to work for low wages than there were jobs, so the owners could fire anyone who supported the union.

Attempts to organize the coal miners had only a little more success. When a United Mine Workers' strike in Sebastian County in

A young lad hauls logs in the family wagon in Gregory, Arkansas, in 1920. (Courtesy of the University of Central Arkansas Archives)

The Coronado Coal Company's Prairie Creek Mine #4 as it appeared in 1913. (Courtesy of the University of Arkansas, Fayetteville, Special Collections)

The Coronado Coal Company's Prairie Creek Mine #4 in ruins following a labor uprising in 1914. (Courtesy of the University of Arkansas, Fayetteville, Special Collections)

1914 turned violent, President Woodrow Wilson sent in U.S. Army troops to stop the strike. Workers in skilled trades, such as printing, were able to maintain unions. The skilled-trade unions usually belonged to the American Federation of Labor, which formed its first Arkansas chapters in 1904.

Arkansas also had a small group of socialists, people who called for the public to own business and industry. They sought equal shares of the wealth for all. They were mainly an outgrowth of the farmers' revolt and the miners' unions. The socialists in Arkansas belonged to more than a hundred local groups. They published newspapers and ran candidates for office. In 1912, the socialist candidate for governor won more than thirteen thousand votes.

NEW DEVELOPMENTS IN AGRICULTURE

Arkansas was still a very rural state, with most of its people involved in farming. And most farmers, without land of their own, were

Fruit growing was especially successful in northwest Arkansas but was not limited to that area. Here, peaches are harvested at Nashville by a crew with a sense of humor (see man seated at far right, and the boy in front) *around 1920.* (Courtesy of the University of Central Arkansas Archives)

sharecroppers or tenants (renters) on someone else's land. The wasteful system of sharecropping now trapped poor white farmers, as well as blacks.

Throughout the first two decades of this century, cotton was still the major crop, followed by corn, hay, oats, wheat, rice, sorghum, and peanuts. Those crops used 95 percent of the farmland in the state. Farmers also produced some fruit, dairy products, eggs and chickens, and hogs.

Rice was a rising new crop. The prairie lands around Hazen and Lonoke were best suited to rice growing, which needed much water. Although the crop required expensive machines to pump water and prepare the soil, it could be very lucrative. These were also good years for fruit growing, mainly apples, in northwest Arkansas.

There were some attempts to make crops more diverse and to use modern methods of farming. The University of Arkansas opened a School of Agriculture in 1906. By 1915 the university, with help from the U.S. government, was sending farm agents and home agents to most of the state's counties.

Despite these considerable improvements, Arkansas remained quite poor. Farm prices were better during these years, and even more so after the outbreak of the war in Europe. But it was still hard to make a living on the farm. Arkansas's major industries, such as timber and mining, paid low wages. Arkansas produced the raw resource, but other places did

As American involvement in war approached, construction began at Camp Pike outside North Little Rock. This photo was taken in 1917. (Courtesy of the University of Central Arkansas Archives)

The building is division headquarters at Camp Pike near North Little Rock during World War I. Notice the cavalry horse and the motorcycles with sidecars. (Courtesy of the UALR Archives and Special Collections)

the higher paying skilled work needed to process the goods. In 1919, the per capita income (the average amount each person made) of Arkansas was $379 a year. That may have been more money than many Arkansans had ever seen, but the national per capita income was $627.

ARKANSAS AND THE GREAT WAR

In August of 1914, Europe stumbled into a large scale war. For more than a generation, national rivalries over economics, colonies, and military weapons had made Europe a kind of powder keg, waiting for a match to touch it off. The spark came with the assassination of a member of the Austrian royal family in Sarajevo. Although no single nation really intended to start a big war, fear, suspicion, and a complicated alliance system quickly brought all the major nations to war. At first, England, France, and Russia joined up against Germany and Austria. But the war soon involved many other nations and became a World War. On the fields of battle in Europe, troops faced each other in the stalemate of trench warfare. As the war went on for years, the young men of an entire generation

Several scenes at the Camp Pike training base near North Little Rock during World War I. On the top, setting up exercises and recruits registering; in the center, infantry troops on a hike; and on the bottom filling the sleeping sacks with straw and cleaning up after a meal. (Courtesy of the UALR Archives and Special Collections)

died in futile charges against entrenched rifles and machine guns.

Most Americans deplored the war and hoped the United States would stay out of it. But as both sides wore each other down, the robust strength of the United States became more important. Then, in the spring of 1917, German submarines attacked American ships.

America came into the war on the side of England, France, and Russia. The nation quickly mobilized itself for war and sent American soldiers to the trenches in Europe. The war ended in November 1918, before American strength could be fully felt. But

America tipped the balance in favor of the British and French side.

In Arkansas, Governor Donaghey formed a Council of State Defense in May of 1917. Its charge was to register young men to serve in the war. It was an involuntary **draft**, and it met with stiff resistance at first, when the war still seemed remote to many Arkansans.

For the most part, Arkansans were patriots who supported the war effort after the United States entered the war. They engaged in "Wheatless Mondays" and "Meatless Tuesdays" and bought nearly two million dollars in war bonds, which helped finance the war effort. Counting **draftees**, volunteers, and three regiments of the Arkansas National Guard, about 72,000 Arkansans served in the armed forces. This number included African Americans and 1,400 women. About 2,000 Arkansas soldiers died, 500 in combat and the rest from diseases and accidents.

At war's end, the commander of the American Expeditionary Force in Europe, General John J. Pershing, named his top 100 heroes of the war. The list named Oscar Franklin Miller of Franklin County and Herman Davis of Manila in Mississippi County. Miller, who was killed in action, received the Congressional Medal of Honor. Ace fighter pilots also came from Arkansas, among them Captain Field E. Kindley of Gravette and John McGavock Grider, who was also killed in action.

Just as the war was nearing its end in 1917, Arkansas and the rest of the nation was struck by a fierce killer. This was an epidemic of a most severe form of the flu. Health care units were swamped by the disease through the fall of 1917. In Arkansas 7,000 men, women, and children died from the flu, far more than the wartime death toll.

Captain Field E. Kindley, from Gravette, was one of Arkansas's Air Aces of World War I. (Courtesy of the University of Arkansas, Fayetteville, Special Collections)

THE ELAINE RACE RIOT

The speed of change and the tensions of the war years produced a new unease in the years right after the war. The **Bolshevik**, or Communist, Revolution in Russia in 1917 sparked a great **"Red Scare"** in the United States. Some saw all kinds of rising revolt at home, mainly in labor unions and among immigrants.

There was also fear of social change, which was reflected most clearly in the concern over the status of African Americans. During the war, African American soldiers served in the armed forces. Many moved north to work in defense plants. A sense that things were changing gave hope to blacks, but provoked fear in some whites.

One result of these fears was an outbreak of race riots, in which groups of blacks and

Sharecroppers, or tenant farmers, worked long days in cotton fields like this one. The entire family had to plant, hoe, and pick the cotton, leaving little time for school. Even then, the family had terrible difficulty working its way out of debt to the landowner. Early efforts of tenants to organize in order to obtain just treatment could result in violence, like the Elaine Race Riot of 1919. (Courtesy of the University of Arkansas, Fayetteville, Special Collections)

Scipio Jones was a bright and fearless lawyer who fought for justice for African American Arkansans. He confronted Jeff Davis on treatment of convicts in the penal system, defended those accused of murder in the Elaine Race Riot, and would later fight in the courts for equal pay for African American teachers. This photo was taken around 1885. (Courtesy of the University of Central Arkansas Archives)

whites clashed, fought, and sometimes killed each other. There were twenty-five race riots in 1919 all over the nation. There were major riots in Longview, Texas, Washington, D.C., and Chicago, Illinois. One of the worst of these, in terms of numbers of deaths, was in the Arkansas Delta town of Elaine in Phillips County.

While the war had brought high cotton prices and some new wealth to Delta planters, African American sharecroppers felt that they had not received their fair share. Many

Booker T. Washington was a national leader in education for African Americans. He founded the Tuskegee Institute in Alabama in 1881, which led the way in technical training. Here, he is shown (center) *visiting Scott Bond and his family in Arkansas in 1911. He died in 1915.* (Courtesy of the University of Central Arkansas Archives)

wished to belong to a new union, the **Progressive** Farmers and Household Union of America.

Although many people then and since have studied the events in Elaine, the complete and true story may never be known. African Americans said that the main purpose of the union was to help blacks get a better deal from the planters. They meant to file lawsuits against whites who had cheated them. Whites believed that the union, a secret society, was giving members guns and urging them to violence.

One night in October of 1919, union members were meeting near Elaine. Because the area was tense with rumors, African American armed guards patrolled outside the building. Then a car drove up. In the car were two armed whites, a deputy sheriff and a railroad agent, and a black trustee from the local jail. The lawmen later said they were hunting for a whiskey runner. Their showing up at the union meeting was an accident, they said

No one knows who fired first, but shots broke out. The railroad agent was killed, and the deputy was wounded.

The sheriff formed a **posse** to hunt down the African Americans involved in the fields and in their homes. As blacks stood their ground, whites and blacks were killed. More whites joined in, among them many from Mississippi across the river. Finally, Governor Brough, who was in Helena himself, called in five hundred U.S. Army soldiers to restore order.

The official report on the two days and one night of the riot said five whites and twenty-five blacks were killed. Other reports put the number of African Americans killed at closer to one hundred or more. The highest estimate is 856.

After the riot, sixty-five African Americans were tried on varied charges. The trials were brief: all-white juries reached **verdicts** in as little as two minutes in some of the cases. Twelve African Americans were sentenced to death for murder. They quickly appealed to higher courts.

The key defense lawyer in the tough and complex legal process was Scipio Jones, Little Rock's leading African American lawyer. The new National Association for the Advancement of Colored People helped finance the appeals. In the end, the higher courts freed all of the men who had been condemned to death.

One of the ironies of the riot was that Governor Brough was as forward thinking on the subject of race as almost any white southerner of the time. In 1912, he had chaired a study group on the "race question" in the South. He held Booker T. Washington of Tuskegee Institute in high regard and honored Arkansas blacks Joseph A. Booker and E. T. Venegar for their efforts to spread Washington's ideas.

Brough once said, "the Negro is entitled to life, liberty, and the pursuit of happiness and the equal protection of our laws for the safeguarding of these inalienable rights." After the Elaine riot, Brough convened a group of whites and blacks to discuss the problems between the races and to search for ways to work together. But he could not control the larger social forces at work.

Arkansas had taken many steps toward the modern world. But it still had a long way to go.

VOCABULARY

anti-trust law (ANT-eye TRUST law) law passed to limit the power of business monopolies, to protect trade and commerce from unfair business practices.

bauxite (BOX-ite) the raw ore from which aluminum is derived.

Bolshevik (BOWL-shuh-vik) a member of the political party in Russia responsible for the Russian Revolution of 1917; commonly used to mean the same thing as Communist.

demagogue (DEM-uh-GOG) a person who gets power by stirring up the fears and biases of the public.

draft government selection of individual young men for service in the nation's armed forces without their having any choice in the matter.

hookworm a parasite that lives in its victim's intestines and that can enter the body through bare feet.

illiteracy (ih-LIT-er-uh-see) the inability to read and write.

initiative (ih-NISH-uh-tiv) the power of citizens to create a new law by obtaining enough signatures on a petition to place the proposed law on the ballot for a popular vote.

manganese (MANG-guh-neez) a hard metal used to strengthen steel.

monopoly (muh-NAH-pull-ee) a company that controls all the business in its industry, operating without any competition; also known as a "trust."

pellagra (pull-LAY-gruh) a chronic disease of the skin and digestive tract caused by deficiencies of protein and niacin (vitamin B).

posse (PAH-see) a band of citizens authorized by law enforcement officers to assist in the search for and arrest of suspected criminals.

Progressive movement social reform movement of the early twentieth century aimed at improving health care, education, working conditions (especially concerning child labor), prisons, and other social institutions.

Red Scare widespread fear of a communist takeover in the United States.

referendum (REFF-er-END-um) the ability of the legislature to place laws or proposed laws before the general public for a popular vote.

suffrage (SUFF-ruj) the right to vote.

tribune (TRIB-yoon) a Roman official who protected ordinary citizens from harmful acts of more powerful, influential members of society; a defender of the people.

verdict in a trial, the jury's judgment about the guilt or innocence of the accused party.

veto (VEE-toh) one vote that overrules the votes of others. A governor may veto acts passed by the state legislature, as the president may veto acts passed by Congress.

"wool hat boys" term Jeff Davis used to describe the common hill folks and farmers who supported him; they wore wool hats instead of stylish and expensive silk or felt hats.

STUDY QUESTIONS

1. What circumstances were the background for the Progressive period?

2. What group of voters did Gov. Jefferson Davis appeal to the most? How and why?

3. Describe the conditions in Arkansas prisons in this period.

4. Discuss the improvements in public education in the Progressive period.

5. What factors made Arkansans interested in building better roads?

6. Explain how Arkansas got its state flag and state flower.

7. Describe the improvements in public health during the Progressive years.

8. What changes took place in the role of women during this period?

9. What were the good and bad points about the lumbering and mining industries?

10. Discuss the Elaine race riots, including the general background, the specific situation in the Arkansas Delta, and the events in Elaine.

8 Hard Times

1920–1940

What to Look for in Chapter 8

The period 1920 to 1940 brought the hope of prosperity and the reality of the Great Depression.

Although most Americans enjoyed a new economic prosperity in the 1920s, Arkansas remained a poor state with slow progress. The discovery of oil and the coming of electricity offered a glimpse of a better future. A deep split over traditional values was revealed in the revival of the Ku Klux Klan and a new attack on Darwinian evolution.

For state government, health, education, and road building continued to be major concerns. In agriculture, more people became tenants or sharecroppers, without land. The Flood of 1927 covered half the state's farm land and made thousands homeless, and was followed by drought.

Like all America, Arkansas was devastated by the Great Depression of the 1930s. Fortunately, the federal government's New Deal brought temporary work programs, such as the CCC and the WPA, and then permanent safety-net measures such as Social Security and agricultural payments.

THE BEGINNING OF MODERN AMERICA

For most Americans, the decade of the 1920s marked the start of modern times. Industry could now produce a startling array and number of **consumer goods**. There were cars and electric lights, refrigerators, and washing machines. There were telephones, radios, and motion pictures. These new machines had the power to reshape the lives of most Americans.

Going where the factory jobs were, Americans were on the move away from the farms. By 1920, more than half the people of the United States lived in cities.

City life meant a whole new realm of ideas and ways of doing things. In the cities, artists produced **abstract paintings**, musicians played jazz music, and poets and authors wrote in new forms and styles. It was a time of rapid and often shocking change.

In Arkansas, all these trends touched the people, but to a somewhat lesser degree than they affected places with larger urban populations. Arkansans were still poor by the standards of the rest of the nation. Most people remained on farms and in rural areas. Because of this, change came slowly to Arkansas.

Arkansans and other Americans could not see that the 1920s would end with the **Great Depression** and that the 1930s would begin with the major social changes of the **New Deal.**

THE OIL BOOM

For one brief moment, Arkansans shared the thrill and hope of prosperous times. The cry of "It's a **gusher!**" rang out in El Dorado in 1921, and Arkansas's **oil boom** was under way. Swiftly the town's size swelled to three times its normal level. Nearby Smackover, where there was a second strike the next year, soon was home to twenty thousand people. Strangers flooded into town each day to seek their fortunes. Like the Gold Rush of 1849, the oil boom of the 1920s spawned wild, frontier-style towns, and, in a few cases, instant wealth.

With output peaking at more than seventy-seven million barrels a year, Arkansas produced

The 1920s Look to the Future: Roads, Electricity, Schools

In one of the history books young people in Arkansas read in 1924, the author demonstrated the bright hopes of the 1920s. John Moore, in *A School History of Arkansas,* offered a prediction of what the state would be like fifty years in the future.

Here is part of his prediction for Arkansas by 1974:

Fifty years from now Arkansas will have a population of 6,482,963; the Diamond Mines will be the most famous in the world; . . . paved highways will extend from one end of the State to the other like so many bands of ribbon; interurban cars will connect every part of the State with every other part of the State; the forests will be preserved and the lumber industry increased for the reason that every man who cuts a tree will be required by law to plant another in its place and see that it has a chance to grow; our rivers will be converted into electric power and every city, village, and country home will have electricity for lighting and cooking; every ounce of cotton grown in the State will be manufactured into merchantable materials RIGHT HERE; there will be a Grammar school and High school within reach of every home in the State and all the children of school age will be attending them; agricultural schools and normal colleges will be sufficient to take care of all the needs for both white and colored . . . and the University of Arkansas will have 25,000 students; the best citizens will be willing to run for all offices of public trust and though there may be some grafters still among us, they will be very still; . . . and Arkansas will be the best place in the world to live, make a living and rear a family of patriotic citizens. Wouldn't you like to be here, *then?*

You can take a look around you and see how close you think he came to being right.

John H. Moore, *A School History of Arkansas* (Little Rock: Democratic Printing and Lithography Co., 1924), pp. 258–59.

Scenes from the boom in the El Dorado and Smackover area in the early 1920s.
LEFT: *A **gusher.***
BELOW: *Oil field workers soaked in oil from a **gusher.***
NEXT PAGE, TOP: *Oil straight from the well was stored in open fields, held in by small **levees***.
NEXT PAGE, BOTTOM: *Main Street in Smackover during the oil boom. Notice the automobile and the saddle horse. One block had a hotel, a drug store, a cafe, a variety story, a boot shop, and an army surplus store.*
(Courtesy of the Arkansas Museum of Natural Resources, UALR Archives and Special Collections)

the fourth largest amount of oil among all the states by 1924. Hopes of yet larger oil strikes faded, though, and the **oil boom** was contained in a small part of south Arkansas. The oil producers did learn that the natural gas from the wells, at first burned off as waste, was also a valued product.

The timber industry, and related work such as furniture making, remained the state's largest moneymaker. Its products equaled four times the value of any other products. Bauxite mining also continued, although below the peak of the war years. Arkansas produced 70 percent of the nation's supply of bauxite in 1923.

Railroads still employed many Arkansans,

and the Missouri Pacific repair shop in North Little Rock had the state's largest single payroll. For a short time, Arkansas was even making cars: the Climber Company of Little Rock produced about two hundred cars and trucks in the early 1920s.

For the most part, Arkansas industry extracted raw resources from the mines or the forests. The raw products were shipped to other places to be processed. There were never many factories in Arkansas that produced finished goods, as there were in the states of the Northeast. Wages paid to workers were very low, close to the lowest in the nation.

Most Arkansas jobs paid very little. As logger Bill McBride put it, "The wages were

(ABOVE AND NEXT TWO PAGES) *In the 1920s, the oil boom brought a period of prosperity to some of the Indians in Oklahoma who claimed Quapaw descent. Vacationing in Hot Springs, several of them posed in a photographer's studio, with an ostrich-drawn wagon and in a mixture of traditional and modern clothing styles.* (Courtesy of the University of Arkansas, Fayetteville, Special Collections)

Scenes from the timber industry in the 1920s.

ABOVE: *A timber camp, somewhere along the Missouri Pacific Railroad.* (Courtesy of the UALR Archives and Special Collections)

BELOW: *The Forester lumber mill in Scott County with the mill in the background and the company town in the foreground.* (Courtesy of the University of Central Arkansas Archives)

FACING PAGE: *The Henry Wrape Stave Company in Little Rock. They made barrels, like the ones in the foregound.* (Courtesy of the UALR Archives and Special Collections)

cheap; the work was hard. But actually it was about the only thing there was in this country to do." Many boys and girls left school some time after the third grade to work for $2.50 a week in Little Rock factories.

THE COMING OF ELECTRICITY

Arkansas joined the electric age largely through the efforts of Harvey Couch. A farmer's son from Calhoun in Columbia County, young Harvey clearly saw the potential of the telephone. He built telephone lines to serve parts of Arkansas, Mississippi, and Louisiana. When he sold his phone systems to American Telephone and Telegraph, he became a millionaire at the age of thirty-four.

Next, Couch started the statewide power system that came to be known as Arkansas Power and Light Company. By the early 1920s, Couch was selling electric power to almost fifty towns in Arkansas. Couch's special skill was his ability to connect many small city electric systems into a large network. He was also able to convince northern bankers to invest money in him and his plans. To produce yet more power, he built dams on the Ouachita River. The first dam formed Lake Catherine, and the second formed Lake Hamilton.

Radio was one of the new users of electric power. In 1921, Couch started the state's first radio station, WOK in Pine Bluff. That first station broadcast scheduled programs only on Tuesday and Friday nights.

Soon radio swept through Arkansas and the nation. Two young men from Mena, Chester Lauck and Norris Goff, became famous across the nation as Lum and Abner. Housed in their fictional "Jot 'Em Down

Chester Lauck and Norris Goff, on the left as themselves and on the right as their popular radio and movie characters, Lum and Abner. (Courtesy of the Lum and Abner Museum, Pine Ridge, UALR Archives and Special Collections)

Store," Lum and Abner were to delight Americans with their gentle down-home humor. Another Arkansan, Bob Burns, also became a famous radio comic. He told jokes, many about his home state, and made raucous music on his home-made **bazooka.** (During World War II, his instrument gave its name to a deadly rocket launcher.)

The decade also brought motion pictures. At first they were silent films with subtitles on the screen. In some movie houses there was also organ music to go along with the film. By 1928, motion pictures with sound had been developed, and they became even more widely enjoyed.

Like their fathers who coined the "New South" slogan in the early 1900s, modern men of business hoped to attract more industry to the state. They combined to create the

Arkansas Advancement Association to sell the good points of the state to out-of-state investors. They brought news and magazine writers to tour the state. They hired former Governor Brough to make speeches all over the nation about the glory of Arkansas.

In 1923, the General Assembly felt that the nickname **"Bear State"** was no longer fitting. They renamed Arkansas the **"Wonder State."**

THE KU KLUX KLAN

Progress and change did not suit everyone. Some were deeply disturbed by the fast pace of motor cars and telephones. They could not adjust to the shock of different cultures they learned about on the radio and in the movies.

To them, the new ideas that seemed to be spreading out of the big cities spelled disaster. Many people went to extreme lengths to turn back the clock to what they believed were "the good old days" of "true Americanism."

One of their outlets was a revived **Ku Klux Klan.** Starting in Georgia in 1915, the new Klan had spread quickly through the small towns of the United States. It had its greatest strength in the Midwest and the South. The Klan started to gain power in Arkansas in 1921, and within a few years claimed to have forty thousand members.

Unlike the Klan of old, the new Klan did not focus solely on African Americans. The new Klan members also attacked and punished those who seemed to differ in any way from the customs and morals of white Protestant Americans. The Klan's victims included **bootleggers**, wife-beaters, and gamblers. The Klan also harassed Jews, Catholics, union members, and "foreigners" of all types. The Klan was very active in the teeming oil boom towns of southwest Arkansas.

While the Klan flourished, from 1921 to 1924, Klansmen controlled the politics of many counties and towns. They were a major factor in the governor's election of 1924. The Klan declined after 1924, at least partly because its members learned that the national Klan leaders were using them to make money for themselves.

*A Klan rally during the revival of the **Ku Klux Klan** in the 1920s, with robed and hooded Klansmen and a burning cross.* (Courtesy of the Taylor Collection, Arkansas Oil and Brine Museum, UALR Archives and Special Collections)

THE CRUSADE AGAINST EVOLUTION

The debate between change and tradition had a forceful impact on religion. Church, then as now, was a key part in the lives of many Arkansans. Some church groups argued that change was part of God's plan. Others saw any change as tearing down moral values. The debate split churches and even families.

Many of those who hoped to maintain the old ways believed in the concept of **fundamentalism.** This belief held that each word in the Bible was the literal truth and that the Bible was the sole guide to life and morals. Those who believed in this concept were strongly opposed to some new concepts in science.

The British scientist Charles Darwin theorized that all life forms changed over time by the process of **natural selection.** When a certain **species** could adapt itself to do better in the struggle for life, that **species** survived. Those that did not change died out. Thus, by **"survival of the fittest,"** life forms changed over a long period of time. He called the process **evolution.**

Applied to humans, **evolution** implied that the rise of the human **species** was a slow process taking place over many millions of years. Darwin's theory was first expressed in the late 1800s and was widely studied and approved of by many scientists.

In the 1920s, though, the theory of **evolution** became a key symbol in the clash of values. Some church leaders believed that **evolution** went against accounts of creation in the Bible's book of Genesis. This belief led to attempts to limit or stop the teaching of **evolution** in the public schools.

The Arkansas General Assembly in the 1920s twice discussed and voted against such a law. However, a neighboring state, Tennes-see, outlawed the teaching of **evolution.** That set the stage for a great showdown between the two groups in 1925.

John T. Scopes, a high school science teacher in Dayton, Tennessee, deliberately broke the law by teaching the theory of **evolution** in his classes with the intent to test it in court. The Scopes trial—the so-called **"monkey trial"**—became a national focus of the debate between change and tradition. Scopes's defense lawyer was Clarence Darrow, famous for his defense of the oppressed. Darrow was an **agnostic,** one who believes that God cannot be known.

The state's key witness was none other than the great speaker and Populist William Jennings Bryan. He was now a champion of moral values. The state found Scopes guilty. The trial was so stressful, though, that Bryan died there in Dayton right after it was over.

The people of Arkansas, perhaps as a way of sending a message to "Yankee meddlers" like Darrow, then put into effect their own anti-evolution law. Passed in 1928 by 63 percent of the public vote, the act outlawed teaching that "mankind ascended or descended from a lower order of animals." The law stayed on the books for forty years, though it was not enforced.

THE STATE AND ROAD BUILDING

Roads were still the focus of Arkansas state politics. The car was changing the way people lived and moved. In 1920 there were 60,000 cars in the state; by 1926 there were 210,000 of them. In Arkansas, local improvement districts were responsible for building roads. Each one of the hundreds of districts planned, built, and maintained roads in its region, with the support of local taxes. There was no central system for planning and connecting roads.

By a series of steps, Arkansas built a state highway system. The first moves came while Thomas C. McRae was governor. He was a lawyer and banker from Union County who had served eighteen years in the U.S. House of Representatives. He was governor from 1921 to 1925. The U.S. government, which offered the states some funds for highways, took the stand that Arkansas must create its own statewide road system. The federal government backed up its demand by cutting off the state's federal highway funds in 1923. At McRae's urging, the Arkansas General Assembly gave the state Highway Department sole power to build and maintain roads.

Also, the legislature shifted the burden of taxes for roads from local property owners to road users. The legislature did this by charging a fee to obtain a car license and by putting taxes on gas and oil. The next step came from Governor John E. Martineau, a lawyer and state judge from Lonoke. He served only briefly as governor, from 1927 until he became a federal judge in 1928. But he was the author of the **"Martineau Road Plan,"** which further involved the state in building roads.

The state government first took over the debts the local districts had built up over the years by having to build roads before there was state or federal help. Then the state began to issue bonds—that is, the government borrowed money in the name of the state—to pay for roads. In the late 1920s, the nation was still seeing good times. Raising bond money for roads did not seem too risky. But

This became a common sight in the 1920s, as the automobile became common. This service station was in Fort Smith. (Courtesy of the UALR Archives and Special Collections)

The automobile age caught Arkansas still in the mud. Above, *a typical road, muddy ruts after a rain.* Below, *what happens when an automobile tries to travel such a road.* (Courtesy of the University of Central Arkansas Archives)

the state was piling up a large debt that would become a big problem in just a few years.

By 1928, Arkansas had 8,716 miles of roads, about a fourth of them paved. Forty-six counties, well over half of the 75 total counties, had no paved roads. Two counties had no roads at all.

EDUCATION

Education in Arkansas suffered from the problems of a poor, rural state. About half the public schools were one-room schoolhouses, in which one teacher taught all grades and all subjects. Of the 10,000 teachers, about 800 were college graduates, and more than 1,600 had not gone beyond the eighth grade.

There were only about 400 high schools in the state. The school term was arranged around the farm schedule. School started in July, dismissed for the harvest in the fall, resumed in December, then ended in time for the spring planting.

Part of the problem was money. In the early 1920s, Arkansas spent about $23 per pupil per year. The amount in Missouri was about $54, and in Oklahoma about $64. The rural nature of the state and the hardships of travel posed other problems. In fact, Governor Martineau's road campaign was pushed forward in part because of its effect on education. Martineau's slogan was "Better Roads to Better Schools."

Education did improve, with the best results in the towns and cities. People (particularly women) trained at the state teachers' colleges pursued real professional careers in teaching. Terms lasted longer. New buildings were built.

The Maple Valley schoolhouse at Muddy Fork in the 1930s. This is the school attended by Ruth Polk Patterson, who wrote a history of her family in The Seed of Sally Good'n. *(Courtesy of the Arkansas History Commission)*

Little Rock High School (later Central High) moved into its new building in 1927. The National Association of Architects labeled it "America's most beautiful High School." It was also America's largest high school until the 1940s.

About 45 percent of black children went to school, compared with 54 percent of whites. African American schools were separate, and they were not equal. By all measures —state and local funding, teachers' wages, buildings—black schools received less than white schools. Only nine counties had high schools for blacks. Fewer than 2 percent of African American youths were able to get as far as high school.

Some black Arkansans built their own schools out of nothing. For example, Floyd Brown borrowed money and supplies to open a school for African Americans at Fargo. From its start in 1920, the Fargo School grew to have 12 teachers, 180 students, and 12 buildings on a 500-acre plot. The school taught technical and farming skills, **home economics**, and music, as well as more traditional academic subjects.

Despite the low number of African American high school graduates, Agricultural, Mechanical, and Normal College, or AM&N (later the University of Arkansas at Pine Bluff) did provide college instruction. In central Arkansas Shorter College in North Little Rock, Arkansas Baptist College, and Philander Smith College in Little Rock were offering classes. In 1927, African American teachers were allowed to take courses by mail from the University of Arkansas and the State Teachers' College. Two thousand teachers enrolled in these courses.

The state acquired Henderson-Brown College at Arkadelphia in 1929 from the Methodist church. In Little Rock, the city school board started a junior college in 1927, using the extra space in the new Little Rock High School and funds from the George W. Donaghey Foundation. The number of students at the university at Fayetteville rose steadily.

Small towns used to support city bands. During the 1920s, the schools tended to take over this function. Sports events in football and basketball gained appeal during this time as well. Each town took great pride in its local teams. The University of Arkansas became a member of the Southwest Conference but still played other Arkansas schools such as Hendrix. AM&N fielded its first football team in 1929.

PUBLIC HEALTH

The Progressive spirit moved the cause of public health forward during the 1920s in Arkansas. Governor McRae started a **tuberculosis sanitorium** for African Americans at Alexander. Maternal health received aid from a federal program in 1920 that offered instruction to rural pregnant women and **midwives.** The University Medical School won increased funding from the General Assembly in 1922 and again in 1925.

Members of the Arkansas Federation of Women's Clubs campaigned to promote physical therapy and prevent crime. They gave support to programs for children in trouble with the law. They set standards of child health that required every child to have "normal vision or properly fitted glasses, normal hearing . . . good teeth and gums, correct posture."

The new standards called for each child to be well nourished and protected against **typhoid, diphtheria,** and **smallpox,** and "be able to show that his birth is of record." The concern over proper nutrition expressed itself in milk and hot lunch programs in the schools. Child-care classes for parents of preschool children and infants were started.

Hunting has always been one of Arkansans' favorite pastimes. These scenes are from the 1920s, a deer camp near Scott and coming home from a duck hunt at Stuttgart. Much of the state's wild game was almost gone by the 1930s, but the creation of the state Game and Fish Commission and careful management allowed most **species** to restore themselves. (Courtesy of the UALR Archives and Special Collections)

In the 1930s, **tuberculosis** was still a serious disease. People who had the disease were put in separated residences called **sanatoriums**. This was the children's building at the Arkansas Tuberculosis **Sanatorium** at Alexander. Improvements in nutrition and medicine have almost eliminated **tuberculosis, and sanatoriums** are no longer needed. (Courtesy of the University of Central Arkansas Archives)

The Reverend Orlando P. Christian raised one hundred thousand dollars to build the first free children's hospital in the state in 1925. This became known as Arkansas Children's Hospital.

AGRICULTURE AND SHARECROPPING

Even though there was a growing level of well-being in Arkansas in the 1920s, it had little direct effect on the farmers. Most Arkansans were farmers. Most farmers still relied upon cotton as their money crop, and cotton prices were not very good in the 1920s. That meant more and more Arkansas farmers became **sharecroppers** or **tenants.**

About eight out of every ten Arkansans were tied to the land for their living. Cotton was the largest single crop. Other major crops were, in order of volume produced, corn, hay, oats, wheat, rice, **sorghum**, and peanuts. The years of World War I had been good years for cotton, with the price reaching thirty-five cents a pound. Right after the war, though, the price began to drop as cotton farmers produced more cotton than the world markets could absorb. The price was twenty cents a pound by 1920, and then declined during the decade. In a way, the **Great Depression** began for Arkansas farmers in 1920.

The decline in prices meant more and more farmers could not make a crop that would pay for their land, so they had to give up their land and rent from someone else.

Because cash for rent was scarce, the renters became **sharecroppers.**

The **tenant** promised the owner a share of his crop in return for the use of the land and, if needed, a house, mules, tools, and seed. Each tenant's contract varied a little, but in almost all cases the system was an economic trap.

The owner charged the costs of growing the crop, plus food and other living costs—they called these costs **"furnish"**—against the proposed profits. In this way, the **tenant** family was always in debt to the landowner. And it was always the landowner who sold the cotton crop. The **tenants** never knew for sure how much the profit was or the exact amount of their debt that would be removed from the profit.

In the early 1900s, **sharecropping** had mostly been a labor system for African Americans. In the 1920s, most black farmers were **tenants** of some kind, but more and more white farmers were having to **sharecrop** too. In 1900, about a third of white farmers in Arkansas had been **tenants.** By the 1930s, after the decline of the 1920s and the Great Depression, more than half (nearly 60 percent) of the white farmers were **tenants.** Of the total number among blacks and whites, nearly two-thirds of Arkansas farmers were **tenants.**

Most **sharecropping** plots were small and

These men are weighing cotton bales at a cotton yard in Conway, about 1930. The metal arms with the curves on the ends are a part of the scale. (Courtesy of the University of Central Arkansas Archives)

*A young girl looks out the window of a **sharecropper**'s cabin. Near the porch are a chopping block, axe, and washtub. And curled up near them is the family's black-and-white cat.* (Courtesy of the Jesse Laurence Collection, University of Arkansas, Fayetteville, Special Collections)

required intense farming even to hope to meet the debt to the landowner. In most cases, the cotton fields came right up to the front door of the house. Everyone worked in the fields: men, women, and children. School was often ignored, because the **tenant** needed his children working to help support the family. Many **tenants** were without roads, and most lacked electric power and running water.

THE FLOOD OF 1927

Nature was hard on Arkansas farmers, too, bringing troubles ranging from the **boll weevil** to the great flood of 1927. After a cold, hard, and wet winter that year, it rained all of April and into May. Yell County got 20 inches

of rain in April. At Little Rock, 8.3 inches of rain fell in 48 hours. A large section of the Baring Cross Bridge across the Arkansas River washed away.

The floods began in mid-April, all along the Mississippi River valley. Arkansas was the hardest hit, with about half the state's crop lands under water. The floods caused the deaths of 127 people and an estimated 50,000 head of **livestock**. Thousands more people were homeless for weeks, camping out on **levees** and other high spots. Near Pine Bluff, about 500 people were stranded for days on a bridge where they had taken refuge.

The American Red Cross and other private groups helped flood victims with food, clothing, and shelter. President Calvin Coolidge named Herbert Hoover to arrange private relief efforts. But farmers' appeals to the U.S. government for help were ignored.

Cotton farmers were not alone in their troubles. The fruit growers of northwest Arkansas came upon hard times, too. Disease attacked many types of fruit trees and ruined the orchards within a few years. Moreover, fruit growers had to compete with new and well-organized growers in states of the Northwest, such as Washington.

New trade in the Pacific Northwest also had its effect on the lumber industry. Timber output in Arkansas in 1925 was half of what it had been in the peak year of 1909 as the big firms began to "cut out and get out."

One firm tried a new approach. In 1925, the Dierks Lumber Company began the practice of **sustained yield forestry.** This meant they kept their lands and planted new seedlings where trees had been cut. They managed the forest's new growth with the intent of growing and cutting trees on the same land for years to come.

THE COMING OF THE GREAT DEPRESSION

All the bright hopes of the 1920s came crashing down in 1929 with the start of the **Great Depression.** Some believe the basic cause of the **Great Depression** was that the American system was able to produce goods much faster than people were able to buy goods. During the 1920s, high profits had been used for building more factories, which further increased output.

While workers' wages increased, wages did not increase as fast as goods were produced. Also, many rural parts of the country, like Arkansas, had never really been a part of the boom of the 1920s. There were signs of

The floods of 1927 reached as far as Fort Smith. (Courtesy of the UALR Archives and Special Collections)

During the great flood of 1927, the Missouri Pacific Railroad bridge between Little Rock and North Little Rock was isolated and almost washed away. (Courtesy of the University of Central Arkansas Archives)

Refugees from the floods of 1927 grabbed everything they could, loaded it on wagons, and headed for higher ground. These refugees were coming into Marianna. (Courtesy of the University of Arkansas, Fayetteville, Special Collections)

Rogers celebrated fruit growing with its annual Apple Festival. This is the Springdale float in the 1926 parade. (Courtesy of the UALR Archives and Special Collections)

business troubles as early as 1926 and 1927, but people refused to believe that the good times could end. Many began to **speculate** on the stock market. That is, they bought stocks on credit in the belief that stock prices would keep going up. The collapse of the stock market in the fall of 1929 was the signal that the economy was failing and marked the start of the **Depression.**

First the banks had to close. Those who had borrowed could not repay their loans. Many who had placed their savings in the banks stormed the banks' doors to withdraw all their money.

Soon factories shortened their work hours or even closed their doors. Hundreds of thousands of men and women were now without jobs, which meant they had no money to buy cars or houses or clothing or food. Therefore, even more firms, including small retail shops, had to close or cut back.

By the early 1930s, about 25 percent of the American labor force was out of work, without any steady income. Through the early 1930s, the **Depression** spread throughout the United States and then the entire world.

In Arkansas during 1930 and 1931, 192 banks failed. Total bank holdings dropped from $137.6 million in 1929 to $41.8 million in 1934. The biggest bank in the state, the American Exchange and Trust Bank, shut down in 1930, taking with it many other banks. Many people who had checking or savings accounts in the banks lost all their money.

Claudia and Dave Schwartz owned and operated this dry goods—or clothing—store in Earle in the 1920s. (Courtesy of the UALR Archives and Special Collections)

Nearly half of the businesses in Arkansas had closed by 1931. Between 1929 and 1933, construction of all types dropped by two-thirds, and the number of workers in Arkansas lumber mills was reduced by about 60 percent. In all, about 245,000 people lost their jobs, more than a third of the state's wage-earning work force.

Those who still had jobs took wage cuts. People worked for 50 cents a day and were glad to get it. The annual income of Arkansans fell from $705 in 1929 to $152 in 1933, with only Mississippi falling further behind.

Local and county governments were with-out funds, and public schools faced disaster. By 1933, lack of money had forced 725 schools to close and another 1,200 to shorten their terms. Teachers, already the lowest paid in the nation, sometimes worked without wages.

On the farms, what was bad to begin with got worse quickly. Cotton that brought 20 cents a pound in 1927 was at 17 cents a pound in 1929, and 5 cents a pound by 1932. That was less than the cost of growing the crop. Nearly 80 percent of the people were farmers, and the farmers' not being able to buy had an impact on almost every business in the state.

THE DROUGHT AND THE DUST BOWL

As if to make things as bad as they could get, nature hit the South and Southwest during the 1930 growing season with the worst drought on record. Arkansas received only 35 percent of its average rainfall. The central part of the state went without a drop of rain for 71 days that summer. The heat stayed around 100 degrees, burning up home gardens along with the state's cotton crop.

Throughout the heartland of America, farmers despaired as their fields turned to dust and blew away in the wind. Farmsteads stood empty as farmers loaded their goods into cars and trucks and headed west to California, looking for food and work. Out in California, they called the displaced farmers **"Okies"** or **"Arkies."**

People later talked and wrote about the **"Dust Bowl"** that hit the Great Plains in the mid-1930s. In truth, Arkansas was harder hit by the combined forces of flood, Depression, and drought than any other section of the nation.

During the winter of 1930–31, many people in Arkansas faced not just want and hunger but real starvation. Neither the state nor the U.S. government had any means for giving relief. Fully one-third of Arkansas's people relied solely upon private relief efforts. They were mostly living on the one meal a day offered by the American Red Cross. In

Black, White, and Blue: The Depression Hits Stamps

Maya Angelou, who later became a famous poet, writer, and singer, lived in Stamps, Arkansas (near Texarkana), for a time when she was a young girl. In her autobiography, she described the white community from the perspective of the black community and the coming of the **Great Depression** of the 1930s.

A light shade had been pulled down between the Black community and all things white, but one could see through it enough to develop a fear-admiration-contempt for the white "things"—white folks' cars and white glistening houses and their children and their women. But above all, their wealth that allowed them to waste was the most enviable. They had so many clothes they were able to give perfectly good dresses, worn just under the arms, to the sewing class at our school for the larger girls to practice on. . . .

The Depression must have hit the white section of Stamps with cyclonic impact, but it seeped into the Black area slowly, like a thief with misgivings. The country had been in the throes of the Depression for two years before the Negroes in Stamps knew it. I think everyone thought the Depression, like everything else, was for the whitefolks, so it had nothing to do with them. Our people had lived off the land and counted on cotton-picking and hoeing and chopping seasons to bring in the cash needed to buy shoes, clothes, books and light farm equipment. It was when the owners of the cotton fields dropped the payment of ten cents for a pound of cotton to eight, seven, and finally five that the Negro community realized that the Depression, at least, did not discriminate.

Maya Angelou, *I Know Why the Caged Bird Sings* (New York: Barton Books, 1971), pp. 40–41.

*One of the **tenant** farm families displaced from the land in the **Great Depression** moves out with all its household goods in a mule-drawn wagon.* (Courtesy of the University of Arkansas, Fayetteville, Special Collections)

Chicot County, 21,912 people out of a total population of 22,646 received Red Cross aid each day. Many others made do with wild game, turnips, roots, herbs, and nuts.

Starving people have little patience, and their anger began to rise to the surface. England, in Lonoke County, almost had a food riot in January of 1931. The town merchants had run out of the Red Cross forms they needed in order to be paid back for the food they gave to hungry farmers and their wives and children. The farmers threatened to take the food by force. The merchants' response was to give them the food and hope the Red Cross would pay them back. The entire nation heard about this event, and before long thirty-two states sent hundreds of boxcar loads of food to Arkansas.

THE REACTION OF STATE GOVERNMENT

The state government seemed neither inclined nor able to give relief. Harvey Parnell, a merchant and owner of a large farm from Chicot County, was governor from 1928 to 1933. At first, while the good times went on, Parnell increased the highway building program and the state debt.

As the **Depression** hit and deepened in Arkansas, Parnell claimed that things would get better soon, with perhaps a little belt tightening. He reduced the wages of state workers by 10 percent. The General Assembly met in special session in 1931 to talk about the crisis, but did nothing to help.

Junius Marion Futrell, a lawyer and judge

Joe T. Robinson: Governor, Senator, Vice-Presidential Candidate

Arkansas's most influential politician on the national level in the 1920s and 1930s was Joe T. Robinson.

Son of a father who was both a doctor and a preacher and a mother who was part Indian, Robinson grew up in Lonoke. Starting when he was seventeen years old he taught in the Lonoke schools for a while, then attended the University of Arkansas for two years, and finally studied law at the University of Virginia.

After one term in the Arkansas legislature, he served in the United States Congress from 1903 to 1913. A supporter of the Populist and Progressive movements, he worked on legislation to limit trusts, lower tariffs, and protect child labor. He was elected governor of Arkansas in 1912. But after he had served only two weeks, the legislature chose Robinson to represent Arkansas in the U.S. Senate. He replaced Jeff Davis, who had died suddenly in office. Robinson served in the Senate until his death in 1937.

By 1923, he was the leader of the minority party at the time, the Democratic Party, in the Senate. His skill and popularity won him the Democratic Party's nomination for the vice presidency in the election of 1928. The presidential candidate, Al Smith, was a New Yorker, a Roman Catholic, and an opponent of Prohibition. The Democrats hoped Robinson would make those characteristics appeal a little more to the South.

Robinson campaigned long and hard. He was especially effective in dealing with the religious issue. Many American Protestants feared the idea of a Catholic president, but Robinson made powerful arguments for religious tolerance. The Democrats lost to the Republican ticket headed by Herbert Hoover, but everyone agreed Robinson had done very well.

After the election, Robinson continued his leadership role in the Senate. With the **Great Depression** underway, the Democrats in 1932 elected Franklin D. Roosevelt to the presidency, and they also helped elect enough Democrats to make the Democratic Party the majority party in both houses of Congress. Robinson, as leader of the Democratic Party in the Senate, was now majority leader. He played a major role in shaping **New Deal** legislation and getting it through Congress. Robinson Auditorium in Little Rock, built by the **New Deal**'s Public Works Administration, is named after him.

from Paragould, became governor in 1932 and won again in 1934. Futrell at first saw no active role for state government to take in the **Depression.** Eager to reduce state expense, he proposed that the state not fund public schools beyond the eighth grade.

The state's chief problem was the huge debt burden acquired during the 1920s, mostly from building roads. By 1934, Arkansas's total debt stood at $174,633,000. Over half of each year's state income was used to pay just interest on the loans.

As the **Depression** dried up tax income, the state borrowed even more to meet its costs. In 1934, Arkansas was forced to **default** on its payments and extend the due date on its bonds. It was the third time in one hundred years of statehood that Arkansas **defaulted** on its state debt.

SOCIAL UNREST

The failure of the economic system signaled by the **Great Depression** led thoughtful as well as desperate men and women to consider other social systems. People were jobless, hungry, and angry, and many voices called out for major changes in the American system.

Commonwealth College at Mena was home for a number of **socialists,** people who believed the government, as an agent of all people, should own all business and industry. Formed in California and moving briefly to Louisiana,

In the 1930s, many Arkansas highways crossed rivers on ferry boats, like this one, Shipp Ferry on the White River, south of Mountain Home. By the 1990s, all the ferries had been replaced by bridges. (Courtesy of the University of Central Arkansas Archives)

Senator Hattie Caraway. (Courtesy of the University of Arkansas at Fayetteville Special Collections)

Commonwealth College moved to Mena in 1925. It only had about forty-five students, and no degrees were offered. It was viewed with suspicion by the local people because of the students' odd dress and rumors of their practice of "free love." The school stayed open until 1940, when the state forced it to close.

The shock of the **Depression** caused many Americans at least to consider ideas that might have seemed radical before. For example, the "Kingfish" Huey Long, the political boss, former governor, and U.S. senator from Louisiana, gained the nation's attention for his "Share the Wealth" plan. He proposed that the wealth should be taken from the rich and given to the poor. He offered a bill in Congress seeking a $100,000 limit on a person's income. Long, who wanted to be president, chose Arkansas as a place to show his vote-getting power.

Hattie Wyatt Caraway had been named to fill the Senate seat of her husband, Thad Caraway, upon his death in November 1931. She then won a special election held in January 1932. To the surprise of all, in 1932 she sought her own full term. She opposed six male party regulars, among them former Governor Brough.

Long helped Caraway, partly because in the Senate she had voted for his $100,000 income bill. He joined her in a 2,100-mile tour of the state, giving thirty-nine speeches in seven days. Long and Mrs. Caraway seemed to draw the poor and hungry into a kind of social protest. Caraway won by a hefty margin, and she carried counties that Long did not even visit. Arkansas thus gave the nation its first woman elected to the United States Senate.

One of Arkansas's industries in the 1930s was the Ward Bus Company, in Conway. Workmen like these built bus bodies on truck chassis, to be used by schools and others. (Courtesy of the University of Central Arkansas Archives)

A NEW DEAL

Real help for Arkansans would come from the U.S. government. So long as Republican Herbert Hoover was president, the government gave no aid to individuals and only some aid to business. In 1932, Hoover was ousted by the Democrat Franklin Delano Roosevelt.

Roosevelt was a distant cousin of former President Theodore Roosevelt and a former governor of New York. He was deeply concerned about people's distress and was willing to try a number of new federal programs. He also had a gift for shoring up the people's confidence.

Arkansans, who gave their votes to Roosevelt by a huge margin, listened to his **inaugural** address over the radio. Roosevelt said: "Let me assert my firm belief that the only thing we have to fear is fear itself."

Roosevelt promised the American people a **New Deal**. The Democrats had also won most of the seats in both houses of Congress. The people were clearly ready for new ideas. At the very beginning of Roosevelt's term, Congress produced a flurry of new programs in what became known as the "**Hundred Days**" of the 1933 session. From then on through the 1930s, the **New Deal** offered relief for the needy, recovery for business and industry, and reform for the economic system.

One of the first measures was a "**bank holiday**" that closed all the banks in the country. Those that were financially sound were later allowed to open, but those that were not closed for good. The Federal Deposit Insurance Corporation (FDIC) was formed to back savings accounts in the future. The Home Owners' Loan Corporation (HOLC) backed thousands of home loans. The Farm Credit

Administration (FCA) did the same for farm loans.

Not all of the early **New Deal** measures were successful or long-lasting. The National Recovery Administration was supposed to restore industry through a series of codes set up in each area of business. The NRA was greeted with fervor. Little Rock staged a huge parade of twenty-five thousand people. But the idea did not work and had to be dropped.

One of the most pressing needs was relief in the form of food and shelter for people without jobs. The Federal Emergency Relief Administration (FERA) gave nine million dollars to needy Arkansans within a few months of its start. Soon, 15 percent of all people in the state were getting relief, one of the highest rates in the nation. The program ran in Arkansas under the forceful guidance of W. R. Dyess of Osceola.

The federal relief program moved from direct relief in the form of handouts to work programs, in which the government paid people to work on useful projects. The Public Works Administration (PWA) hired skilled workers to build major public buildings, such as Robinson Auditorium in Little Rock.

A very popular work program was the Civilian **Conservation** Corps (CCC). The CCC hired mostly young men, gave them a military form of life, and put them to work on outdoor projects. In Arkansas, the CCC built the state park system. Although the state had approved state parks before, nothing had been done with them.

Civilian **Conservation** Corps crews built the cabins, lodges, and trails at Petit Jean Mountain, Mount Nebo, Buffalo River, Lake Catherine, Crowley's Ridge, and Devil's Den. They built well, and most of their projects are still in use.

By 1935, the work relief concept had grown into the Works Progress Administration

FDR Visits Arkansas

President Franklin D. Roosevelt made a brief visit to Arkansas in 1936. It was the state's centennial year, the anniversary of one hundred years of statehood. It was also a presidential election year, and Roosevelt was assured of Arkansas's vote.

Arriving by train, Roosevelt visited the army-navy hospital in Hot Springs and then traveled to Little Rock to speak to thirty thousand people at Fair Park. The talk in Little Rock was preceded by a historical pageant put on by the Federal Theater Project, one of the **New Deal**'s work programs. Eleanor Roosevelt, the President's wife, accompanied him to Arkansas. She toured the Dyess Colony agricultural cooperative.

Harvey Couch, the founder of AP&L, was in charge of the centennial celebration. While in Hot Springs, Roosevelt visited Couch's eight-room log cabin on nearby Lake Catherine. To make sure Roosevelt got the best impression of Arkansas, Couch persuaded the governor to pave the highway from Hot Springs to the lakeside house. Couch then sent AP&L employees with free paint to persuade every homeowner along the route of the president's motorcade to paint their houses.

*The Works Progress Administration, which everyone called the WPA, was one of the **New Deal** agencies that provided jobs for people during the **Great Depression** of the 1930s.* (Courtesy of the University of Central Arkansas Archives)

(WPA). Because its goal was to hire as many people as it could to get them off relief and put money into the economy, almost no project was beyond the scope of the WPA. Through the 1930s, WPA workers in Arkansas built thousands of miles of roads and more than seven hundred new buildings. The buildings were hospitals, airports, fire stations, almost three hundred schools, and even houses for the animals at the zoo in Little Rock. Among the smaller projects were thousands of badly needed outdoor toilets and **septic tanks.**

The WPA also ran reading programs for thirty thousand people and served hot lunches in the schools. The WPA hired actors, painters, and writers. The WPA Writers' Project produced *Arkansas: A Guide to the State,* first published in 1941 and still a fine account of history and folklore. At its peak, the WPA was spending two million dollars a month on wages in Arkansas. As late as 1941, the WPA was the largest single source of jobs in Arkansas, with thirty-three thousand people on its payrolls.

THE NEW DEAL AND AGRICULTURE

For Arkansas, a major **New Deal** program with long-range impact was the Agricultural Adjustment Administration (AAA). During the 1920s, it had become clear that the root of the nation's farm problems was putting too much of a product on the market. This was most clearly evident with major crops, such as cotton.

Aviation came to Arkansas in the 1920s and 1930s. Louise Thaden of Bentonville (left) won the 1936 Bendix Transcontinental Air Race, against both men and women pilots. Helen H. Arlitt (below) with her open cockpit biplane, was the first woman pilot in Jefferson County in the 1920s. (Courtesy of the UALR Archives and Special Collections)

Composer William Grant Still of Little Rock was well known for both his blues-influenced popular pieces and his operas and symphonies. This picture, with his cello, was taken in 1920. (Courtesy of the University of Central Arkansas Archives)

American farmers produced more crops than the American and world markets could absorb. The result was the low prices that had plagued farmers through the 1920s. Neither local nor state action could deal with the problem. Arkansas and other southern states had tried to reduce the cotton crop in the early 1930s, but had no success.

The answer was a national program that required farmers in the major crop areas to take land out of production. The goal was a crop that would meet demand at a fair price to the farmers, called "**parity**." The AAA was designed to achieve **parity** by paying farmers to take as much as a third of their land out of production. Farmers were eager to try the new program and rushed to sign up.

When the AAA was first passed, in the late spring of 1933, there was a problem. Planting time was past, and crops were in the ground. For that year only, farmers plowed up a quar-

ter of their crop, a shocking sight. Farmers swapped stories about how hard it was to get a mule to plow through the cotton plants instead of around them as they had been trained to do.

In the years after that, farmers in the AAA planted only part of their land. The AAA reached its goal of reducing the crop and thus raising the price the farmer was paid, and it became a long-term program.

THE SOUTHERN TENANT FARMERS' UNION

In the end, the program to reduce crops made life even worse for **tenant farmers** and those who **sharecropped.** The government payments for farmers went to the landowners, not the tenants who really farmed the land. The landowners were supposed to share the money

Family homes at the Lakeview Resettlement Project. The Federal Resettlement Administration, one of the New Deal agencies, tried to provide homes and land for tenant farmers who lost their holdings in the Great Depression. (Courtesy of the University of Arkansas, Fayetteville, Special Collections)

with their **tenants**, but few did. Also, since less land was being used to grow crops, the owners needed fewer people to **sharecrop**. Landowners with large tracts of crop land also used part of their payments to buy tractors and other machines, which further reduced their need for labor. Many **tenants** were forced to leave the land and faced an economy with few jobs. In Arkansas, one out of every five **tenant families** left the land between 1933 and 1940.

Two young white men in Tyronza, in northeast Arkansas, thought the times of crisis called for bold action. H. L. Mitchell was a former **sharecropper** who owned a dry-cleaning shop, and H. Clay East ran a service station. They had read **socialist** literature and also knew about the work of labor unions. With their help, a small group of **sharecroppers**, black and white alike, formed a union in 1934. They called it the Southern **Tenant** Farmers' Union (STFU). Their goals were a fair share of the government payments, higher

Arkansas in the 1930s As Seen by the WPA Writers' Project

During the 1930s, unemployed writers and historians were put to work by the **New Deal**'s Works Progress Administration (WPA). Among other projects, they produced a series of guides to American states. The remarkably detailed Arkansas guide included suggested tours, a description of almost every town in the state, and topical sections on subjects such as history, agriculture, industry, the arts, and others.

Here, for example, is part of the section on recreation:

The climax of the sportsman's year is the deer hunting season, at present five days in November and five in December. In the thick timber of the flatlands dogs are sometimes used to run deer, though there is a growing sentiment against the practice. . . . The typical deer hunter leaves camp just before daylight and takes his stand at a "crossing," which may be a ford in a river, a gap in a ridge, or a fork in an old logging road. While he waits the sun touches the hilltops, and the hollows begin to stream with early morning mists. . . . The hunter glances casually at the crossing and is suddenly electrified: a buck is stealing by, antlers laid back on his neck. . . . There is time for just one shot as the deer clears the open space—and the hunter has downed or missed his buck of the season. . . .

Fox hunting, still fairly common in the State, is a sport for dogs rather than for their masters. . . . The men lounge in the glow of a campfire on a hilltop and listen to the blended, echoing chorus of running dogs. . . . The "start dog" is released in fox territory to pick up a trail, and the pack rallies at his long-drawn notes. The listeners know from experience which points the quarry will probably include in his circle, so that by leaving the campfire they sometimes see the fox flash by, the pack boiling in his wake.

And here is a sampling of the town descriptions:

[Harrison] The Boone County Courthouse, in the town square, is a two-story red brick structure trimmed with white flagging. . . . The return of legalized liquor in 1933 brought

wages for hired hands, and a better deal for **tenants**. Within three years, the STFU had more than eleven thousand members, mostly in the five counties of the northeast Arkansas Delta.

The union was despised, harassed, and accused of being led by Communists from outside the state. But its actions caused the nation to focus on the plight of the **share-cropper.** The very idea of a mixed black and white union caused a great stir. Writers came to visit the state, and filmmakers produced a movie about the STFU.

The STFU helped inspire President Roosevelt to create the Farm Security Administration (FSA). This agency aimed at moving displaced farmers onto new lands. One model the FSA used was a program that had been tried in Arkansas. W. R. Dyess, the state's Federal Emergency Relief chief, had used FERA funds to create an ideal farm community for Arkansas's relief clients. Called the Dyess

about a boom in [barrel stave milling at Harrison, and for a time 5 such plants were running, some of them 24 hours a day. . . . The town is a shipping center for red cedar and hardwood taken from Ozark forests. Other industries include a cheese factory owned by the Cudahy Packing Company, a flour mill and grain elevator, and produce houses that handle poultry and eggs brought in from near-by counties. . . .

[Hope] is a leading fruit-shipping point and the "watermelon capital" of the State. Melons as big as hogsheads are grown hereabouts, the champion (1939) being a 195-pound whopper. . . . Raising a giant watermelon requires as much art as growing a rare orchid. The farmer selects an exceptionally strong vine and clears the field around it. When the melons first appear he chooses the most promising and culls all the others. At this point solicitude begins in earnest. Castor beans and other plants are set around the pampered melon for shade; the soil is enriched with nitrogen-charged water from the manure trough or with commercial fertilizers; the melon is force-fed from shallow pans of water through lengths of wool yarn driven into the stem. . . .

[Little Rock] Capitol Avenue, once called Fifth Street, links Main Street to Broadway, another north-south artery, and continues ten blocks westward to the Capitol. The slight elevation on which the Capitol stands is an outpost of the hills of Pulaski Heights, where terraced lawns, hedges, evergreens, and curved drives typify one of the community's newer residential sections. Higher and cooler than the rest of the city, Pulaski Heights attracts home owners and visitors who like the suburban atmosphere of pine-studded hillsides and ravines. . . . Chromium-trimmed store fronts, air-conditioned buildings, and sleek buses give Little Rock its modern metropolitan aspects, but the city still stays fairly close to the earth. Mockingbirds sing in downtown districts on early summer mornings, and nighthawks wheel low over the streets at dusk.

Arkansas: A Guide to the State, compiled by workers of the Works Progress Administration (New York: Hastings House, 1941), pp. 78-79, 170, 215, 269.

A fishing party at Mountain Home, just back from a good day on the White River. (Courtesy of the University of Central Arkansas Archives)

Sharecropping in Arkansas: "The Dee Ducks Got It All"

H. L. Mitchell—his friends called him "Mitch"—lived in Tyronza when he was a young man. This is the way he described a plantation farmed by **sharecroppers:**

> The gravel road ended at the company store. . . . Down the muddy road back of the plantation store were the **sharecropper** shacks. Each had two rooms, one for cooking and the other for sleeping. . . .Cotton grew almost to the door of the shacks. There was no evidence of a vegetable garden anywhere. . . . The **sharecropper** houses were all made of green lumber, and the siding had warped in the hot delta sun. About twenty feet away was the water supply for two houses. This consisted of a three-inch steel pipe driven in the ground, with a hand pump attached. . . .
>
> For a **sharecropper** the day started before dawn. The plantation bell was the first sound he heard upon awakening. His wife was soon getting a fire going in the cookstove. A cup of cheap strong coffee started the day off. She put biscuits in the oven to be eaten with molasses and fatback meat by the adults. There was cornmeal mush for the young ones. First the man would go to the plantation barn where the hostler assigned a mule to him. He harnessed it and was in the cotton field before sun was up. The day's work was well underway by sunrise, and it didn't end until after sundown. The plantation riding boss would be in the field supervising the croppers' work. Usually the riding boss was also a deputy sheriff. In eastern Arkansas in the 1930s, such men wore khaki hunting coats that barely concealed the Colt revolvers they carried. In addition to seeing to it that each **sharecropper** was in the field and plowing his rows straight, the rider represented the law to both black and white **sharecroppers** alike. . . .
>
> After the crop was all about picked out, usually just before Christmas, "settlement time" came. . . . The verdict would be handed down something like this: "Well, you had a good year. You raised twenty bales of cotton. We sold it for seven cents a pound, that comes to $35 a bale, or a total of $700. Half of that is yours—$350. But you owe $200, plus interest of $80 on the **furnish.** You know we had to get a doctor when your wife was sick, and we deducted the doctor's calls and the medicine he gave, and then you bought some clothes for the children, too. The amount due to you is $49.50. At least you got some Christmas money." The **sharecropper** usually left the office grumbling to others waiting hopefully: "The Dee Ducks got it all."

H. L. Mitchell became one of the founders of the Southern **Tenant Farmers'** Union.

H. L. Mitchell, *Mean Things Happening in This Land* (Montclair, NJ: Allanheld, Osmun & Co., 1979), pp. 17–22.

Colony, it was near Wilson in Mississippi County. The Dyess Colony parceled out sixteen thousand acres into five hundred farmsteads for three thousand people. The Colony was a new town with a post office, cafe, stores, school, hospital, and cotton gin.

The Farm Security Administration formed more such farm colonies at Plum Bayou, Lake Dick, Lakeview, Trumann, and Clover Bend.

Also, fifty thousand Arkansas farmers received loans to acquire farms and homes. The FSA program helped many move from being **tenants** to owning their own land. In the late 1930s, still more federal programs helped to reshape Arkansas. Loan programs like the **Commodity** Credit Corporation became the basic source of funds for farmers. A new Soil **Conservation** Service taught farmers ways to

John Gould Fletcher

An important voice from Arkansas in the 1920s and 1930s was that of poet John Gould Fletcher.

Fletcher, the son of a wealthy banker, cotton merchant, and frequent candidate for governor, grew up in the house in Little Rock built by Albert Pike in 1844. (Today it is open to the public as the Arkansas Decorative Arts Museum.) It was a privileged and often lonely life for a little boy.

After a few years at Harvard University, Fletcher visited Italy and France and then settled down in London. There he was influenced by Ezra Pound and other modern poets. As Fletcher developed his own poetic style, he was closely associated with the Imagist poets, emphasizing a simple, lyrical, and musical style of poetry. He published many books of poetry. In 1939, after the publication of *Selected Poems,* he was awarded the Pulitzer Prize for his lifelong work.

Although Arkansas and the South were not often the subjects of his poetry, Fletcher increasingly came to believe that the Old South of the years before the Civil War represented something gracious and fine that was lacking in the modern world. Like many who were offended by the emphasis on materialism in the 1920s and shocked by the collapse of the economy in the 1930s, Fletcher liked to recall (or invent) a time when life was simpler. He was associated with a group of writers at Vanderbilt University, called the Agrarians or the Fugitives, who shared Fletcher's longing for a pre–Civil War past. Fletcher contributed an essay on education to a collection of the Agrarians' essays, *I'll Take My Stand* (1930).

Fletcher was also a leader in reviving interest in Arkansas folklore and folk songs. His major prose work, *Arkansas,* is a history of the state that was published in 1947 and is still good reading.

Fletcher's second wife was Charlie May Simon, an author of books for young people. They built a house they called Johnswood in the hills west of Little Rock. As he grew older, Fletcher suffered severe attacks of depression. In 1950, in the pond near Johnswood, he drowned himself.

protect the land against soil **erosion**. The Rural Electrification Administration gave low-interest loans to local groups to bring electric lines, and later phone lines, to even the most remote rural areas. Before the REA, fewer than 10 percent of Arkansas farms had electric power.

A new law set a minimum wage for most urban workers. And, in the act Roosevelt himself saw as the greatest of his four terms as president, the United States created a Social Security system to provide **pensions** for retired older people.

The **New Deal** was not meant to be a civil rights movement, but it did in fact affect the lives of all black Arkansans. **New Deal** programs such as the WPA were segregated, and most relief payments were not equal, with blacks getting less than whites. Even the first minimum wage law did not apply either to farm laborers or **domestic workers**. These were two major sources of jobs for African Americans in Arkansas. But most major **New Deal** programs, such as Social Security, did apply to African Americans. The **New Deal** helped the poor, and, in Arkansas, African Americans were among the poorest.

THE STATE GOVERNMENT AND THE NEW DEAL

While the U.S. government was putting massive amounts of money into Arkansas, the state itself was giving very little. When Arkansas teachers were added to the FERA rolls, the state's response was to cut back its share of school spending. Then the U.S. government threatened to withdraw federal relief funds if the state did not share at least part of the costs.

In the end, Governor Futrell asked the General Assembly to create a Department of Public Welfare and to raise new taxes. In 1935, Arkansas made the sale of liquor legal and put a tax on it. The government also made gambling on dog races in West Memphis and horse races in Hot Springs legal and taxed the betting money. The state also put into effect its first sales tax, a 2 percent tax on retail buying, except for food and medicine.

By the late 1930s, the **New Deal** was having an impact on state politics. Some felt the **New Deal** had gone too far. Local bosses feared the power of the national government. White **racists** feared the power that government programs might be giving blacks. But other whites became liberals who gave support to the **New Deal** programs and the concepts behind them. Young men emerged as new state leaders. Brooks Hays served a distinguished career in the U.S. House of Representatives. Carl Bailey, like Hays a supporter of the **New Deal**, served as governor from 1937 to 1941. Under his leadership the state created a state civil-service system and reorganized the state welfare department.

In a major and long-term change, the **New Deal**, because of the aid and recognition it gave to African Americans, began to convert African Americans from the Republican Party of Abraham Lincoln to the Democratic Party of Franklin D. Roosevelt.

By 1939, the **New Deal** had spent $474,986,972 in Arkansas. The government had also loaned $244,767,279 to Arkansans. Arkansas had not fully emerged from the **Great Depression**, nor was the state close to national standards by most measures. But the relief programs had allowed many people of Arkansas to survive a time of grave crisis. They were better off than they had been in 1928 before the **Depression**. The long-term reforms, from the farm programs to Social Security, promised a better future for all.

The relationship of the people of Arkansas to the U.S. government would never be the same. Also, Arkansas state government had taken steps to respond to the needs of all the people in a way it never had before.

Against this background, Arkansans faced a different crisis: the world was once again headed toward war.

Selected Census Data for Arkansas 1920 to 1940

	1920	1930	1940
Total population	1,752,204	1,854,482	1,949,511
White population	1,279,757	1,375,315	1,466,084
Black population	472,220	478,463	482,578
Total urban population	290,497	382,878	431,910
Percent urban population	16.6	20.6	22.2
Number of farms	232,604	242,334	216,674
Average acres per farm	75	66.2	83.3
Value of farms	$753,110,666	$547,828,250	$456,848,156
Cotton bales produced	869,350	1,398,475	1,351,209
Bushels of corn produced	34,226,935	27,388,105	33,762,323
Bushels of rice produced	6,797,126	6,958,105	7,651,231
Manufacturing Establishments	3,123	1,731	1,178
Wage earners	49,954	44,205	36,256

Notes:

The figures for black and white population for each year will not add up to the exact figure for the total population. The difference is the small number of other races in the population.

The "number of farms" includes sharecropping or tenant plots.

VOCABULARY

abstract painting showing reality as the artist sees it, not necessarily as it appears to others.

agnostic (ag-NOSS-tik) one who does not profess to believe in God but who does not necessarily deny God's existence.

Arkies (ARK-eez) the name given to 1930s refugees from Arkansas who traveled to California seeking work.

"bank holiday" the forced closing of all banks by Roosevelt to stem the nationwide run on banks.

bazooka (buh-ZOO-kuh) Bob Burns's radio trademark, a comical musical instrument; WWII G.I.s named a rocket launcher after it.

"Bear State" Arkansas's frontier-era nickname.

boll weevil (BOHL WEE-vuhl) a destructive beetle that infested southern cotton crops during the 1920s, causing great damage.

bootleggers people who sold and, in some cases, made liquor illegally, particularly during Prohibition.

commodity (kum-MAHD-it-ee) an agricultural product of value.

conservation (KAHN-ser-VAY-shun) saving something, such as farm soil through contour plowing, windbreaks, and rotating crops.

consumer goods merchandise designed for home or personal use.

default (dee-FAWLT) to fail to make payments on a loan.

diphtheria (dif-THEER-ee-uh) a bacteria-caused contagious disease resulting in inflammation of the heart and nervous system.

domestic workers maids, housekeepers, and others who perform labor in the home of someone else for pay.

Dust Bowl the ruinous condition of drought during the 1930s that caused horrible dust storms.

erosion (ee-ROH-zhun) the wearing away of soil through the action of wind and water.

evolution (EV-oh-LOO-shun) the gradual change of a species over time to better adapt to existing environmental conditions.

fundamentalism (FUN-duh-MENT-uhl-izm) the literal interpretation of the Bible.

furnish the means of a sharecropper's survival, including seed, tools, draft animals, food, etc.

Great Depression global economic collapse from 1929 through 1942; businesses came to a virtual standstill, resulting in high unemployment.

gusher oil rushing out of a new oil well as it is struck by drilling equipment.

home economics (HOHM EE-kuhn-AHM-iks) the study of managing and operating a household, including cooking, sewing, etc.

"Hundred Days" the first one hundred days of Roosevelt's administration when many relief and recovery bills were enacted.

inaugural (in-OGG-yoo-ruhl) upon the taking of office, as an inaugural address given by a brand new governor or president.

Ku Klux Klan (KOO KLUKS KLAN) a group of white Protestant supremacists known for its violent, terroristic activities directed against other groups.

levee (LEH-vee) an earthen wall extending a river's natural banks upwards to contain high water so that it will not flood.

livestock farm animals, especially cattle, sheep, horses, and hogs.

Martineau Road Plan (MAR-tin-oh ROHD PLAN) the ambitious highway-building program Governor Martineau began in 1927.

midwives women who assist other women in delivering their babies.

"Monkey trial" newspapers' name for the Scopes trial, which involved the teaching of biological evolution in the public schools.

natural selection the gradual improvement of a species through survival of the fittest.

New Deal President Roosevelt's programs aimed at alleviating the effects of the Great Depression and preventing another depression.

oil boom rapid population and economic growth following the discovery of oil in an area.

Okies (OH-keez) the name given to refugees from Oklahoma during the Depression who traveled to California seeking work.

parity (PAIR-it-ee) as used in New Deal agricultural programs, the goal of setting prices for farm products that would give the farmer a fair share of the national income.

pension (PEN-shun) money set aside for use in retirement and old age.

racist (RAY-sist) the belief that one race is superior to another, or a person who holds this belief.

sanitorium (SAN-ih-TOR-ee-um) a hospital created for the long-term treatment of one particular ailment.

septic tank (SEP-tik TANGK) an underground tank used for the disposal and treatment of sewage, usually in rural areas.

sharecropper (SHAIR-krahp-er) one who rents farmland and pays for its use by sharing his crop with the property owner.

smallpox (SMAHL-pahks) an acute viral disease characterized by skin eruptions with pustules and scar formation.

socialists (SOH-shull-ists) those who believe in government ownership rather than private ownership of business and industry.

sorghum (SOAR-guhm) a cane-like tropical grass that produces sweet sap that is made into syrup.

species (SPEE-sheez) a group of animals similar enough to one another to reproduce, e.g., *Homo sapiens*, or human beings.

speculate (SPEK-yoo-layt) to assume a business risk in the hope of gain, especially buying and selling stocks.

survival of the fittest the theory that the best and strongest examples of a species live and reproduce themselves.

sustained yield forestry to manage forests for economic uses by planting new trees as others are cut.

tenant farmer (TEN-uhnt FAR-mer) one who lives and works on rented farmland, usually meaning the same as sharecropper.

tuberculosis (too-BERR-kyoo-LOH-sis) a bacteria-caused lung disease which is highly contagious.

typhoid (TIE-foyd) a contagious disease caused by bacteria with symptoms resembling the flu with very high fever.

"Wonder State" Arkansas's nickname during the early decades of the twentieth century.

STUDY QUESTIONS

1. What were some of the industrial and cultural changes going on in the United States by the 1920s, and why were they slow to develop in Arkansas?

2. Describe the oil boom in southern Arkansas.

3. What were Harvey Couch's accomplishments?

4. What circumstances contributed to the revival of the Ku Klux Klan in the 1920s?

5. Describe the major efforts of state government in this period in roads, education, and health.

6. What changes occurred in agriculture doing this period?

7. Describe the impact of the Flood of 1927 and the drought that followed.

8. Describe the effect of the Great Depression on Arkansas.

9. Describe the operation of the New Deal work programs the Civilian Conservation Corps (CCC) and the Works Progress Administration (WPA).

10. What were the long-term effects of the New Deal in Arkansas?

World War II and the Postwar World

1940–1955

What to Look for in Chapter 9

The period 1940 to 1955 began with another war, World War II. The war started in Asia in 1937 and in Europe in 1939, but the United States did not join until the Japanese attacked Pearl Harbor in 1941. The United States, along with Great Britain, the Soviet Union, and others, was at war against Germany, Italy, and Japan.

Arkansans—black and white, men and women—served in the armed forces, many with distinction. At home, large amounts of government money created whole new industries, and jobs, in areas such as aluminum and munitions.

The war to defend democracy focused attention on some of America's inequities. African Americans in Arkansas and in the United States made some gains in civil rights, but there was still a long way to go.

When war ended in 1945, it was clear that things were going to be different. Returning soldiers—"G.I.s"—entered politics and swept out some of the old politicians. One G.I. leader, Sid McMath, became governor.

Land owners were able to buy machines to replace workers, and sharecropping was on its way out.

WAR ONCE AGAIN

As the 1940s began, neither Arkansas nor the nation had fully recovered from the Great Depression. The New Deal had prevented disaster and begun the process of recovery and reform, but there was still a long way to go. Times were still tough, especially in rural agricultural states such as Arkansas, and change seemed to come very slowly.

Meanwhile, events in Europe and Asia were moving toward global war. For the second time in the twentieth century, distant warfare would change the face of the entire world. Arkansas would change along with it.

Arkansans, like most Americans, had not been much concerned about the rest of the world since the end of the first World War in

A classroom at St. Bartholomew's, a school for African American children operated in Little Rock by the Roman Catholic Church. The picture was taken in the 1940s. (Courtesy of the Arkansas History Commission)

1918. Without many Americans fully knowing it, the world had become a very small place in which events in one place affected events in many other places.

The American Great Depression, for instance, was a worldwide event, causing severe problems in all the European countries. Some nations, such as Britain and France, coped with their problems in a peaceful way, as the United States had. Other nations, though, tried to relieve their own problems by causing trouble for their neighbors. In Europe, Germany and Italy turned to **fascism**, which combined an extreme national pride with strong central control. Although Italy came under the control of Benito Mussolini's Fascist Party early in the 1920s, Germany grew to be

a more deadly threat. There Adolf Hitler formed the **National Socialist Party**—"Nazi" for short.

Part of Hitler's message to the German people was that they had been tricked and denied their rightful place as rulers of the world. He blamed Germany's economic troubles and other problems on the Jewish people. Because the Germans were the pure master race of **"Aryans,"** Hitler said, they could do as they wished with the Jews.

As the Depression worsened in the 1930s, many Germans listened, approved, and gave support to Hitler and his Nazis. Those who did not became the victims of brutal Nazi gang-war tactics. In 1933, the year Franklin D. Roosevelt became president of the United

States, Germany voted to make Hitler its leader. Hitler quickly declared himself supreme ruler for life, the "**Führer**" (leader) of what he called the German Empire.

Hitler began building for war. He built a huge and modern German war machine, with guns, tanks, and airplanes as well as soldiers. Within Germany, the Nazis began to mistreat the Jews and stripped them of their legal rights. Hitler allied Germany with Mussolini's Italy. They planned to aid each other in conquest and to share the spoils. The rest of the world, preoccupied with economic problems and memories of the First World War, watched as if in a daze as Hitler moved closer to war.

Meanwhile, in Asia, the leaders of Japan were on the same course toward war. The only major nation in Asia to achieve modern levels of industrial development, Japan made it clear that it meant to rule the Pacific area. By the 1930s, Japan, under its emperor, had been taken over by military leaders. They intended to use force if needed to take what they wanted.

THE AXIS POWERS

Germany, Italy, and Japan joined forces as the **Axis Powers.** They had little in common except the intent to take what they wanted. They also shared the same enemies, the other nations of Europe and the United States. In 1935 Italy attacked Ethiopia in Africa. Japan took over nearby nations, including Korea and Manchuria. Then, in 1937, Japan attacked China.

In 1938 Hitler issued a demand for part of Czechoslovakia. The leaders of Britain and France met with Hitler at Munich in Germany. They took Hitler at his word when he promised that he wanted only a small part of Czechoslovakia. Then Hitler took over all of Czechoslovakia, and next he wanted Poland. At long last, Britain and France said they would fight if Hitler took Poland.

World War II in Europe began in September 1939, as German forces drove into Poland. Britain and France declared war against Germany and Italy, but there was little fighting until the spring of 1940. Then, Hitler struck quickly in Denmark and Norway, then in Belgium, the Netherlands, and France. All of these nations fell before the *Blitzkrieg*— lightning warfare—of the new German army with its fast-moving infantry and tanks supported by airplanes and artillery.

By June of 1940 France was taken, leaving Britain alone in the fight against Hitler and Mussolini. Hitler attacked the Soviet Union in June of 1941, which put the Russians in the war on the side of Britain.

Hitler's army was only part of the threat he posed to the world. His mad belief in the supreme rule of "**Aryans**" led to **heinous** crimes. Hitler threw Jewish men, women, and children into slave-labor camps. Also, people with mental impairments, **gypsies**, and leaders who opposed the Nazis were all herded into the camps. The captives there were worked to death or murdered outright. They were killed by the millions during the war, as the Nazis processed trainloads of people at a time through factories of death, the gas chambers.

THE UNITED STATES ENTERS THE WAR

Even after war started, in Asia in 1937 and in Europe in 1939, most American people did not want to get involved. Many Americans had convinced themselves that our fighting in World War I had been a mistake. To them, it seemed that affairs on the other side of the world were none of America's concern.

But the rise of the **Axis Powers** did convince President Roosevelt and Congress to strengthen American armed forces. They arranged to produce fifty thousand airplanes a year and a navy big enough to patrol both the Atlantic and the Pacific oceans. In 1940, Congress passed (for one year only) a **Selective Service Act** to draft young men into the armed forces.

The German march across Europe, and most of all the fall of France in 1940, shifted the public's will toward aiding Britain. In 1941 Congress approved Roosevelt's **Lend-Lease Act**, which allowed the United States to give weapons and other supplies to Britain. In support of **Lend-Lease**, President Roosevelt said the war against Germany was a struggle to defend the **"Four Freedoms."** These were freedom of speech, freedom of worship, freedom from want, and freedom from fear.

In Arkansas, as in the rest of America, some people began to fear German spies. Governor Carl Bailey ordered the state police to explore any signs of Nazi plots within the state. He called upon Arkansans to report any pro-German actions.

Some people were more than ready to **denounce** things that had a German flavor. At least one German immigrant, Frank Lewis of Danville, was killed. He had made a public attempt to distinguish between the Nazi Party and the German people as a whole. As much

World War II soldiers wait at a railroad station with their duffle bags. Winthrop Rockefeller, the future governor of Arkansas, is on the far left. (Courtesy of the Winthrop Rockefeller Collection, UALR Archives and Special Collections)

Governor Carl Bailey, on the right, *with then Vice President Harry Truman.* (Courtesy of the Bailey Family Collection, UALR Archives and Special Collections)

as they disliked the Germans and the Japanese, most people in Arkansas still opposed U.S. entry into the war.

America's sense of distance from world events was shattered on December 7, 1941. Early that Sunday morning (it was mid-afternoon in Arkansas), Japanese airplanes bombed the American fleet at Pearl Harbor in the Hawaiian Islands. The surprise attack was a direct blow against American ships and men on American soil. The attack resulted in awful losses. Nearly one-third of the Pacific Fleet was destroyed or badly damaged.

The next day, Arkansas schoolchildren listened to radios in their classrooms as President Roosevelt spoke. He described the attack as "a day that will live in **infamy**." He asked Congress to declare war against Japan. A few days later, Germany and Italy declared war on the United States. Americans were once again at war in Europe and in Asia. The Second World War would last until 1945.

Young men in Arkansas rushed to sign up for the war effort. In Lepanto, the entire football team volunteered for the navy. Before the war was over, two hundred thousand Arkansans—more than 10 percent of the state's people—served in the nation's armed forces. The number would have been even higher except that many people failed to pass their physical exams. Thirty-five percent of the would-be recruits had severe health problems ranging from chronic malaria to malnutrition. Others could not read and write well enough to meet the army's standards.

Black Arkansans joined in large numbers, although the armed forces still put them in all-black units with white officers. Women, too, served in all branches of the armed forces.

Arkansas troops did battle in both Europe and the Pacific. Examples of individuals who saw action include Lieutenant Samuel H. Marett, a pilot from Little Rock who fought in defense of the Philippine Islands. After leading his **squadron** of fighter bombers against the Japanese, Marett died when he flew his airplane into a Japanese ship.

Major Pierce McKennon of Clarksville was a famous flying ace who shot down more than twenty enemy airplanes. Colonel William Darby of Fort Smith helped create the

Bravery "Above and Beyond the Call of Duty": Footsie Britt and the Medal of Honor

Maurice L. Britt was born in Carlisle, but he grew up in Lonoke, where his family moved when he was very young. When he was still young, he was delighted to win a pair of shoes in a contest, then dismayed to discover they were baby shoes. His friends called him "Footsie" from then on.

At the University of Arkansas, Britt majored in journalism and lettered in basketball and football. After graduation, he briefly played professional football for the Detroit Lions. But the United States was at war by then, so twenty-two-year-old Footsie Britt went into the army as a lieutenant.

From bases in North Africa, Britt's unit went with the American and British forces that in 1943 invaded the island of Sicily and then the mainland of the Italian peninsula. The Italian government surrendered almost immediately, but German forces dug into the mountains, determined to resist.

Britt was in the tough fighting to take Naples. There he earned the Silver Star for bravery and the Purple Heart for being wounded.

Then, at Mount Rotundo, Britt and his men were ordered to hold a position between two high points. About one hundred German soldiers moved into the area. With eight men, Britt attacked the Germans. With rifles and hand grenades, Britt and his men knocked out a machine gun and killed thirty-five of the Germans. Britt was wounded again, but he held the ground until other American forces moved in and Britt was ordered to get medical aid.

For that action, the British awarded him the Military Cross and the Americans awarded him the **Congressional Medal of Honor.** This is our nation's highest decoration for bravery in combat "above and beyond the call of duty." The medal was actually presented at a ceremony during the 1944 commencement day at the University of Arkansas. As he received the medal, Britt asked that it be considered an award for all Americans who had fought and were still fighting in the war.

Britt went on to do more fighting, including one engagement in which he lost his arm. He later became lieutenant governor of Arkansas in the administration of Governor Winthrop Rockefeller.

Members of the Women's Army Corps—the WACs—in World War II smile from their train windows. They were arriving in Arkansas for training. (Courtesy of the University of Central Arkansas Archives)

army **Ranger battalions.** Captain Maurice L. "Footsie" Britt of Carlisle won the **Congressional Medal of Honor** for his brave deeds in fighting against the Germans in Italy.

Families who sent sons and husbands to war put a little white banner with a single star on it in their windows. A gold star meant the loved one had been killed. During the four years of war, 4,611 Arkansans died. Of those, 3,814 were in the army or the air force (then a part of the army) and 797 were in the navy or marine corps.

At home, Arkansans joined in the war effort any way they could. One way was to buy **war bonds,** a kind of loan to the United States to help pay for the war effort. Schoolchildren bought bonds at the rate of twenty-five cents for a "stamp" until they had enough for a twenty-five-dollar bond. Children also helped collect scrap metal and rubber to be made into war weapons. Women, like the all-black MacArthur Knitting Club of Pulaski County, went home from ten- to twelve-hour days at work to knit sweaters for soldiers.

Families planted **"victory gardens"** to help raise enough food to see the country through the war. Coffee, tea, sugar, meat, gas, and tires were in short supply and were rationed. People could buy only a small amount of each of those things each month. The government issued **ration** books, with **coupons** that had to be turned in with each purchase.

William Darby and the Rangers

When he was a twelve-year-old boy in his home town of Fort Smith, William O. Darby read a book about West Point, the United States Military Academy. From that point on, he knew what he wanted to be: a soldier.

Darby did go to West Point, graduating in 1933. That was the year Adolph Hitler came to power in Germany and the world began to move toward war.

Soon after the United States entered World War II, Darby was given an important assignment. The United States Army wanted to create a **Ranger Battalion**, a unit modeled on the British Commandos. The **Rangers**, like the Commandos, were to be a small group of highly trained men who would conduct daring raids, damage the enemy, then get away.

Darby set high standards. Thousands of soldiers applied for the new **Ranger Battalion**, but only five hundred were selected. They had to be the best. Darby's **Ranger** training program included endurance marches and mountain climbing. The **Rangers** also trained under combat conditions with live ammunition.

The main **Ranger Battalion** went into battle with the American landings in North Africa in the fall of 1942. The American army, with their British allies, then invaded Sicily and Italy in 1943. In almost all the amphibious landings and attacks in these campaigns, the **Rangers** were the first soldiers into battle. Darby, now a colonel, was often at the head of his troops. His men called him "El Darbo."

Darby came back to the United States in 1944 to work in army headquarters. He was called back to Italy in 1945, as assistant commander of an army mountain division. He was in action with that unit when he was killed, only two days before the German forces in Italy surrendered. He was thirty-four years old.

WARTIME INDUSTRY

The all-out war effort required new factories and new army bases. Arkansas's share of U.S. war industries was less than 2 percent of the total in the nation, but that was enough to have a major impact on the state.

Arkansas had been a major source of bauxite, the raw ore for aluminum, for decades. The lightweight metal was used for the outer skin of most airplanes. During the war years, bauxite mining increased twelvefold. The government built new plants at Jones Mills and at Hurricane Creek and leased them to the Aluminum Company of America to run.

The process used to produce aluminum requires huge amounts of electric power. Arkansas's own energy sources could not keep up with the new plants. The government helped build dams to produce more power at Blue Mountain, Lake Catherine, and Lake Norfork. Even then, almost 70 percent of the electric power had to be brought in from other states.

Major defense plants were built at Camden, Jacksonville, Maumelle, and Pine Bluff. These all made some form of arms, bombs, or chemicals for the war effort. At Hope, the army carved a huge testing range out of the farmland. It even had its own airport.

Camp Robinson in North Little Rock became a training camp for soldiers, as it had been in World War I. The United States had begun building Camp Chaffee, near Fort Smith, just before Pearl Harbor. After the United States entered the war, it was enlarged to train soldiers by the thousands. Other army bases were at Blytheville, Newport, Stuttgart, and Walnut Ridge.

Defense plants in Arkansas hired almost 28,000 people. The payrolls at the plants plus the spending at the army bases put about $400 million into the Arkansas economy during the war years. Many Arkansans moved to other states to work in still more defense plants.

Cities near the defense plants and bases quickly increased in size. Little Rock grew by 25,000 people in six months during 1940. Hope grew from 7,475 in 1940 to 15,475 by the end of 1941. There were not enough houses to go around, and sometimes people had to live in tents, garages, or warehouses.

Every public service unit, from school systems to fire departments, had to do more work with fewer people. Their workers were leaving in droves to take jobs with the better-paying defense plants.

Colonel William Darby, of Darby's **Rangers.** (Courtesy of the UALR Archives and Special Collections)

*Maurice "Footsie" Britt.
Around his neck is the
**Congressional Medal of
Honor.** (Courtesy of the
University of Arkansas,
Fayetteville, Special
Collections)*

*These Fayetteville women are doing their share for the war effort in 1942, by preparing bandages
for the Red Cross. (Courtesy of the University of Arkansas, Fayetteville, Special Collections)*

WOMEN IN THE WAR EFFORT

One of the biggest changes brought by the war was the presence of women in the work force; they replaced men who had joined the armed forces. In the nation as a whole, women at work outside the home increased from 13.9 percent of American workers in 1940 (the same as it had been in 1910) to 31 percent. In Arkansas, where there were fewer defense plants, the number of women workers was only 20 percent of the total number of workers, but that was a major increase from the past.

Women were sought by the **munitions** plants as line workers making **fuses, boosters,** and **primers** for weapons. Women worked in machine shops. They were also called upon to operate radios, **rivet** aircraft, and do sheet metal work, woodwork, and drafting.

Across the United States, "Rosie the **Riveter**" became the symbol of all women in defense work. (But in fact, women trained in Arkansas as aircraft **riveters** had to leave the state because there were no airplane plants here.) Women also managed farms. The International Harvester Company sponsored a national "**tractorette**" training program for them.

Defense plants were not alone in hiring women for the work force. Private business also had a labor shortage. Women for the first time became bank tellers, newspaper reporters, cab and bus drivers, and mechanics in auto repair shops.

The war meant many women had gone through relocation, boom-town stress, and war-forced separations. Many achieved financial independence, public recognition, and renewed self-esteem. All this changed their lives and changed the American family. When the war ended in 1945, most wartime women workers returned to their roles as housewives. But many had acquired a taste for wider options.

THE SCHOOLS

Schools in the South had trouble during the war years. More students flocked to city school districts. At the same time, many teachers and principals left to join the armed forces or to take high-paying jobs in the war plants. More than half of the prewar teaching staff had left the schools by 1945. At one time during the war, almost 60 percent of Arkansas's teens had dropped out of school due to the lack of teachers.

Congress proposed special help for the schools, but southern Congressmen refused federal aid. They feared accepting federal aid might threaten school segregation. The Arkansas General Assembly also considered a bill designed to raise the sales tax to give the schools more money, but the measure failed to pass.

JAPANESE INTERNMENT CAMPS AND WARTIME PREJUDICE

The Japanese attack on Pearl Harbor shocked and surprised the people of the United States. Many Americans took out their anger on the Japanese people living in America. In 1941, thousands of Japanese Americans lived on the West Coast, many of them in California. They had begun coming to that area early in the 1900s. Most of those first to arrive were now U.S. citizens. Their children, called **Nisei**, were U.S. citizens by birth.

Through hard work and skill, many Japanese in America had achieved success in their

Robert Leflar in 1942. The longtime dean of the University of Arkansas, Fayetteville, Law School, Leflar was also active in the attempts at constitutional reform in Arkansas. (Courtesy of the University of Arkansas, Fayetteville, Special Collections)

new homeland. But after Pearl Harbor, their neighbors turned against them. Many Americans feared, without good reason, a Japanese landing on the West Coast. Many also hated the Japanese Americans for racial reasons.

The fear and hatred of Japanese Americans grew so strong that President Roosevelt agreed to round up 117,000 of these citizens as a military measure. They were removed from the West Coast and transferred into the interior of the country. In the process, the Japanese Americans lost their homes, their businesses, and most of their worldly goods.

The Japanese Americans did not commit any crimes or acts of disloyalty to their country. Yet they were herded onto trains and moved thousands of miles away from home. They were locked up and "**interned**" in quickly built "**relocation centers.**"

Two of the Japanese American centers were in southeast Arkansas. One was at Rohwer in Desha County and the other was at Jerome in Chicot County. About eight thousand people lived in each center beginning in the summer of 1942. Families were able to stay intact but were crowded into

A Young Girl Arrives at the Rohwer Internment Camp

Many of the Japanese Americans who came to the camps in Arkansas were young people. At Rohwer, for example, 40 percent of the Japanese Americans were under nineteen years old; 30 percent were school-aged children.

One young girl wrote in her diary about her arrival at the Rohwer camp by train from the West Coast. Her first memory was "seeing the points of the barbed wire fences with droplets of rain stuck on them." Then she wrote:

It must have been after 1:30 A.M. when they finally decided to let us off the train—we wanted to sleep in the car—most of the children were asleep or grouchy for the need of it. We were herded off the cars—MP's [military policemen] grabbed our arms as we slipped into the soft mud. . . .

"Our home"—38-1-E. Fujinos to the right and the block office to the left. Ought to be quiet—unit looks good—and empty, also. An ugly black stove and a suggestion of clothes closet—shelves and rod very low. They must think we are midgets.

Well, we were led into our quarters wading through mud. . . . We struggled with cots only to discover that one was torn and terribly underslung. Sneaked into the next unit and did a quick exchange job. Had to wait for blankets.

The young people managed to act like American young people everywhere. At Rohwer the teenage students had school officers, honor societies, clubs, a newspaper, and an annual. Athletic teams were organized for games between classes or between the two schools at the camp. In Rohwer and Jerome together, there were 256 weddings.

Quoted in Russell Bearden, "Life Inside Arkansas's Japanese-American Relocation Centers," *Arkansas Historical Quarterly,* Vol. XLVIII (Summer, 1989), p. 177.

*Japanese American children arrive at the Rohwer **Internment Camp**, each with his or her name on a tag.* (Courtesy of the Library of Congress)

wooden buildings. The government supplied housing, food, schools, and medical care.

The Japanese Americans worked hard at clearing land for farming. They raised much of their own food and ran small factories within the camps.

Some Arkansans were not pleased to host the Japanese Americans and were hostile to them. A few churches, particularly the Methodist church, did offer a hand of welcome. Two hundred preachers at the Arkansas Pastors School at Hendrix College believed it was their Christian duty to greet the newcomers in friendship.

The Japanese Americans were not allowed to leave the camps for any reason, partly for their own safety. A United States soldier of Japanese descent from Camp Robinson, in uniform, was shot and badly wounded in a Dermott cafe. He had been on his way to visit relatives at Rohwer.

The United States Army recruited soldiers from the camps in Arkansas and other camps around the country. These Japanese American soldiers served with honor in the war in Europe.

Forty years after the war, the United States offered a small payment and a formal apology to the Japanese Americans whose civil rights had been so abused during the war. Justice was done to some extent in the end. But there was no way to make up the losses to those Japanese Americans who had spent their childhood or teen-age years penned up in the camps.

Toward the war's end, Arkansas also housed German prisoners of war. About twenty-three thousand Germans and a few Italians were

*Japanese American men at work at the Rohwer **Internment Camp**. (Courtesy of the Library of Congress)*

*A children's program at the Japanese **internment camp** at Rohwer in 1943, during World War II. The children, almost certainly born in America and therefore American citizens, are in the camp only because they are of Japanese descent. Notice the American flag, the picture of Abraham Lincoln on the back wall, and the stars and stripes decorations. (Courtesy of the University of Central Arkansas Archives)*

This group of German prisoners of war at Camp Chaffee during World War II had its own band. They are playing at the funeral of one of the prisoners. (Courtesy of the UALR Archives and Special Collections)

shipped to Arkansas. To make a place for them, the Japanese Americans were moved from the Jerome camp to Rohwer and to other states. Captured German and Italian soldiers were also housed at Camp Robinson, Camp Chaffee, and Dermott. There were smaller "branch camps" in the Delta and the Grand Prairie. During these days of farm labor shortages, many of these men were used for extra labor by Arkansas farmers.

When the war was over, the soldiers were sent back to Germany and Italy, and the Japanese Americans were freed. Almost all the Japanese Americans left Arkansas, never to return. Only a very few remained to make their homes in Arkansas.

Other Americans were also denied their civil rights during the war years, among them **Jehovah's Witnesses.** This church group literally interpreted the Bible's commands of "Thou shalt not make unto thee any graven image" and "Thou shalt not kill." As a result, they would not salute the flag, nor would they join the armed forces. This was viewed as being unpatriotic. As a result, they were abused all across the country and became the objects of vicious mob attacks.

The **Jehovah's Witnesses** of Arkansas tried to meet in Little Rock in 1942. As they gathered, seven **Witnesses** were shot and others beaten with lead pipes while a crowd stood by and cheered. When the police arrived, they put the **Jehovah's Witnesses** under arrest. The police even arrested those who were badly wounded, instead of those who had attacked them. A sixty-five-year-old lawyer, Oscar Winn, was himself badly beaten after he agreed to defend the **Witnesses** in court. It took direct action by President Roosevelt and two U.S. Supreme Court rulings to protect the **Witnesses** and give them some peace.

WARTIME CIVIL RIGHTS

In the armed services, African Americans were well aware that they were fighting a war to secure freedoms for others that they did not enjoy themselves at home. In the defense plants, they got the worst jobs and the lowest pay. African Americans began to demand their full rights as citizens.

Both the methods and goals of the future civil rights movement had their roots in the war years. In New York, the brilliant A. Philip Randolph took the lead. He was head of the Brotherhood of Sleeping Car Porters, an African American labor union, and the highest ranking African American in the American labor movement. He began to insist that President Roosevelt order tax-financed defense plants to hire and pay blacks on an equal basis with whites.

When Roosevelt balked, Randolph planned a great march on Washington to display support for equal employment and pay. He

John Watson of Little Rock (left) *in front of the head-quarters of his company, with the U.S. Army in Germany during World War II.* (Courtesy of the Arkansas History Commission)

The "King Biscuit Time" radio program over KFFA in Helena gave Arkansas blues musicians a chance to express their distinctive style. (Courtesy of the Arkansas History Commission)

promised that he would have a hundred thousand people come to Washington. The president, with the help of his wife Eleanor, got Randolph to agree to cancel the march. In exchange, the president ordered a halt to unfair job practices in public programs throughout the nation.

President Roosevelt issued **Executive Order 8802.** This outlawed hiring on a racial basis in public job training programs and in private industries that received U.S. contracts. Roosevelt also formed a Fair Employment Practices Commission to make sure business firms followed the new rules.

Job options for African Americans began to improve dramatically. The wartime labor shortage helped to speed the hiring of African American workers. But Roosevelt's rules on

the hiring practices of private business set the pace for future civil rights laws. And Randolph's plans for a march did not go to waste. The basic plan was revived in 1963 at the height of the civil rights movement when the Reverend Martin Luther King, Jr., took part in a famous march on Washington, D.C.

While business began to integrate, the armed forces did not. All-black units assigned to Arkansas for training were made to follow the legally sanctioned racial rules of the South, both on and off the army bases. For many of the African American soldiers from the North, it was their first taste of legal segregation.

In March 1942, Sergeant Thomas B. Foster, a black soldier stationed at Camp Robinson, was shot and killed by a white police officer on Little Rock's Ninth Street. Daisy and L. C. Bates's *Arkansas State Press,* Arkansas's only African American newspaper at that time, then led a campaign for the hiring of African American police officers. Under pressure from the *Press* and the Negro Citizens Committee of Little Rock, the Little Rock City Council agreed to hire eight black patrolmen.

These first African American police officers could work only in the black areas of the city. They could not arrest whites without the help of a white officer, and they did not get the pensions all other officers received. Still, their hiring was a major step forward, and it helped reduce tension between black soldiers and white police in the city.

African American leaders also made some gains in seeking equal pay for public school-teachers. In 1941, white teachers in Arkansas earned $625 a year, compared to $367 for blacks. After the U.S. Supreme Court held in favor of an African American teacher in Virginia, Arkansas lawyer Scipio A. Jones filed a suit on behalf of Susie Morris to obtain equal pay. She was a teacher at Little Rock's Dunbar High School. Thurgood Marshall, a lawyer with the National Association for the Advancement of Colored People, also helped in the case. This was a time when 22 percent of the white teachers in Arkansas had less than one year of college training. Susie Morris had a B.A. degree from Talladega College in Alabama and grades of "A" in master's-level English courses from the University of Chicago. She had been teaching for seven years. The school board's defense in court was that "regardless of college degrees and teaching experience no white teacher in Little Rock is inferior to the best Negro teacher."

Believe it or not, Judge T. C. Trimble was swayed by this blatant racist statement. He found in favor of the school board. But his finding was struck down by the U.S. Court of Appeals in 1945. Susie Morris had won a major victory but was promptly fired from her job. In the end, she was hired back, but not until 1952.

The "separate but equal" doctrine handed down by the 1896 *Plessy vs. Ferguson* Supreme Court decision had been weakened as early as 1937 in a Supreme Court finding on rail travel. Arthur W. Mitchell was an African American Democratic member of the U.S. House of Representatives from Illinois. He was thrown off a Pullman car in Arkansas on the way from Chicago to Hot Springs. The court ruled in Mitchell's favor, despite many briefs filed in defense of segregation from the states of Arkansas, Alabama, Florida, Georgia, Kentucky, Louisiana, Mississippi, Texas, Tennessee, and Virginia.

A major part of the struggle for racial justice involved the right to vote. In Arkansas, the main issue was the right to vote in the Democratic Party primary. The winner among the Democrats always won the election, because the Republican Party was still weak. A Texas case, **Smith vs. Allwright,** challenged the all-white primary. The Supreme Court in 1944 ruled that the all-white primary vote was illegal.

Arkansas blacks were then able to vote in the primary in the summer of 1944. They also voted in the runoff and in the general elections.

The white-controlled Democratic Party of Arkansas rallied and imposed new rules for joining the party. Once again, African Americans were kept out. The new rules called for holding two sets of elections, one national and one state. That meant taxpayers had to cover the costs of four elections, two primaries and two general elections. The march to the polls proved to be a long and rugged journey for black Arkansans.

THE ELECTION OF 1944

During the war, Arkansas chose two U. S. senators who served the state for many years to come. When Senator John E. Miller resigned to become a federal judge, John L. McClellan won his Senate seat in 1942. When Senator Hattie Caraway's term expired in 1944, a number of men entered what would be called the "million dollar race."

Among those in the race was Governor Homer Adkins, who had once given support to Mrs. Caraway. Others were T. H. Barton, head of Lion Oil Company, and Congressman J. William Fulbright. Fulbright was a former president of the University of Arkansas who had been fired by Adkins. They all spent so much money on the campaign that a special committee of the U.S. Senate was set up to look into their campaign records.

The field narrowed to a runoff between Fulbright and Adkins. Congressman Fulbright beat Governor Adkins with 58 percent of the vote. Thus began a thirty-year career for Fulbright in the Senate. There, he gained worldwide respect and fame for his knowledge of foreign affairs and his efforts for world peace. McClellan and Fulbright would be strong voices for Arkansas in Congress for decades to come. A third leader was Representative Wilbur Mills, who was elected to the House in 1937.

William Fulbright when he was first elected to the U.S. Senate. (Courtesy of the University of Arkansas, Fayetteville, Special Collections)

The Arkansas artist John Howard, in 1946, with one of his still life paintings. (Courtesy of the Arkansas History Commission)

THE G.I. REVOLT

The war ended in Europe in May 1945 and in Japan that August. The end of the war revealed its full horrors. As American and **Allied** forces moved through Europe, they found the few who had survived the **Holocaust** of the Nazi death camps. They learned that six million Jews had been killed in the name of the German master race. The war against Japan ended with the cities of Hiroshima and Nagasaki laid waste by the world's first atom bombs.

As Arkansans mustered out of the armed forces to return home, many of them resolved that things would have to change at home. They had been exposed to the wide world and had risked their lives on the battlefield in the name of the **four freedoms**. They wanted Arkansas to have those **four freedoms**, too. In what became known as the **"G.I. Revolt,"** these young former soldiers took on those in the seats of political power. They started at the local level and later moved onto the statewide scene.

In Hot Springs, Mayor Leo P. McLaughlin had been running a corrupt **political machine** for nearly thirty years. He allowed the town to be a national center for gambling in open scorn of state laws. Young men bent on reform challenged McLaughlin's power. They were led by Sidney S. McMath, a former marine and war hero, who ran for prosecuting attorney of Garland County.

Movements like this also occurred in Crittenden and Yell counties. The G.I.s joined forces to make election judges obey the laws, to challenge phony poll tax receipts, and to expose **nepotism**, the practice of giving public jobs to relatives. The **G.I.**s offered the voters slates of honest candidates in place of those who were corrupt.

McMath won his race. His efforts in Hot Springs did not end gambling there, but he did become known statewide. That made him a leader in the 1948 governor's race. He won in a runoff.

As governor, McMath placed black Arkansans on state boards for the first time since Reconstruction. African Americans also made

Sid McMath, in the center, *celebrates an election victory. On the right is Henry Woods, then an aide to McMath and later a federal judge.* (Courtesy of the J. N. Heiskell Collection, UALR Archives and Special Collections)

gains in local races, earning seats on city councils in Malvern and Hot Springs. McMath sponsored laws to end lynching and bills to end the poll tax, but the members of the General Assembly refused to pass many of his reforms.

The General Assembly did support McMath's highway program. Much work was needed after neglect during the hard times and heavy use during the war years. Arkansas was known throughout the nation for its bad roads. One carmaker touted its cars as having "passed the Arkansas mud test." In 1949, the state borrowed money through a bond issue to pay for repairs and new highways. Nearly eighty million dollars, both state and federal funds, were spent to improve roads.

The schools faced the new problem of crowding on top of the old funding problems. Thousands of veterans enrolled in colleges. The United States paid their way through the **G.I. Bill**, a "thank you" from a grateful nation. An increase in the birth rate (the **"baby boom"**) began right after the end of the war. Those children arrived at the public schools in the early 1950s, flooding the classrooms grade by grade.

Meanwhile, Arkansas's teacher pay and spending per pupil were at the bottom of the country's scales. One reform that did meet

As Others See Us: Arkansas in 1946

John Gunther, a well-known American author, set out just after the end of World War II to visit all the American states. He recorded his observations in his book *Inside USA*. Here are some selections from his comments on Arkansas in 1946:

> Arkansas is a curious and interesting community . . . it is probably the most untouched and unawakened of all American states, as well as one of the poorest. Its . . . backwoods are inaccessible and primitive in the extreme; yet . . . it contains such a notably fashionable resort as Hot Springs, cotton land as rich as the Mississippi Delta, gambling dens of almost Pompeiian splendor, and a senator as good as James William Fulbright. . . .
>
> Little Rock, the capital (population 101,387) is a clean, modern-looking town with a lively spirit that does much to dispel the state's reputation for provincialism. . . .
>
> The west, a region of open plains, is cow country, and resembles Texas; the Ozark area in the north seems to be a carry-over from Missouri, with small truck and chicken farms and a 100 per cent Anglo-Saxon population, very poor and thrifty. The other great division is the Delta region along the Mississippi, which is pure "old South"—a district of huge plantations (you scarcely count as a cotton farmer unless you have 10,000 acres), and a social system still mostly feudal. . . .
>
> The war shook things up. From being a backwater, Arkansas found itself with 400 million dollars worth of war production orders. . . . Arkansas had a vivid and successful veterans' revolt in 1946. . . .

John Gunther, *Inside USA* (Revised edition, New York: Harper Brothers, 1951), pp. 842–43, 846–48.

with success was an effort to **consolidate** school districts in 1948. In 1921, there had been 5,112 school districts. In 1948, there were still 1,598. With the passage of the new law, these were further reduced to 424.

African Americans made some gains at the college level right after the war. For years, the state had paid to send African American students to other states to become doctors and lawyers. This practice changed, partly because of the expense of this custom and partly under threat from the Supreme Court. Silas Hunt and Jackie L. Shropshire entered the University of Arkansas Law School in 1948. Edith Irby entered the University of Arkansas School of Medicine in Little Rock.

The McMath years saw industry expand in the state, with 509 new or enlarged plants bringing $209 million dollars into the state.

The United States went to war again in 1950. This time it was in Korea. Even before the end of World War II, it became clear that the aims of the United States and its World War II ally, the Soviet Union, were at odds. The Soviet Union seemed intent on gaining control of people and lands all over Europe and the rest of the world. This led to a **"cold war"** between the two nations. In the United States, an intense fear of Communism arose.

In 1950 North Korea, an ally of the Soviet Union, attacked South Korea, an ally of the United States. President Harry S Truman ordered American armed forces to protect South Korea. It was not declared a war but was called a **"police action"** by Truman. The purpose was to prevent the Communists from taking over South Korea. The United Nations called on its members to help stop the Communist aggression.

Many Arkansas veterans of World War II who had joined the Army Reserve or the National Guard found themselves called up to fight again. Younger men, eighteen-year-olds, learned that the **"cold war"** had led the United States to start the draft again. The fighting stopped in 1953, with the border between North Korea and South Korea where it had been when the fighting started. In this undeclared war, 461 Arkansans died.

Governor McMath Speaks Up for Arkansas

Governor Sidney McMath worked at being a good ambassador for Arkansas. He was active in national Democratic politics, as a close associate of President Harry S Truman. He also spoke frequently to audiences all over the country, describing the progress he saw in Arkansas and the South. This is part of a speech he made to a northern audience in 1949, soon after he became governor:

> We are not spending all our time on white-columned verandas sipping mint-juleps, and plotting to keep our people in economic slavery. In fact, there is abroad in all the southland a vigorous progressive movement—a growing demand for the development of the human and economic resources of our region.

Jim Lester, *A Man for Arkansas: Sid McMath and the Southern Reform Tradition* (Little Rock: Rose Publishing Company, 1976), p. 129.

This postcard during World War II showed the old federal arsenal in Little Rock and, in an inset, General Douglas MacArthur. MacArthur, who was one of the war's major leaders, was born at the arsenal while his father was stationed there. (Courtesy of the UALR Archives and Special Collections)

THE CHANGING AGRICULTURAL ECONOMY

The Depression, New Deal, and World War II, along with new farm machines and techniques, had made sweeping changes in the way Arkansans farmed.

The number of farmers all over the state—and, indeed, all across the country—had dropped sharply during the war. There were 1,113,000 Arkansans living on farms in 1940, but only 595,000 by 1954. The New Deal farming programs were still in effect. They favored large land holdings and gave the large landowners enough money to buy new machines, such as cotton pickers. The use of machines allowed fewer farmers to work more land.

Most of the people who left the land were those who had been sharecroppers or tenants. These workers not only left the farm: they left the state. Arkansas lost 10.9 percent of its people, costing the state one of its six seats in Congress after the 1950 census.

With the advent of larger farms using modern machines came changes in the types of farming. In the hill country, small farms switched to cattle or poultry. In the Delta, soybeans began to replace cotton as the chief cash crop. Rice growing also increased greatly during the war years and after.

THE RISE OF ORVAL FAUBUS

Governor McMath got into a dispute with C. Hamilton Moses of Arkansas Power and Light. At issue was a rural electrical **cooperative**

As World War II ended, cotton was still a major crop. These boys are grinning over a bale at a cotton gin in Conway in 1945. (Courtesy of the University of Central Arkansas Archives)

in northwest Arkansas. AP&L thought that the **co-op**, which could get government loans, could compete on an unfair basis. McMath was in favor of the **co-op**. When McMath ran for a third term in 1952, AP&L and others in business opposed him.

Also, the way some highway contracts had been given to friends of McMath caused a scandal that hurt his **G.I. reform** image. The unknown Francis Cherry ran a clever, non-stop "radio talkathon" campaign that won over enough voters to defeat McMath.

Cherry only lasted one term. His administration coincided with a hefty rate increase by AP&L and caused a decrease in welfare coverage. He proved an easy target for the eager

Orval E. Faubus. Born in Huntsville in the Madison County Ozarks, Faubus was the poor son of a man with populist and socialist ideas. After high school, Faubus briefly went to Commonwealth College in Mena. Known as **"The Little Red School House,"** the college was later closed by the state because its staff was thought to have Communist leanings.

A schoolteacher for a time, Faubus joined the army as a private soon after Pearl Harbor. He rose to the rank of major during the war. Upon coming home, he was named postmaster and he bought the local newspaper. McMath named him to the Highway Commission. Faubus managed to emerge untouched by the scandals there.

In a four-way Democratic race, Faubus forced Cherry into a runoff. Cherry tried to beat Faubus by bringing up Commonwealth College. Communism was now a major issue all across the country. But the attack backfired against Cherry. People felt sorry for the "poor boy" being picked on by the rich man. Faubus won the runoff by a narrow margin.

In the general election, Faubus faced the stiffest opposition the Republicans had mounted since Reconstruction. Their man was Little Rock Mayor Pratt Remmel, a handsome, clean-cut man who campaigned on moral values and stressed his religious beliefs. Remmel polled a mighty 127,004 votes, but Faubus won with 208,000 votes.

During his first term, Governor Faubus proved to be a strong spokesman for the common man. He managed to keep a dog racing track from starting in West Memphis that would have promoted gambling. He rolled back an AP&L rate increase that refunded $9 million to taxpayers. He stopped an Arkla Gas rate increase. He also had success in luring industry to the state.

ARKANSAS AT MID-CENTURY

The war years brought major changes to Arkansas's way of life. People shifted from rural to urban settings, and many displaced farm workers left for other states. Women gained their first access to decent jobs and wages. African Americans made slow but large

Governor Francis A. Cherry. (Courtesy of the University of Arkansas, Fayetteville, Special Collections)

strides in both jobs and civil rights. The public at large had a taste of the good life for the first time in thirty years.

The corrupt politics that had so often been a part of Arkansas life began to change under public review and demands for reform. Industry began to come to Arkansas. Some of it was short term, but much of it, such as the bauxite industry, stayed after the war was over. Farming changed from small, family farms to huge businesses. Farm products changed from cotton to rice, soybeans, and poultry. **Food processing** became a major industry in the state.

A strong team served Arkansas in Congress, and bright young leaders held public offices throughout the state. Arkansas still lagged far behind other parts of the country in education and many other sectors. But the state was well on its way to joining the mainstream of American life in the new postwar era.

Or so it seemed.

Selected Census Data for Arkansas 1940 to 1950

	1940	1950
Total population	1,949,511	1,909,511
White population	1,466,084	1,481,507
Black population	482,578	426,639
Total urban population	431,910	630,591
Percent urban population	22.2	33
Number of farms	216,674	182,429
Average acres per farm	83.3	103.4
Value of farms	$456,848,156	$1,135,671,000
Cotton bales produced	1,351,209	1,584,307
Bushels of corn produced	33,762,323	21,626,026
Bushels of rice produced	7,651,231	19,889,614

		1954
Manufacturing establishments	1,178	2,428
Wage earners	36,256	79,052

Notes:

The figures for black and white population for each year will not add up to the exact figure for the total population. The difference is the small number of other races in the population.

Governor Orval Faubus at the Gator Bowl Parade in 1960. (Courtesy of the University of Arkansas, Fayetteville, Special Collections)

VOCABULARY

Allied Powers, or Allies (AL-eyed POW-erz) Great Britain, the United States, France, China, Russia, and others allied against the Axis Powers in World War II.

Aryans (AIR-ee-unz) blonde, blue-eyed Germans who, according to Hitler, were a superior "race" of people destined to rule.

Axis Powers (AKS-iss POW-erz) the combined forces of Nazi Germany, Fascist Italy, and Japan during World War II.

baby boom a population explosion in the United States in the years following World War II.

Blitzkrieg (BLITS-kreeg) the German army's "lightning war" that mowed down European defenses with horrifying speed at the beginning of World War II.

booster a device that increases force, power, or pressure.

cold war tension and confrontation short of total war between the Communist and the Free World beginning after World War II.

Congressional Medal of Honor the highest award given in the United States for military valor.

consolidate to combine, as in consolidating two or more school districts into one.

cooperative, co-op (koh-AHP-er-uh-tiv, KOH-ahp) a business that is owned cooperatively by producers (e.g., farmers who collectively sell their produce) or consumers (e.g., homeowners who collectively buy their electricity).

coupons (KYOO-pahnz) during World War II, tickets entitling the holder to purchase a rationed item, such as meat or gasoline.

denounce (dee-NOWNSS) to accuse, to pronounce guilty or evil.

Executive Order 8802 issued by President Roosevelt during World War II to ban discrimination among federal contractors in hiring on the basis of race.

fascism (FASH-izm) political belief in one's nation and race as superior to all others and upholding highly centralized government under an all-powerful dictator.

food processing turning raw food into a packaged product suitable for shipping and storage and easy consumer use.

Four Freedoms according to President Roosevelt, the freedom of speech and worship, and freedom from want and fear.

Führer (FYIR-er) title assumed by Hitler as all-powerful ruler of Nazi Germany; "the Leader."

fuses detonating devices to set off bombs or torpedoes.

G.I. a member or former member of the armed services, especially an enlisted man.

G.I. Bill enacted following World War II, the law provided a government-sponsored free college education to veterans.

G.I. Revolt movement against corruption in government spearheaded by veterans returning to Arkansas from service in World War II.

Gypsies (JIP-seez) wandering tribal people, originally from India, who live in Europe and the United States.

heinous (HAY-nuss) hatefully, shockingly evil.

Holocaust (HALL-uh-kawst) name later given to Hitler's "Final Solution for the Jewish problem," the execution of at least six million Jews and many other "undesirables" in the Nazi extermination camps.

infamy (IN-fuhm-ee) evil reputation brought about by grossly criminal, shocking, or brutal acts.

internment camp (in-TURN-munt KAMP) a compound resembling a small village established to confine "enemies" during wartime.

Jehovah's Witnesses (jeh-HOH-vuhz WIT-ness-ez) a fundamentalist religious sect that was persecuted during the war for its pacifist beliefs.

Lend-Lease Act law under which the United States sent weapons and supplies to Britain despite an official policy of neutrality.

Little Red School House nickname for Commonwealth College, referring to its Communist, or "red," leanings.

munitions (myoo-NISH-unz) weapons, ammunition.

National Socialist Party Hitler's fascist party, known as the Nazi party.

nepotism (NEH-poh-tizm) using the power of public office to offer government jobs to relatives.

Nisei (nee-SAY) second-generation Japanese-Americans, U.S. citizens by birth.

police action a substitute term for war, used to describe the Korean War, which was never declared a war by Congress.

political machine a tightly controlled organization headed by a political boss that determines the outcome of elections and the distribution of political jobs and favors which often operates outside the law.

primer (PRY-mer) percussion cap used to ignite an explosive charge.

Ranger Battalions special forces formed during World War II by Colonel William Darby; known as "Darby's Rangers."

rationing (RASH-uhn-ing) distributing rare commodities on a limited basis to share limited supplies fairly among the people.

relocation centers the term used to describe internment camps for Japanese Americans during World War II who were "relocated" by force from their homes into prison-like settings.

rivet (RIH-vet) to join two pieces of metal together with a bolt; the bolt so used.

Selective Service Act law which re-established the draft, requiring young men to serve in the armed forces.

Smith vs. Allwright Supreme Court case (out of Texas) which outlawed the all-white Democratic primary.

squadron (SKWA-drun) a unit of military organization in the Air Force, bigger than a flight but smaller than a group.

"tractorette" (TRACK-tor-ET) a term coined by International Harvester to refer to farming women whom the corporation was training to use heavy machinery when able-bodied men were away at war.

victory gardens home vegetable gardens promoted to boost U.S. agricultural output for the war effort.

war bonds citizen loans to the U.S. government to aid in the war effort.

STUDY QUESTIONS

1. Explain the origins of World War II, including how the United States got involved.

2. Describe the war-time heroics of Arkansans such as Footsie Britt and William Darby.

3. What was the effect of the war on people at home?

4. Describe the new industries brought to Arkansas by the war.

5. Discuss the role of women in the war effort.

6. Discuss the removal of people of Japanese descent to the internment camps.

7. Evaluate any changes in race relations during the war.

8. Discuss the "G.I. Revolt" in Arkansas right after the war.

9. What changes were underway in agriculture after the war?

10 How did Orval Faubus become governor?

10

Conflict and Change

1955–1975

What to Look for in Chapter 10

The years from the mid-1950s to the mid-1970s were a time of change for most Arkansans as many people left the farms and the state for jobs in the north. One response was the beginning of a major attempt to attract industry to Arkansas.

When the civil rights movement and the end of racially separate schools became a major movement, a crisis at Central High in Little Rock focused national attention on Arkansas.

The Little Rock school board had a prepared a plan that would put nine African American students in the all white Central High School. Then the governor, Orval Faubus, used the National Guard to keep the black students out. President Dwight Eisenhower responded by sending in federal troops to escort the "Little Rock Nine" to school. Little Rock and Arkansas got national attention in the worst way.

Faubus went on to serve twelve years as governor. He was replaced by the Republican Winthrop Rockefeller.

One of the major steps toward equality for all was the change for the better in the role of women.

INDUSTRIAL DEVELOPMENT

As Arkansas entered the last half of the twentieth century, the rise of industry became a major goal for the state. It was clear that more jobs were needed to provide for Arkansas's people, even to keep people in the state. The changes in farming were swiftly slashing the number of rural jobs. In the decade of the 1950s, the number of people living in rural areas dropped by almost 50 percent.

Many people had to leave the state to find jobs, at a rate of about forty thousand a year.

Arkansas lost 6.5 percent of its people between 1950 and 1960. The population loss, among other things, meant that Arkansas lost another Congressional seat, leaving the state with only four members in the U.S. House of Representatives. In addition, Arkansans were poor by the country's standards. The average income per person in the state was $1,142 in 1955, or 60 percent of the United States average. Factory jobs tended to pay more than most farm work.

Lumbering and wood products remained important industries in Arkansas in the 1950s. These are workers at the Union Company Mill at Huttig. (Courtesy of the Arkansas History Commission)

Some efforts to attract business had begun in the 1940s, under the guidance of the Arkansas Power and Light Company. Its head, C. Hamilton Moses, drew up an **"Arkansas Plan"** to urge industry to move to the state. Moses and other leaders toured the nation touting the virtues of Arkansas. By the mid-1950s, business leaders were ready for the state government to take a major role. When Orval Faubus took office, he endorsed the idea of state action. The result, in 1955, was the start of the Arkansas Industrial Development Commission, the **AIDC.**

To head the new body, Faubus chose Winthrop Rockefeller. A grandson of John D. Rockefeller, founder of the Standard Oil Company, Rockefeller had just moved to Arkansas. An army buddy from Arkansas had told Rockefeller that he could find a good home for himself in Arkansas and many opportunities to do good things for the state.

An enormously wealthy man, Rockefeller started a large ranch on top of Petit Jean Mountain and became active in civic and cultural affairs.

Under Rockefeller, the **AIDC** hired a staff and began to seek industry. Arkansas could offer its central location, its rich resource base, and its willing labor force. In Arkansas, there were plenty of workers so badly in need of jobs that they were willing to work for about 30 percent less than the nation's average wage.

The General Assembly and local cities and towns also offered enticements to new industry. In some cases, they allowed new businesses to be **exempt** from taxes. To help prepare workers, the state started the Vocational Technical Educational Program.

Over the next ten years, hundreds of factories with thousands of jobs moved into the state. Jobs increased by 57 percent, and income

International Paper Company became one of the state's big industries in the 1950s. Its Camden mill made paper. Here a roll of paper is being loaded on a boxcar for shipment from the plant. (Courtesy of the Arkansas History Commission)

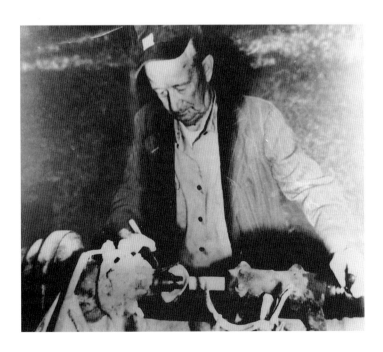

One of Arkansas's early industries lingered into the 1950s. This man at Black Rock is operating a simple machine that cuts buttons from White River mussel shells. (Courtesy of the University of Central Arkansas Archives)

By the 1950s, tourism was a big business in Arkansas. Above, one of the state's scenic roads. Below, the view from Highway 7, in Newton County. (Courtesy of the University of Central Arkansas Archives)

increased by 65 percent to $1,888. That was 68 percent of the U.S. average. Many of the new jobs were in small towns and rural areas where they were most needed. The drive for industry continued into the 1990s.

THE END OF SCHOOL SEGREGATION

Although blacks and whites were still kept apart in almost all aspects of life, there were starting to be signs that change might come. In the early 1950s, the major stores in Little Rock removed the "white" and "colored" signs on their drinking fountains. The Rock Island Railroad stopped seating people by race on its trains. Whites, as well as blacks, were starting to discuss both the wrongs in the system and plans for solving them. The black and white public school systems were still separate but, as all were aware, not equal. In 1952, the Little Rock Council on Education, which contained members of both races, pointed out that the black schools were worse than the white schools in every way. The Council concluded, "the only practical, realistic, and ethical answer is integration."

With a genuine American faith in learning, African American leaders throughout the United States believed that equal education was the answer to many of the problems of black people. With the help of the National Association for the Advancement of Colored People, the NAACP, African Americans began to bring lawsuits to challenge the separate school systems. A number of these cases, combined as *Brown vs. the Topeka Board of Education,* reached the U.S. Supreme Court.

In 1954 the Supreme Court heard the *Brown* case and ruled that because separate education was not and could not be equal, it was not in keeping with the U.S. Constitu-tion. In a second *Brown* decision the next year, the Court said that school districts must integrate "with all deliberate speed."

Across the South, the first response to this decision was mixed. In some places, people moved quickly to change their schools. In other regions, white leaders in public office said openly that they would never allow blacks and whites to go to the same schools.

As time went on, those opposed to change grew more vocal with public leaders saying the Supreme Court could be ignored. In the U.S. Congress, almost all the members from the South signed a **"Southern Manifesto"** against school integration. All of Arkansas's members of Congress signed it.

In Arkansas, a number of groups arose that gave active support to integration. The Arkansas Council on Human Relations was headed by Ozell Sutton and Ruth Arnold. Then came the Urban League, which had the support of Winthrop Rockefeller and Congressman Brooks Hays. In Little Rock, church leaders formed the Interracial Ministerial Alliance.

A few school districts complied with the *Brown* decision quickly and without trouble, particularly in sections of the state with few African American students. Fayetteville, for instance, was integrated immediately but had only six African American high school students. Before integration, Fayetteville had sent them sixty-three miles by bus to a high school in Fort Smith. In 1955, the state colleges started to admit African American students.

The first signs of trouble were at Hoxie in Lawrence County in northeast Arkansas. The school board in 1955 started to move the twenty-one black students living there into the white public schools. After the school term had started with no problems, **segregationists** from outside Hoxie formed a group to begin a protest.

The leaders were James D. Johnson of Crossett and Amis Guthridge of Little Rock.

Rather than give in to the pressure, the Hoxie school board took the matter to court. The court ruled that integration should go forward.

THE SITUATION IN LITTLE ROCK

Meanwhile, the Little Rock school board drew up a plan to integrate. Named the **Blossom Plan**, after Superintendent Virgil Blossom, the plan was voted in only ten days after the *Brown* decision. It was designed to integrate the schools very slowly, starting at the high school level.

To begin, Little Rock Central High School would accept a few African American students in the fall of 1957. Horace Mann, a new high school opened in 1956, would remain all black. Hall High School, to be finished in 1957, would be all white. The second phase of the plan would open white junior high schools to a few blacks in 1960. The third phase would open white grade schools to a few blacks at some unspecified date in the future.

The **Blossom Plan** had major flaws. Putting off any action until 1957 allowed time for opponents of integration to organize. Instead of spreading the changes throughout the entire city, the plan focused on Central High. This was in a lower-income, working-class section of the city. The plan would allow richer whites living in the western part of the city to send their children to all-white Hall High.

From the standpoint of many African Americans, the **Blossom Plan** was both too little and too slow. In 1956, the parents of

Jim Johnson, after his election as a justice of the Arkansas Supreme Court. (Courtesy of the J. N. Heiskell Collection, UALR Archives and Special Collections)

Daisy and L. C. Bates in the 1950s. Together they founded and operated the Arkansas State Press; *she became head of the National Association for the Advancement of Colored People in Arkansas.* (Courtesy of the Arkansas History Commission)

more than thirty African American school-children filed suit against the school board. They said their children had been denied entry into their neighborhood all-white schools.

The NAACP, headed by its state president, Daisy Bates, aided in the suit. The lawyer for the African American parents was Wiley Branton of Pine Bluff. Branton was one of the first African American graduates of the University of Arkansas Law School. (He went on to a long career as a nationally respected civil rights lawyer.)

In this case, *Aaron vs. Cooper,* Federal Judge John Miller ruled that the **Blossom Plan** should be carried out. The judge also said the court would supervise the plan,

meaning that any opponents to the plan in Little Rock would be opposing the U.S. courts.

And the forces against change were growing. In Little Rock and other towns, **White Citizens' Councils** were formed to oppose integration. Jim Johnson, who had opposed integration at Hoxie, proposed to amend the state constitution. His aim was to defy the Supreme Court's *Brown vs. the Board of Education* ruling. Johnson also ran against Faubus for governor in 1956.

Although Johnson was soundly beaten in the governor's race, his proposed amendment won by a vote of 185,374 to 146,064. The amendment required the General Assembly to take action against the *Brown* ruling. This was to be done by "interposing the **sovereignty** of the State of Arkansas to the end of **nullification**" of the decision. In fact, the American system grants no state the right to **nullify**, or cancel, an action of the United States. The outcome of the Civil War settled that issue.

Governor Faubus began to be concerned about the growing **segregationist** strength. Up to this point, Faubus's position on race matters had been moderate to liberal. Soon after the *Brown* ruling, Faubus had declared himself neutral on the question. He said it was a matter for local school districts to handle. But during the campaign of 1956, Faubus began to feel the political power of the **segregationists.** He thought he needed their support to get his programs passed and to win the next race for governor.

In the next session of the General Assembly in the spring of 1957, Faubus proposed a tax increase. Much of the new money would

Faubus and Little Rock: An Editor's View of the Governor's Motives

After Governor Orval Faubus defied the federal government to prevent the integration of Central High School, many people tried to understand his motives.

Harry Ashmore was editor of the *Arkansas Gazette* in 1957. The *Gazette*'s support of integration at Central High won it two Pulitzer Prizes, the highest honor for newspapers. One was for the *Gazette*'s general coverage, and the other was for Ashmore's editorials.

Later, in a history of Arkansas, Ashmore wrote about Faubus's reasons:

> Many of Faubus's supporters accepted him as a racist ideologue, and he was usually so portrayed in the national media, but few of his antagonists in Arkansas ever did. The *Gazette* contended from the outset that he had no real concern with racial matters, one way or the other, but was exploiting the highly charged school desegregation issue to maintain himself in power. . . .
>
> The man who knew Orval Faubus longest was convinced that he was untouched by simple race prejudice. Old Sam Faubus [Orval's father] the self-educated hill farmer . . . never abandoned the populist faith. . . .
>
> Orval, Sam Faubus recalled, had never even seen a black until he was grown . . . and he knew of nothing that had happened since to cause him to reject his father's teaching that racial equality was essential to progress as well as justice. His son went off the track, Sam Faubus thought, because he could never stand to be looked down on, and Orval believed that the leading citizens of Little Rock had done just that. . . . This personal resentment reinforced his suspicion that the Little Rock school desegregation plan was deliberately designed to discriminate against poor whites, requiring those in the downtown area to mingle their children with blacks, while the schools in the upper-income precincts . . . would remain segregated. . . .

Harry Ashmore, *Arkansas: A Bicentennial History* (New York: W. W. Norton & Co., and Nashville: American Association for State and Local History, 1978), pp. 153–55.

go to schools and would provide equal pay for African American teachers. In return for support of the tax increase, Faubus agreed to support east Arkansas **segregationists** in the passage of their laws.

These laws ended compulsory school attendance and gave state aid to districts threatened with court suits. **Segregationists** also wanted to require the NAACP to publish its list of members and to create a State **Sovereignty** Commission protecting Arkansas from the U.S. courts. But once Faubus's tax increase was passed, the governor seemed to ignore the demands of the **segregationists.**

THE CENTRAL HIGH CRISIS

In Little Rock, the school board went forward with its plans to integrate Central High in the fall of 1957. Superintendent Blossom asked African American students to apply for entry into Central. With the help of African American teachers and principals, Blossom chose nine African American students to be the first to attend Central. The school officials and the city's white leaders assumed that all was going well.

But throughout the summer of 1957, whites who opposed integration were gaining strength. The **White Citizens' Council** brought Marvin Griffin, the governor of Georgia, to Little Rock. He urged them to defy the *Brown* ruling, then stayed with Faubus in the governor's mansion.

The Mothers' League of Central High, a **segregationist** group, filed a court suit in an attempt to prevent the school from opening. Governor Faubus was their only witness. He said that he knew that black and white students had guns. He had learned that gangs were forming to threaten students at the high school. No one else, then or since, has been able to find any proof to support the governor's claims. A local court agreed to delay the opening of school, but the federal court insisted that the plan proceed.

School was scheduled to start on September 2. The day before, Faubus ordered units of the Arkansas National Guard to surround Central High. He told the Guard to prevent the African American students from coming into Central High. Drawn by the Guard and urged on by the governor's actions, a crowd of whites gathered at the school. Many of them were from outside the city. Reporters from all over the nation rushed to Little Rock.

On September 4, eight of the nine African American students went to school and the Guard turned them away at a side door. The ninth African American student, Elizabeth Eckford, did not get the word to join the others. She came to school alone, went to the walk leading to the front door, and was told by a Guardsman to leave. She then had to walk from the school back to the bus stop.

All by herself, with her books clutched in her arms and fighting back tears, the fourteen-year-old girl walked a long block past the mob of whites. There were now about one thousand people lining the street. They screamed and shouted at her, but she kept her head held high. Pictures and stories of her ordeal were national and worldwide news within hours.

It was an awful moment, and Little Rock and Arkansas would pay dearly for the pain of it. But it was in fact a beginning. It was a moment in which the effects of racism became embodied in the fear and courage of one teenaged girl. Americans were shocked at the sight, and they began to change. In a very real sense, "Little Rock 1957" was a major step forward in the civil rights movement.

The African American students waited. Meanwhile, the courts, the school board, the

*Elizabeth Eckford, one of the "**Little Rock Nine**," on the first day she tried to enter Central High School. She's walking in front of Central toward the bus stop, while members of the mob scream at her. In the background is an Arkansas National Guardsman.* (Courtesy of the University of Central Arkansas Archives)

Elizabeth Eckford's First Day at Central High: "It was the longest block I ever walked in my whole life."

For many, the most dramatic moment of the integration crisis at Central High School in 1957 was fourteen-year-old Elizabeth Eckford's lonely walk in front of an angry mob after she had been turned away from entering the school by the Arkansas National Guard.

Soon after, Elizabeth described her day to Daisy Bates, the head of the NAACP in Arkansas, who was a friend and advisor to the **"Little Rock Nine"** during the whole ordeal. Here are some of Elizabeth's recollections:

> You remember the day before we were to go in, we met Superintendent Blossom at the school board office. He told us what the mob might say and do but he never told us we wouldn't have any protection. He told our parents not to come because he wouldn't be able to protect the children if they did.
>
> That night I was so excited I couldn't sleep. . . . Before I left home Mother called us into the living room. She said we should have a word of prayer. Then I caught a bus and got off a block from the school. I saw a large crowd of people standing across the street from the [National Guard] soldiers guarding Central. As I walked on, the crowd suddenly got very quiet. . . .
>
> The crowd moved in closer and then began to follow me, calling me names. I still wasn't afraid. Just a little bit nervous. Then my knees started to shake all of a sudden and I wondered whether I could make it to the center entrance a block away. It was the longest block I ever walked in my whole life.
>
> Even so, I still wasn't too scared because all the time I kept thinking that the guards would protect me. . . . So I walked until I was right in front of the path to the front door.
>
> I stood looking at the school—it looked so big! Just then the guards let some white students go through. . . . When I was able to steady my knees, I walked up to the guard who had let the white students in. He . . . didn't move. When I tried to squeeze past him, he raised his bayonet and then the other guards closed in and they raised their bayonets.
>
> They glared at me with a mean look and I was very frightened and didn't know what to do. I turned around and the crowd came toward me.
>
> They moved closer and closer. Somebody started yelling, "Lynch her! Lynch her!"
>
> I tried to see a friendly face somewhere in the mob—someone who maybe would help. I looked into the face of an old woman and it seemed a kind face, but when I looked at her again, she spat on me. . . .
>
> I turned back to the guards but their faces told me I wouldn't get help from them. Then I looked down the block and saw a bench at the bus stop. I thought, "If I can only get there I will be safe." I don't know why the bench seemed a safe place to me, but I started walking toward it. I tried to close my mind to what they were shouting. . . .
>
> When I finally got there, I don't think I could have gone another step. . . . Then, a white lady—she was very nice—she came over to me on the bench. . . . She put me on the bus and sat next to me. . . . I can't remember much about the bus ride. . . .
>
> [Elizabeth went to the Arkansas School for the Blind, where her mother was a teacher.] Mother was standing at the window with her head bowed, but she must have sensed I was there because she turned around. She looked as if she had been crying and I wanted to tell her I was all right. But I couldn't speak. She put her arms around me and I cried.

Quoted in Daisy Bates, *The Long Shadow of Little Rock* (1962; reprinted, Fayetteville: University of Arkansas Press, 1987), pp. 72-76.

governor, and even the president of the United States wrestled with the problem. Congressman Brooks Hays arranged a meeting between Governor Faubus and President Dwight D. Eisenhower. It failed to produce results. In the end, the federal court ordered Faubus to end the state's involvement at Central. Governor Faubus withdrew the National Guard.

On September 23, the nine African American students tried again to enter Central High. By this time, the white mob at the school was very large and unruly. The Little Rock police said they could not protect the students if they remained in school. The African American students left under police escort after only a few hours. Mayor Woodrow Mann called upon President Eisenhower for help.

President Eisenhower had to uphold the authority of the federal court system. The president removed the Arkansas National Guard from the governor's command and put it under command of the U.S. Army. Then the president ordered units from the U.S. Army's 101st Airborne Division into Little Rock. The combat troopers swiftly set up guard posts around the high school and a command post on the field behind it.

Then, an army station wagon with jeeps full of armed troops before and after it picked up the nine African American students. The army brought them to Central High, and they walked up the steps to the front door with an armed escort. Little Rock Central High was now an integrated school, and it was clear to all that the United States would enforce the *Brown* ruling.

Inside Central High School during the 1957–58 school year, most of the white students ignored the **"Little Rock Nine."** Some students and many teachers were very help-

Congressman Brooks Hays with a group of University of Arkansas students, about 1955. (Courtesy of the University of Arkansas, Fayetteville, Special Collections)

Two of Arkansas's great women, about 1968. Adolphine Fletcher Terry (left) led the movement that restored local control of the schools in Little Rock in 1958–59. Lily Peter of Marvell (right) was among the first to abandon the use of chemicals on her farm, in order to protect the environment. Noted for her gifts to the arts, she once personally arranged for the Philadelphia Symphony Orchestra to play in Arkansas. (Courtesy of the University of Central Arkansas Archives)

ful. But a small number of white students set out to make life rough for the black students. They tried to provoke them with words and sometimes physical abuse. One of the black students hit back and was expelled along with the white student who had started the fight. The others tended to their studies.

The army units were withdrawn after a few weeks. The National Guardsmen remained to patrol the halls. At the end of the school year, Ernest Green became the first African American graduate of the Little Rock school system. There to see him graduate was the Reverend Martin Luther King, Jr., who had been in Pine Bluff to speak at Arkansas AM&N College.

THE END OF THE CRISIS

Things in Little Rock got worse before they got better. Acting under a law passed in a special session of the General Assembly, Faubus closed the public high schools in Little Rock for the 1958–59 school year. Although the football teams played their schedules, the students either had to give up school or go to new, all-white private schools. Black students and whites too poor to pay had no choices. Half the members of the new Little Rock school board were now **segregationists.**

The turning point came when the **segregationists** on the school board tried to fire forty-four teachers and officials. In response, the Women's Emergency Committee to Open Our Schools, headed by Mrs. David D. Terry, took the lead. Their **STOP** (Stop This Outrageous **Purge**) campaign called for a special election in the spring of 1959. The vote removed the **segregationists** from the school board.

The Little Rock high schools opened again in the fall of 1959, and some African American students attended Central High while others attended Hall High. Complete integration of the Little Rock schools at all grade levels did not come until the early 1970s, with court-ordered busing.

THE FAUBUS YEARS

Faubus's role in the crisis had gained him widespread public support, which probably had been one of his motives for taking that role. He won six elections to the governorship. His twelve years in office increased power in the Arkansas governor's office as never before.

In that length of time, Faubus was able to appoint the members of all the boards and commissions in the state. This gave him control over all the state agencies. He also mastered the state budget process, which gave

Senator J. William Fulbright (left), *and Governor Orval Faubus.* (Courtesy of the Arkansas History Commission)

Governor Winthrop Rockefeller (just right of center, waving the hat) *always opened his political campaigns in Winthrop, Arkansas. Mrs. Jeannette Rockefeller is walking next to her husband. The picture isn't backwards; the sign "Winthrop Welcomes Winthrop" is facing the other direction.* (Courtesy of the J. N. Heiskell Collection, UALR Archives and Special Collections)

him virtual control over the General Assembly. The results, in many cases, were good for the state. State programs expanded, schools and colleges received more money, and highway building increased.

But Faubus also forged close ties with special interest groups. He allowed gambling houses to stay open at Hot Springs. Scandal touched him in the form of pay raises and bonus money given to favored state workers.

Faubus's control of the Democratic Party kept any serious threats to his power from forming within that party. A challenge finally appeared in the form of Republican Winthrop Rockefeller, who had fallen out with Faubus over the Central High crisis.

As head of the **AIDC**, Rockefeller knew how much the crisis had hurt the drive to bring industry to the state. Eight new plants opened in Little Rock in 1957, before the crisis. For the next two years, not one new firm moved to Little Rock. Rockefeller also truly believed that competition between two political parties produced healthier politics and government than did domination by one party.

Rockefeller's family had always been Republican. One brother, Nelson, would later become vice-president of the United States under Republican President Gerald Ford. The Arkansas Republican Party was weak, but a Rockefeller could do something about that. His name and his wealth carried great power. Also, many Democrats could be counted on to oppose Faubus.

Rockefeller ran for governor against Faubus in 1964, getting 254,561 votes to Faubus's 337,489. Rockefeller promised to run again in 1966. Faubus, for his part, chose not to run again that year.

THE ROCKEFELLER YEARS BEGIN

Arkansas Democrats, lulled by years of Faubus's rule, went through a hard primary in the 1966 governor's race. The winner was Jim Johnson, now called "Justice Jim" after a term on the state supreme court. The **segregationist** leader of the 1950s had not changed his platform.

Rockefeller brought Arkansas political campaigns into the modern age. Rockefeller spent lots of money, and he used computers, polls, and radio and TV ads. Rockefeller himself traveled the state from end to end. Never at ease in public settings, the wealthy man from the East tried his best to be one of the boys. Johnson focused on personal attacks against Rockefeller, criticizing him for his wealth, his drinking, and his divorce from his first wife.

African Americans in Arkansas were starting to vote in large numbers. Rockefeller welcomed the African American vote. Johnson did not even try for it.

Rockefeller won, 306,324 to 257,203, a

Elijah Coleman, a veteran of World War II, became active in civic and governmental affairs in the postwar years. (Courtesy of the Arkansas History Commission)

John Gammon of Gammonville: at the Fish Fry

John Gammon of Gammonville, in Crittenden County, thought part of racial integration was inviting whites to previously all-black events.

A graduate of Arkansas AM&N, Gammon became an important leader among Arkansas black farmers. In addition to operating his own farm, he organized the African American branch of the American Farm Bureau in 1948. He was president of that organization until 1965, when the Farm Bureau merged its white and black branches.

In the 1940s, Gammon began holding an annual fish fry and wild game dinner for blacks. Then he began inviting whites. By the late 1960s, the guest list was about evenly white and black. It was one of those gatherings that no politician could afford to miss.

Gammon also used the dinner to collect money for his John Gammon Foundation, which provided college scholarships for African American young people.

John Gammon died in 1988. He was eighty-five.

---

majority of 54 percent. Rockefeller won in the cities and the Republican mountain counties of the northwest. Johnson had many of the white voters, but Rockefeller got 90 percent of the black vote, assuring his win. The voters also chose a Republican lieutenant governor, World War II hero "Footsie" Britt. Most voters were really voting either for Rockefeller and his integrity or against Johnson. Some were simply turning their backs on the Faubus years. In any case, it was not really a lasting win for the Republican Party.

Rockefeller found that out when he met his first session in the General Assembly. With 132 Democrats and 3 Republicans, they were in no mood to put up with a Republican governor. Even after Rockefeller's second win in 1968, over Democrat Marion Crank, the General Assembly blocked most of his proposed laws.

His terms did see passage of a **"sunshine law"** that opened the state's business to public view. The state also got its first **minimum-wage law.** Rockefeller also started the Division of Mental Retardation Services, which was the state's first program to offer housing and training options to people who have mental retardation.

Most of what Rockefeller achieved was the enforcement of existing laws. Rockefeller enforced the laws against gambling in Hot Springs, closing the gambling houses there at last. Soon after taking office, Rockefeller received a report from the state police about the brutal treatment of inmates in the state prison system. The report revealed grim living conditions and downright torture of inmates. Long-term inmates really ran the prisons. Known as **"trustys,"** they held all the important jobs and sold favors to the others.

Rockefeller brought in a professional prison director, Tom Murton. Murton brought the national spotlight to Arkansas by digging up what he said were the bodies of murdered inmates. It was later learned that he was digging in the site of an old graveyard. Murton was replaced by Robert Sarver, who worked to improve the prisons in a more discreet fashion.

Neither the public nor the General Assembly had much interest in prison reform.

At last, in the 1970s, a U.S. court declared the entire Arkansas prison system unconstitutional. The judge called it a "dark and evil world." The courts supervised the running of the prisons for thirteen years. Just before he left office, Rockefeller changed the sentence to life in prison for all fifteen people then on Death Row.

THE CIVIL RIGHTS MOVEMENT

In 1955, the year after the *Brown* decision on schools, African Americans in Montgomery, Alabama, began a boycott to force an end to segregation on city buses. They refused to ride the buses. A young African American minister, the Reverend Martin Luther King, Jr., led this effort to success.

*Bobby Brown, a student at Philander Smith College, was one of the organizers of the student **sit-in** movement to protest segregation in public facilities in the early 1960s.* (Courtesy of the Arkansas History Commission)

President Kennedy Visits Arkansas: Greers Ferry Dam

President John F. Kennedy visited Arkansas to dedicate the Greers Ferry Dam and Reservoir in 1963.

The Corps of Engineers built the dam at the Little Red River to provide flood control, hydroelectricity, and recreation. It cost more than $46 million.

Kennedy flew into Little Rock Air Force Base on Air Force One, then went to the dam site by helicopter. In his brief talk, he praised the Arkansas congressional delegation and defended federal projects such as the dam. After the speech he talked to people who had gathered at a barbecue lunch and shook hands with schoolchildren.

Arkansas had voted for the Democrat Kennedy in the 1960 presidential election, but many whites had since become displeased with Kennedy's support of civil rights activities. There were, however, no demonstrations at his speech.

Kennedy visited Arkansas on October 3, 1963. On November 22, 1963, on a visit to Dallas, John F. Kennedy was assassinated.

From that campaign grew the Southern Christian Leadership Conference, or **SCLC**. In many places in the South, King and the **SCLC** began to challenge segregation and unfair voting systems. They used the technique of nonviolence: they refused to fight back when they were attacked by white mobs or the police.

Young African Americans, most of them college students, joined the movement by starting "**sit-ins**." They went to whites-only stores or lunch counters and asked for service. When they were denied service, they refused to leave. Their movement was called the Student Nonviolent Coordinating Committee, or **SNCC**. African Americans had taken charge of their own drive for freedom. The civil rights movement was on. Although many southern whites resisted, the movement gained great support all across the country.

President John F. Kennedy, who came to office in 1961, gave his moral support to the movement. In 1963, while Congress delayed action on a civil rights bill, blacks and whites held a huge march in Washington. More than 250,000 people gathered in peaceful protest. Among the speeches given there was King's famous "I have a dream" speech.

Kennedy was assassinated in November of 1963. Vice President Lyndon B. Johnson took his place. A master of the lawmaking process and a strong supporter of civil rights, Johnson helped direct the passage of major new laws. The Civil Rights Act of 1964 opened stores and public buildings to all races. The Civil Rights Act of 1965 called for fair and equal voting rights. Although some whites resisted for years to come, race relations in the nation began to be transformed.

The civil rights movement in Arkansas also moved faster than whites would have believed could be true. It was also slower than blacks would have liked. In Little Rock, Philander Smith College students staged **sit-ins** and marched on the state capitol. In 1962, some African American leaders, among them Dr. William Townsend and Dr. Jerry Jewell, filed a lawsuit to integrate city-owned buildings and programs in Little Rock.

In Pine Bluff, the local **SNCC** group staged protests to achieve equal hiring practices. By 1964, the city's major stores agreed to hire blacks on the same basis as whites. Even after the passage of the 1964 civil rights laws, Ozell Sutton of the Arkansas Council on Human Relations was thrown out of the State Capitol Building dining room. Sutton filed a complaint that opened the dining room to African Americans.

African Americans had begun to gain voting rights in Arkansas before the Civil Rights Act of 1965. The state gave up the poll tax and began a fair system to register voters. The use of voting machines in many places improved the chances for honest vote counting. In 1940, around 3 percent of black adults in Arkansas were registered to vote. By the 1970s, the number had risen to 72 percent, about the same as for white voters. Still, in the 1980s there were only six African American members of the Arkansas General Assembly.

Governor Rockefeller named African American people to high state offices, including the pardons and parole board, county boards of welfare, and state college boards. Rockefeller also formed a Governor's Council on Human Resources to foster hiring African American workers in public and private business. He named Ozell Sutton to head it.

In April 1968, the Reverend Martin Luther King, Jr., was shot and killed by a white man in Memphis, Tennessee. All over the nation, cities erupted in riots and burned in flames. In Arkansas, there was some property destroyed in some cities. But most people, black and white, paid peaceful tribute to the great civil rights leader. Thousands gathered at the steps of the State Capitol Building. There Governor and Mrs. Rockefeller led them as everyone joined hands and sang the anthem of the civil rights movement, "We Shall Overcome."

THE IMPACT OF THE FEDERAL GOVERNMENT

In the 1960s and 1970s, major federal programs were changing the face of Arkansas. One project was the Interstate Highway System, which built four-lane highways to connect Arkansas to other markets of the region and nation. The state road-building program, also with U.S. aid, replaced dirt roads with paved roads.

An old dream of Arkansans came true in 1970 when the McClellan-Kerr Arkansas River Navigation Project was finished. The project built a series of locks and dams to create a year-round water level. Boats and barges could now go 445 miles from the mouth of the Arkansas River to Catoosa, Oklahoma, near Tulsa. It cost $1.2 billion. At the time, it was the largest job ever done by the U.S. Corps of Engineers.

The federal government also built many lakes in Arkansas, including Norfork, Table Rock, Bull Shoals, Beaver, and Greers Ferry. The lakes offered Arkansans great fishing, boating, and other forms of water sports. They also enhanced the tourist business.

President Johnson's "**Great Society**" program greatly increased U.S. aid for social problems. Partly a "**War on Poverty**," the programs offered help with education, housing, health care, social services, job training, and the problems of cities. In 1956, 9.3 percent of state and local revenues came from the federal government. By 1966, that figure reached 18.1 percent and continued to rise.

The federal Interstate Highway System in the 1960s and 1970s dramatically improved highway transportation in Arkansas. Above, workmen are pouring concrete at an overpass near West Memphis, as the four-lane interstate stretches to the horizon beyond them. Below, the Interstate 30 bridge between Little Rock (foreground) and North Little Rock (background) as it neared completion. Notice that wide areas of land had to be cleared to allow the interstate highway to go through the cities. (Courtesy of the University of Central Arkansas Archives)

In the second half of the twentieth century, Arkansas once again became nationally famous for its hunting and fishing. Above, a fishing scene in Faulkner County. Below, ducks by the hundreds descending upon an Arkansas lake. (Courtesy of the University of Central Arkansas Archives)

Arkansas at the Elections of 1968: Rockefeller, Fulbright, and Wallace

In the elections of 1968, Arkansas voters showed just how independent—or contrary—they could be.

That year Arkansans re-elected Republican Winthrop Rockefeller to a second term as governor, re-elected Democrat J. William Fulbright to the U.S. Senate, and gave their electoral votes to George Wallace for president.

Wallace, running as the American Independent Party candidate, had made himself a symbol of opposition to integration, support for the Vietnam War, and disgust with **hippies.** Fulbright, long a leader in America's international involvement, had begun to oppose the war in Vietnam.

Thus in the same year Arkansans voted for a reform Republican governor, a progressive, anti-war Democratic senator, and a conservative, pro-war Independent presidential candidate.

LIFE IN THE 1960S

All across the country, the decade of the 1960s was a time of rapid change. Many young people rebelled against the ways of parents, some styling themselves as **"hippies"** who **"dropped out"** of the American middle class. They showed their social freedom with new styles of hair (worn very long), casual clothing, and their support of rock and folk music. Arkansans as a rule were not very keen on **hippies,** although some college students adopted their style for a time.

Cutting across the 1960s and 1970s was the deep scar of the Vietnam War. The cold war emphasis on stopping the spread of Communism caused the United States to commit itself to the defense of South Vietnam. That country was fighting a civil war against Communist North Vietnam.

At first, American military advisors worked to train the military of South Vietnam. But, starting in 1965, the United States sent large numbers of American armed forces to fight the war themselves. Arkansans again went to war in a far-off place.

The U.S. armed forces did not call up its Guard and Reserve units in large numbers. That meant that most of the fighting was done by eighteen- or nineteen-year-olds who were either drafted or volunteered in order to avoid the draft. Before the American forces were withdrawn in 1973, more than 580 Arkansans died in Vietnam, more than the death toll in the Korean War.

As the years of the war dragged on, more and more Americans came to feel that the costly struggle in Vietnam was none of America's business. All over the country, open protest of the war was staged on a steady basis, week after week. Voices within the government began to object as well, especially the voice of Arkansas's U.S. senator and chairman of the Foreign Relations Committee, J. William Fulbright. Arkansas saw very little of the **protest movement** until the last years of the war.

The men and women who came home

Senator John L. McClellan. (Courtesy of the University of Arkansas, Fayetteville, Special Collections)

Clarence Young of Little Rock served in Vietnam in 1966 with the First Cavalry Division. (Courtesy of the Arkansas History Commission)

Senator John L. McClellan (center), with C. G. "Crip" Hall, longtime Arkansas Secretary of State. (Courtesy of the Arkansas History Commission)

George Howard was the first African American to become a justice of the Arkansas Supreme Court. (Courtesy of the Arkansas History Commission)

from Vietnam received little of the thanks and praise that had greeted their fathers' return from World War II. Their service was not fully honored until the 1980s when the Vietnam Veterans Memorial was built in Little Rock on the State Capitol grounds. Like the bigger Vietnam Memorial in Washington, it displays the names of Arkansans who died in the war.

These years also saw the advance of the modern wave of the feminist movement in Arkansas. Although he did not intend to do so, State Representative Paul Van Dalsem of Perry County moved the women's cause forward greatly. In the mid-1960s, a group of women campaigned to defeat a bill sponsored by Van Dalsem. He complained about it in a speech to the Optimist Club of Little Rock.

There, he explained how men in his county kept women from "poking around." "We get her an extra milk cow," he said. "If that doesn't work, we give her a little more garden to tend. And then if that's not enough, we get her pregnant and keep her barefoot." The voters, men and women, handed Van Dalsem a sound defeat in his bid for a General Assembly seat in a newly drawn district which united Perry and Pulaski counties.

Meanwhile, his **"barefoot and pregnant"** remark became a rallying cry for Arkansas women to unite and lobby. They worked to improve their lives as they had in the late nineteenth century and the early years of the twentieth. Women the world over began to pursue more and better jobs. Many more women became doctors and lawyers, and they

How 'Bout Those Hogs! Arkansas and the Razorbacks

One of the major developments of the 1960s was Arkansas's fascination with the football team of the University of Arkansas at Fayetteville, the Razorbacks. The university had played its first football games in 1894. That year the team beat Fort Smith High School twice, but lost to the University of Texas, 54–0. The team was first called the Cardinals, then after 1909, the Razorbacks.

Under Frank Broyles, the head coach from 1958 to 1976, the team began to win regularly, not just in its own Southwest Conference, but also big games against nationally regarded opponents. During those years Arkansas won the Southwest Conference championship seven times, went to ten bowl games, and once, in 1964, was national champion. (Ken Hatfield, a future head coach, played on that 1964 team.)

The Razorbacks became a statewide mania. Thousands followed the team to wherever it played, dressed in Razorback red. Thousands more followed it by radio and television.

In 1969 came "the Game of the Century." Texas, ranked number one in the nation, traveled to Fayetteville to meet Arkansas, ranked number two. The game attracted national attention. President Richard M. Nixon even flew in by helicopter for the game.

Texas won, 15–14, making the winning score in the last minutes of the game. But Arkansans continued to love those Hogs.

filled top jobs in private business and public agencies they had never held before.

In 1975, Elsijane T. Roy became the first woman on the Arkansas Supreme Court. When she moved up to a federal judgeship, African American civil rights lawyer George Howard took her place. (He, too, later became a federal judge.)

Not everyone approved of women's gain-ing their share of political and social power. Arkansas had promptly passed the Nineteenth Amendment that granted women the right to vote in 1920, and the state had sent the first elected female member of the U.S. Senate to Washington. But the Arkansas General Assembly of the 1980s repeatedly refused to ratify the proposed **Equal Rights Amendment** to the U.S. Constitution.

Coach Frank Broyles.
(Courtesy of the J. N. Heiskell Collection, UALR Archives and Special Collections)

VOCABULARY

Aaron vs. Cooper the lawsuit brought against the Little Rock School Board by the NAACP to integrate the schools.

AIDC Arkansas Industrial Development Commission, a state agency established by the legislature in the administration of Orval Faubus to encourage industry to locate in Arkansas.

Arkansas Plan a design by which C. Hamilton Moses of AP&L intended to draw new industry to Arkansas.

"barefoot and pregnant" a politician's remark that came to symbolize male chauvinism to the feminist movement of the seventies.

Blossom Plan the Little Rock School District's original desegregation plan.

dropped out having foregone the typical middle-class style of life, creating a "counter-culture" among young people during the sixties; often associated with drug use.

Equal Rights Amendment a proposed constitutional amendment acknowledging rights for American women equal to those of men.

exempt (eggz-EMPT) to exclude from bearing the same responsibilities as others; for instance, not having to pay taxes when others do.

Great Society the programs of Lyndon Johnson aimed at bringing African Americans and poor citizens into the mainstream of American life.

hippies (HIP-eez) young people who wore their hair long and dressed unconventionally to distance themselves from a mainstream culture they considered violent and destructive.

Little Rock Nine the nine black students admitted to Central High School in 1957.

minimum wage law law making it illegal to pay wages below a certain amount for any job.

nullify (NULL-if-eye) to throw out, to undo, to declare void.

protest movement a nationwide call to end the war in Vietnam.

purge (PERJ) to remove in a drastic fashion, even by force.

SCLC Southern Christian Leadership Conference, the organization founded and led by Dr. Martin Luther King, Jr.

segregationists (SEG-gruh-GAY-shun-ists) those driven by racial prejudice to keep the races separated at all costs.

sit-in taking a seat in and refusing to leave an establishment from which one is excluded in order to protest the exclusion.

SNCC (SNICK) Student Nonviolent Coordinating Committee, the wing of the civil rights movement made up of college students and other young people.

Southern Manifesto (SUTH-ern man-if-EST-oh) a written protest from southern members of Congress in response to the *Brown vs. Board of Education* decision to integrate schools.

sovereignty (SAWV-runt-ee) independence; the power to make one's own laws without interference from other powers.

STOP Campaign the movement organized by Little Rock women to "Stop This Outrageous Purge"; it returned schools to normal operation.

sunshine law Freedom of Information law, which opened state business to public scrutiny.

trusty (TRUSS-tee) a long-term prison inmate entrusted with the oversight of other prisoners.

War on Poverty Lyndon Johnson's programs aimed at raising the standard of living among America's poorest citizens.

White Citizens' Councils segregationist groups organized in Arkansas to fight school integration.

STUDY QUESTIONS

1. What were Arkansas population trends during the 1950s and the 1960s? What were the causes? What were the effects?

2. What was the role of the Arkansas Industrial Development Commission?

3. What were some of Orval Faubus's plans to improve the economy?

4. Before *Brown vs. Board of Education,* what steps had been taken in Arkansas towards social integration?

5. What were some of the reactions to *Brown vs. Board of Education?*

6. What was wrong with the Blossom Plan?

7. What was the effect of the crisis at Central High School in 1957 on Arkansas?

8. How was the Republican Winthrop Rockefeller able to get elected governor?

9. What were some of the accomplishments of the Rockefeller Administration?

10. What was the role of women in Arkansas by the 1970s?

Arkansas Today

1975–Present

What to Look for in Chapter 11

During the period from 1975 to the present, the population of Arkansas began to grow, and Arkansas became urban, meaning that more people were living in cities than in the countryside.

There was more interest in the arts, theater, music, and writing. As the signs of the past began to disappear, Arkansans began to get serious about historic preservation.

Dale Bumpers and David Pryor served the state for many years, first as governor, one after the other, then as the two U.S. senators.

This period saw the rise of Bill Clinton, who was state attorney general for one term, governor for twelve years, then president of the United States for eight years.

As the twentieth century became the twenty-first century, the major political trends in Arkansas were term limits for legislators and the governor, and the rise of the Republican Party, as indicated by the governorship of Mike Huckabee. Another important trend was the increasing diversity in the state, especially in the growth of the Hispanic population.

MORE CHANGES TO COME

As Arkansas and the United States saw the end of the twentieth century and entered a new century, its people would see more change, mixed with a continuation of old trends. And it is during this period that an Arkansan, Bill Clinton, would serve two terms as president of the United States.

Arkansas stopped losing people in the 1960s, then started to grow again. By 2000, the year of the national **census**, the population was 2,673,400, nearly 40 percent more than in 1970. About two-thirds of the growth was in newcomers to the state. Within the state, the continuing population trends were a decline in the Delta and south Arkansas, an increase in the smaller cities around Little Rock, and a rapid increase in the northwest corner. All over the state, the movement of people from the countryside into cities continued. During the decade of the 1970s, in an important milestone, the population of Arkansas became **urban**, meaning that a majority of the people were living in cities.

The Historians Pick the Most Important Events and People of the Past

The Arkansas Historical Association at its annual meeting in the spring of 2000 asked the two hundred people who attended these two questions:

What were the most significant single events in Arkansas history?
What people were most important in Arkansas history?

Here are the results, in order of importance:

Most Significant Events

1) the 1957 desegregation crisis at Little Rock Central High School; 2) the Louisiana Purchase; 3) the election of Bill Clinton as president; 4) the Great Depression of the 1930s and the impact of the New Deal on Arkansas; 5) the impact of the Civil War and Reconstruction; 6) the founding of Arkansas Post; 7) the rise of Wal-Mart; 8 and 9, a tie) the flood of 1927, and the impact of cotton culture; 10) the preservation of the Buffalo River as a National River.

Most Important People

1) Bill Clinton; 2) J. William Fulbright; 3) Orval Faubus; 4) Sam Walton; 5) Daisy Bates; 6) Winthrop Rockefeller; 7) Joe T. Robinson; 8) William E. Woodruff; 9) Hattie Caraway; 10) Dale Bumpers; 11) Hernando De Soto; 12) David Pryor; 13) Adolphine Fletcher Terry; 14) Vance Randolph; 15) E. Fay Jones.

CULTURE IN ARKANSAS

Urbanization, prosperity, and better education contributed to a real cultural revival in Arkansas. Where once rural Arkansas had found almost all its entertainment at home, the world began to open up to Arkansans. By 2001, there were about 230 radio stations in the state, almost half of them specializing in country-western music. The first television station went on the air in 1953. By 2001 there were nineteen commercial television stations, and a state-wide educational television network. Cable systems and satellite dishes also brought television to almost every home in the state.

Winthrop Rockefeller and his wife, Jeanette, took the lead in establishing the Arkansas Arts Center in Little Rock. Public and private funds from all over the state contributed to the Arts Center. Under director Townsend Wolfe, the Arts Center housed and displayed its own permanent collection as well as national exhibits, offered a wide range of classes in visual and dance arts, and sponsored a Children's Theater. In 2001, the Arts Center opened a major new addition to the building, and achieved national recognition for its collection of works on paper, or drawings. The Arts Center also took its traveling arts exhibitions all over the state.

Almost every college in the state offered

theater performances, and several towns had a local amateur community theater. The Arkansas **Repertory** Theater in Little Rock, created by Cliff Baker, offered professional plays.

In the 1960s, musicians in Little Rock formed an **amateur** orchestra, under the direction of Dr. Francis MacBeth of Ouachita Baptist University. This organization grew into the **professional** Arkansas Symphony Orchestra. Eventually there were five orchestras in the state.

In the 1960s Congress created the National Endowment for the Arts and the National Endowment for the Humanities. They were matched in Arkansas by a state Arts Council and the Arkansas Endowment for the Humanities. These agencies provided federal financial support (plus state money for the arts) to a wide variety of cultural and historical enterprises in every community in the state.

ARKANSAS WRITERS

Arkansas has produced an impressive roster of writers. Some of the authors of distinction, and a sample of their works, include historian and novelist Dee Brown *(Bury My Heart at Wounded Knee)*, novelists Crescent Dragonwagon (young people's stories), Donald Harrington *(The Architecture of the Arkansas Ozarks)*, Bill Harrison *(Roller Ball Murder)*, Doug Jones *(The Court-Martial of George Armstrong Custer)*, Charles Portis *(True Grit)*, James Whitehead *(Joiner)*, and many others. The state produced a number of mystery writers, including Joan Hess (the Claire Malloy series), Charlaine Harris (the "Shakespeare" series), and Grif Stockley (the Gideon Page series).

Poet Miller Williams *(Some Jazz a While: Collected Poems)* received the 1976 Prix de Rome award of the American Academy of Arts and Letters, the only Arkansan ever to receive that honor. Williams read one of his poems at

Maya Angelou, who grew up in Stamps, Arkansas, became internationally famous as a writer and performer. She wrote about her childhood in Arkansas in her autobiography, I Know Why the Caged Bird Sings. (Courtesy of the University of Central Arkansas Archives)

Maestro Kurt Klipstatter conducting the Arkansas Symphony Orchestra. (Courtesy of the University of Central Arkansas Archives)

Dee Brown of Arkansas, author of Bury My Heart at Wounded Knee *and many other books about the American West and Native Americans.* (Courtesy of the University of Central Arkansas Archives)

President Bill Clinton's second **inauguration**, but some know him best as the father of folk singer and songwriter Lucinda Williams.

The University of Arkansas creative writing program was nationally known. Arkansas also had three book publishers: August House, Rose Publishing, and the University of Arkansas Press.

THE PAST IN THE MODERN WORLD

The log cabin life of the Ozark hills gradually passed away. Now, cattle dotted the hillsides and poultry houses occupied land that once produced subsistence crops. One room school houses disappeared as districts **consolidated**, and hand-crafted objects became "folk art."

The traditions of the fading Ozark way of life were assured a place in the memory of Arkansans with the establishment of the Ozark Folk Center at Mountain View in the early 70s. There, traditional crafts and music were practiced, taught, and displayed with pride to thousands of visitors from all over the country. In the 1980s the Department of Arkansas Heritage created the Delta Cultural Center in Helena, to celebrate the history and folk art of south and eastern Arkansas.

Arkansas also developed an interest in the preservation of historic buildings. The oldest block of buildings in Little Rock became the Arkansas Territorial Restoration, and later,

Vance Randolph, the major collector of Ozark folklore. The message written on the photograph is his joke. (Courtesy of the University of Arkansas, Fayetteville, Special Collections)

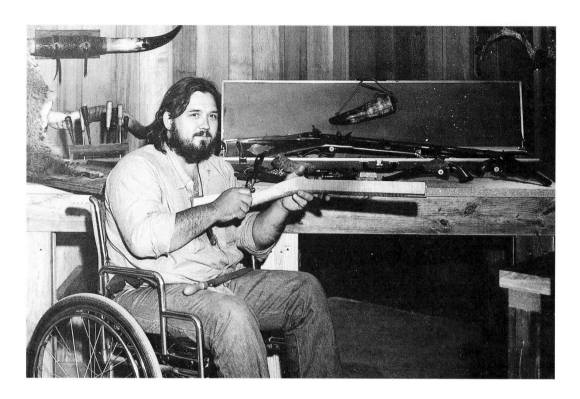

The Ozark Folk Center at Mountain View displays and preserves the old crafts and the old ways of the Ozarks. This is Sloan Lessley, who makes rifles. (Courtesy of the University of Arkansas, Fayetteville, Special Collections)

with the addition of a major museum building, the Historic Arkansas Museum. Preservationists organized the Quapaw Quarter Association in Little Rock. Similar efforts were soon underway at Old Washington, which became a state historic park, and at Helena, Batesville, Fayetteville, and many other communities. The entire town of Van Buren became a showplace of **Victorian** restoration. A statewide organization was formed, the Historic Preservation Alliance of Arkansas. There is also a state **Historic Preservation** Program, which administers Main Street Arkansas, a program that assists local communities in restoring and revitalizing their business districts.

A long but successful battle in the 1960s saved the Buffalo River in northern Arkansas as a wild river. The Buffalo had been slated to be dammed for **hydroelectric** and recreational purposes. Instead, thanks to the Ozark Society and other individuals and groups, the Buffalo became the first National River, owned and operated by the federal governmen. That preserved the free-flowing river for canoeists, kayakers, back-packers, hikers, and campers.

NEW FACES IN POLITICS

The election for governor in 1970 brought a new face to Arkansas politics. Dale Bumpers of Charleston first beat Orval Faubus in the Democratic primary run-off, then beat Winthrop Rockefeller in the general election.

Progressive and free of ties to special interests, Bumpers helped the state continue to develop.

Bumpers enacted a state government reorganization plan that Rockefeller had proposed, combining more than one hundred agencies into thirteen major departments. Bumpers also persuaded the legislature to enact tax reform that established a more progressive tax scale, increasing taxes on higher incomes while reducing the rates on lower incomes. An increase in tax revenue allowed state support for kindergartens, free textbooks in the public schools, and the creation of community colleges. First Lady Betty Bumpers created a statewide immunization program to save children from suffering preventable diseases.

Bumpers was a popular governor, and easily won a second term in 1972. In 1974, he defeated J. William Fulbright for the U.S. Senate. Replacing Bumpers as governor was former congressman David Pryor of Camden, who defeated yet another attempt by Orval Faubus.

By the late 1970s, there seemed to be a clear changing of the generations. Orval Faubus and Jim Johnson appeared to be retired. Wilbur Mills left the U.S. House of Representatives, overcoming a serious problem with alcoholism, to become an effective worker against alcohol and drug abuse. Senator John McClellan died in 1977. Pryor appointed Kaneaster Hodges to fill out McClellan's term, then won the Senate seat himself in 1978.

Although the Democrats were still the dominant party at the state and local level, Arkansans increasingly voted Republican in presidential elections. From Richard Nixon in 1972 until the election of Bill Clinton in 1992, only one Democratic candidate for

Arkansas subjects have been used on U.S. postage stamps several times. Here is a sample, on a postcard printed by the Arkansas Postcard Club.

Governor, later Senator, Dale Bumpers. (Courtesy of the Arkansas History Commission)

Governor, later Senator, David Pryor. (Courtesy of the Arkansas History Commission)

president got the electoral votes of Arkansas. That was Jimmy Carter of Georgia in 1976, when Arkansans apparently liked the idea of a southerner in the White House.

CLINTON BECOMES GOVERNOR

In 1978, the Arkansas governorship was won by Bill Clinton, a former **Rhodes Scholar** and state attorney general. At thirty-two, he was the youngest governor in the nation. He started an ambitious program of educational reform, highway construction, and economic development. The voters became unhappy, however, when he increased car license fees and when Fort Chaffee became home to thousands of refugees from communist Cuba. In the "car tags and Cubans" campaign of 1978, Republican Frank White defeated Clinton.

The White administration was marked by the passage of a state law that would have required schools teaching biological **evolution** also to teach the **creationist** view of the origin of mankind. The creationist view, following the book of Genesis in the Bible, holds that the earth and all life was created in a very brief period and have not changed. A federal judge declared the law unconstitutional, as an attempt by state government to dictate a

Governor Frank White (right) *helps Elizabeth Ashly, the cook at the Governor's Mansion through many different governors, celebrate her sixty-fifth birthday. On the left is Mrs. Gay White; next to her is former governor Orval Faubus.* (Courtesy of the Arkansas History Commission)

Governor Bill Clinton.
(Courtesy of the Arkansas
History Commission)

specific religious concept in the public school **curriculum.** The conservative mood of the state was also reflected in the rejection of a proposed new state constitution, the second in a decade.

Clinton was reelected governor in 1982. With reelection and a change in the governor's term to four years, he would continue as governor until the early 1990s. Anyone from the past would have recognized the major issues. They were still education, highways, and economic development. Clinton was especially interested in education. He appointed a special committee, headed by his wife, Hillary Rodham Clinton, to suggest changes in the public school system. The legislature then enacted significant reforms aimed at improving teaching, student performance, course offerings, and teacher training. Although the reforms quickly began showing some effect, getting the legislature to increase funding became a problem.

Clinton's emphasis on education was related to his strong push for economic development in the state. International corporations and international investments made the Arkansas economy a genuinely global economy. Arkansans needed to get a decent education, learn to speak foreign languages, and increase their understanding of the world beyond their borders if they were to stand a chance at making a living in the competitive marketplace.

THE ARKANSAS ECONOMY

By the beginning of the twenty-first century, Arkansas had finally achieved the goal of diversity in its economic enterprises. About one-fourth of the workers in the state were in service jobs. That included teaching, banks, restaurant work, and other activities that provide some sort of service to people, rather than making something to sell. The other leading areas of employment were manufacturing, about 21 percent; retail sales, about 18 percent; and state and federal government, 16 percent.

The most important manufacturing area, in terms of value, was food processing. Most of that involved **poultry**, also the state's number-one agricultural product. Food processing converted chickens into grocery store products, including chicken parts and prepared meals. Second in manufacturing was electric and electronic products, such as motors, transformers, lamps, television sets, microwave ovens, missiles for the U.S. government, and home appliances such as refrigerators and television sets. Other manufacturing areas included paper products, rubber and plastics, chemicals, cosmetics, and lumber and wood products.

The leading agricultural product, **poultry**, had an annual value about three times as high as the next leading agricultural product, rice. The **poultry** industry involved thousands of small producers, raising chickens for the big processors. Arkansas was still the leading rice grower in the nation, producing

A symbol of changes in agriculture in the 1950s and 1960s. This cropduster is spraying the field with chemicals. (Courtesy of the J. N. Heiskell Collection, UALR Archives and Special Collections)

almost half the country's rice. Riceland Foods, a cooperative marketing association, was one of the state's largest businesses.

Other important agricultural products, in order of their value, were soybeans, cotton, and cattle. Soybeans, rice, and cotton were raised mostly on huge farms, relying on machinery and irrigation. In 1970, Arkansas had about 72,000 farms, with an average size of 244 acres. At the end of the twentieth century, there were about 49,500 farms, with an average size of almost 300 acres.

A new enterprise was fish farming, raising catfish for grocery stores and restaurants, and minnows for bait. Much of this activity was in the area around Lonoke. Arkansas was the second largest producer of catfish, after Mississippi.

Tourism was also a major industry. In a good year more than fifteen million visitors came to Arkansas, spending almost two billion dollars. Partly in tribute to the state's major tourist appeal, in the 1980s "The Natural State" became the latest in Arkansas's series of official nicknames.

BIG BUSINESS

One of the exciting stories in Arkansas was the success of Arkansas businessmen who created major national corporations, and kept their headquarters in Arkansas. Bill Dillard started with one country store and built a major department store chain. Sam Walton of Bentonville created the Wal-Mart stores. For several years Walton was the richest man in the United States.

Tyson Foods produced many of the **poultry** products in the nation. Alltel was a major nationwide operator of regular and wireless telephone systems. Alltel also acquired Systematics, which produced computer sys-

tems on an international scale. Arkansas was also home to several major trucking companies, and Stephens, Inc., was the largest bond trading business outside of New York. Arkansas was behind the rest of the nation in some important areas, such as high-tech jobs involving computers and communication.

The **median** annual income per person in Arkansas by end of the twentieth century was $32,714, or 78 percent of the national median. That was a considerable improvement over the previous generation, when Arkansas's median income had been 70 percent of the national median. Arkansas's growth rate in areas such as investment in manufacturing, new jobs, and personal income tended to be higher than the national average growth rate, but much of that was because the state started from such a low base. For example, Arkansas still ranked near the bottom of the states in **per capita** income.

DEVELOPMENTS IN EDUCATION

All those who had worked so hard to improve education would have been proud of demonstrated improvement in areas such as test scores, high school graduation rate, college attendance rate, and teachers' salaries. Special programs like Gifted and Talented Education became common, and the state created in Hot Springs a residential high school for math and science students. The legislature merged the community colleges and the vocational-technical schools, leading to more efficient management, a wider variety of programs, and increased enrollment. This offered a meaningful path for education beyond high school.

In many areas Arkansas made significant improvement, but still lagged behind national **averages.** For example, by the end of the cen-

Arkansas state parks effectively began with the WPA and CCC projects of the 1930s, then grew into a statewide system. The national government also created parks, especially at historic sites. ABOVE AND BELOW: At Toltec Mounds Archeological State park near Scott, a park ranger teaches a touring school group the art of flint-knapping, or chipping sharp points from a hard stone like flint. PAGE 340: These people, representing Union cavalry and Confederate infantry, are part of a large reenactment of a major Civil War battle in Arkansas, at Pea Ridge National Military park near Fayetteville. PAGE 341: Old Washington, near Hope, once a flourishing stop on the Southwest Trail to Texas, is now a state park with many renovated and preserved buildings, including the Royston House, built about 1835. Old Washington State Park also has an annual daffodil festival. (All pictures courtesy of A. C. Haralson, Arkansas Dept. of Parks and Tourism)

The Arkansas River at Little Rock. (Courtesy of William Mills)

*Map of Arkansas, U.S.
Department of Interior,
Geological Survey*

tury the high school graduation rate increased to about 84 percent, close to the national average of about 86 percent. The number of Arkansans with a college degree increased by almost one-fourth in just the last decade of the twentieth century, to about 16 percent of everyone over twenty-five years old. But Arkansas was still far behind the national average of 24 percent college graduates. From 1970 to 2000, average public school teachers' salaries in Arkansas increased by about 16 percent, while the national average was increasing only 6 percent. Still, Arkansas teacher salaries as the new century began were only about three-fourths of the national average.

There was the continuing problem of unequal funding among school districts. School funding still relied on local property taxes, with additional money from the state. Some districts, with a major industry or a large population within their boundaries, had reasonable funding. Other districts, especially in poor rural areas, had far less money. In May 2001 a state court judge declared the funding of the school system unconstitutional, because of differences in facilities, **curriculum**, and teacher pay among the 310 school districts. That was the third time in eighteen years a similar court ruling had been made. The governor and the legislature began searching for additional revenue or different ways of paying for the schools.

THE PASSING OF THE ARKANSAS GAZETTE

There was by the 1990s a sense that the old institutions were passing. Former Governor Orval Faubus died in 1994, at the age of eighty-four; former Senator William Fulbright died in 1995, at the age of eighty-nine. Each of them, in different ways, had brought Arkansas national and even world attention.

Almost like a death in the family for many Arkansans was the passing of the *Arkansas Gazette*. In the late 1970s, Walter E. Hussman, Jr.'s WEHCO company bought the *Arkansas Democrat,* for years the second daily newspaper published in Little Rock. The *Democrat* and the *Gazette* began a fierce newspaper war, competing for readers and advertisers. By 1986, the Hugh Patterson family (kin to longtime owner J. N. Heiskell) sold the *Gazette* to the Gannett Co., publisher of *USA Today* and many local newspapers throughout the nation.

The newspaper rivalry continued until, without warning, Gannett announced on October 18, 1991, that the *Gazette* had published its last edition. Within days, Hussman's company bought the remains of the *Gazette*. He changed the name of his newspaper to the *Arkansas Democrat-Gazette,* now the only major statewide daily newspaper. It was probably a lesson in the modern economics of newspapers: few cities could support two major, independent daily newspapers.

The Razorbacks of the University of Arkansas at Fayetteville were involved in major changes. In 1992 the sports teams shifted from the Southwest Conference to the Southeastern Conference. Under coach Eddie Sutton in the 1980s, the basketball team began to attract the fan excitement once reserved only for football. In 1994, now with coach Nolan Richardson, the basketball Razorbacks reached the peak of college basketball. They won the **NCAA** tournament to become the national champions.

WAR AGAIN

Arkansans went to war again in the 1990s. When Iraq invaded the neighboring country of Kuwait, the United States put together a

Family, Community, and Success

John Johnson was born in Arkansas City, where his family was poor but happy. An African American, he recalled much later that race relations were generally peaceful. "The only problem, dim at first but constantly growing clearer," he said, "was a feeling that we were not in control of our own destiny, that a word or a frown from a white person could change our plans and our lives."

His mother saw another problem: the black school at Arkansas City went only through the eighth grade; there was no high school for blacks. So, during the Great Depression, when John was fifteen years old, she moved with him to Chicago, where John could get an education.

John Johnson made the best of it. In 1942 he founded his first magazine, *Negro Digest,* with five hundred dollars borrowed on his mother's furniture. He went on to create *Ebony* and *Jet* magazines, Fashion Fair Cosmetics, and Supreme Beauty Products. He also bought Supreme Life Insurance Company, where he had once worked as an office boy. By the 1980s, he was one of the wealthiest men in America.

In his autobiography, Johnson gave much of the credit for his success to his mother and to the African American community:

> I was born into a strong family and reared in a strong community where every Black adult was charged with the responsibility of monitoring and supervising every Black child. I was reared in a community where every Black adult was authorized to whip me, if I needed whipping, and to send me home for a second whipping from my mother, whether I needed it or not.
>
> Sixty years later, I attended a meeting . . . with, among others, Sam Moore Walton, the richest man in America. We discovered with surprise and delight that we had six things in common. We were nonsmokers and nondrinkers who were born into poverty. We grew up in small southern towns and were reared by strong and loving parents who spared neither hugs nor rods. . . .
>
> I didn't have a lot of toys. I didn't have a lot of clothes. But I had a lot of love. . . .
>
> [My mother] had known pain and discouragement and fear. Out of all this came a special kind of dignity. The dignity of a person who'd seen a lot and survived and wasn't afraid of the future.

John H. Johnson, with Lerone Bennett, Jr., *Succeeding Against the Odds* (New York: Warner Books, 1989), pp. 41, 37-39.

coalition of nations to push them back. After an intensive military buildup in the Middle East, the coalition forces, mostly American, struck in January 1991, in the Persian Gulf War or Operation Desert Storm. The war was a massive air attack followed by a swift ground attack. It was over in six weeks, with the loss of very few American lives.

This time the U.S. Armed Forces made extensive use of Reserve and National Guard units, including many from Arkansas. For example, from Marshall in Searcy County, 73 residents went to the war with the 224th Maintenance Company of the Arkansas Army National Guard. That was more than 6 percent of the town's 1,100 population, the state's highest per capita contribution to the war effort. Because the war ended quickly and most of the Guard and Reserve soldiers came home as units, many small towns in Arkansas got to have "welcome back" parades. The marching units included Vietnam veterans, whose war service had not been recognized by parades.

PRESIDENT WILLIAM JEFFERSON CLINTON

Most of his friends thought Bill Clinton had been preparing to run for president of the United States all his life. Still, it was something of a surprise when he did—and got elected. Even Bill and Hillary, on the day after the election, said they felt like the car-chasing dog that finally caught one.

Clinton was re-elected governor of Arkansas in 1986 and again in 1990, both times convincingly defeating his Republican opponent, in spite of the growing Republican Party in the state. (The voters in 1984 had approved changing the term of the governor and other state-wide officers from two years to four.)

He considered running for president in 1988, but waited until 1992, when several strong contenders for the Democratic nomination decided to sit out the race that year. They felt that George H. W. Bush, the incumbent Republican president, would be too hard to beat.

Over the winter of 1991–1992, Clinton ran in state primaries against several other candidates for the Democratic nomination. By the summer of 1992, he had the votes needed to win the Democratic nomination. He was running against Bush, the Republican candidate, and Ross Perot, an independent candidate, who came from the Texas side of Texarkana.

In spite of controversies over his personal life and lack of service in Vietnam, Clinton touched a sympathetic chord with many voters. They liked his youth, his enthusiasm, and his newness to the national scene. Most of all, they liked his sympathy with their problems. The collapse of the Soviet Union and the end of the Cold War made it seem as if foreign policy, Bush's special interest, was no longer a major issue. Instead voters were concerned about the economy as it touched them personally: jobs, salaries, security. Clinton seemed to understand this more than his two opponents, both millionaires. Clinton, in a play on his Arkansas birthplace, reminded voters that "I still believe in a place called Hope."

THE ELECTION CAMPAIGN

It was a different campaign, too. Little Rock, instead of Washington or another major city, was the campaign headquarters. Clinton and his candidate for vice president, Albert Gore of Tennessee, campaigned thorough small-town America by bus. One of the televised presidential debates, a kind of town meeting with ordinary people, showed Clinton at his best. Clinton also appeared on the MTV network and played his saxophone on a popular late-night talk show.

On election day, November 3, 1992, the eyes of the world were on Little Rock. The city was jammed with television transmission trucks, reporters from all over the world, and stars from television, movies, and politics. Late that night, Clinton, with Hillary, their young daughter Chelsea, and the Gore family, stood on the steps of the Old State House to accept his victory.

Clinton had won convincingly in the electoral college. He received 357 electoral votes (thirty-one states) to George H. W. Bush's 168 (eighteen states). In the popular vote, with the independent candidate Ross Perot drawing votes away from both major-party candidates, it was Clinton 43 percent, Bush 38 percent, and Perot 19 percent.

Clinton resigned as governor in January of 1993. The new governor was Jim Guy Tucker, who as lieutenant governor had actually been acting governor through most of the presidential campaign. Tucker, elected in his own right in 1994, was a former state attorney general and member of Congress.

The election of Bill Clinton put our state on the national stage. Arkansans reacted with excitement and enthusiasm. About thirty-five thousand of them arrived in Washington for the festivities surrounding **Inauguration** Day, January 20, 1993. William Jefferson Clinton of Hope, Arkansas was sworn in as the forty-second president of the United States. Standing with him were Hillary Rodham Clinton, who would play an active role in the Clinton administration, and Chelsea Clinton, who would be in the eighth grade in a new school in Washington. Arkansas native Maya Angelou read one of her poems to the assembled crowd and the television audience.

Clinton's inaugural address expressed his hopes for the future. "I challenge a new generation of young Americans to a season of service," he said. "In serving we recognize a simple but powerful truth—we need each other. And we must care for one another. Today, we do more than celebrate America; we rededicate ourselves to the very idea of America."

THE NEW ADMINISTRATION

Clinton put together an executive branch of government headed by long-term Arkansas friends and business leaders such as Thomas F. "Mack" McClarty, who took the job of chief of staff in the White House, and Carol Rasco who headed up the White House Domestic Policy Council. James Lee Witt won high praise for his handling of the Federal Emergency Management Agency, the government agency that helps people in natural disasters like floods and hurricanes. The new president also brought in seasoned veterans of the Carter administration like Secretary of State Warren Christopher.

Twelve years had passed since the Democrats had been in the White House, though, and the new administration got off to a shaky start. Some early nominations were awkwardly withdrawn under fire, and clumsy handling of problems in the White House travel office resulted in much bad publicity.

Clinton came through strongly on his promise to make government "look like the face of America." His many appointments of women, people of all **ethnic** groups, and people with disabilities to key positions of leadership throughout the federal government brought a new kind of balance to power. Arkansans and African Americans Rodney Slater, Secretary of Transportation, and Bob Nash, Director of White House Personnel, were among those who served all eight years.

Health care reform was first on the Clinton agenda. The cost of health care was soaring, and many working Americans could not get health insurance to pay for even basic care. The president asked First Lady Hillary Clinton to put together a broad-based work group to find solutions to the problems that would satisfy patients, medical staff, hospitals, and insurance companies.

Putting the First Lady to work on complicated policy problems had worked in Arkansas for education reform. In Washington, the strategy proved to be a mistake. People resented having someone who had not been elected to office or approved by Congress placed into such a prominent leadership role. Furthermore, the health care proposals coming out of the work group proved to be too radical for Congress to adopt at that time. Clinton's first big plan failed.

CONTROVERSY

Almost from the very beginning, the Clinton years were marked by controversy, like the Whitewater investigations. In the 1980s, Bill and Hillary Clinton and the owners of an Arkansas savings and loan association, had been partners in a land development project in the White River valley. Although the Clintons lost money and the savings and loan association collapsed, the whole "Whitewater" situation became the subject of a long, detailed investigation by a federal special prosecutor.

Blameless of any wrongdoing in the financial dealings that started the investigation, the Clintons would be plagued throughout the administration by the continuous probing of

them and their associates. The special prosecutor kept an office in Little Rock for years, and other Arkansans were swept up in the investigations, although there were only a few minor convictions.

In the 1994 mid-term elections for Congress, the Republicans took control of the House of Representatives for the first time in decades. Their "Contract for America" proposed sweeping changes, calling for tax cuts, reduced spending, and shifting control of programs from the federal government to the states.

The now-experienced president responded in a defensive mode. The battle between the House and the White House resulted at one point in Congress refusing to pass funding bills so that the U.S. government actually closed its doors for a brief period.

ACCOMPLISHMENTS

The divided government managed, however, to get some very important work done. Clinton had promised during his campaign to reduce the size of government, a task he assigned to Vice President Al Gore. Gore was given an office in the White House and was entrusted with the important mission of "Reinventing Government." He worked hard with agencies all across government to trim staff, reduce budgets, and send work out to private businesses. Operating the government in more businesslike ways reduced costs, and therefore helped to make a balanced federal budget possible.

Welfare reform was another major Clinton project. Since the New Deal of the 1930s, the federal government had provided financial assistance to the children of needy families. Offering small cash payments did little to lift people out of poverty.

Some states had been experimenting with different approaches to the problem. The governors had shared their ideas with Clinton when he headed the National Governors Association, and in his presidential campaign, Clinton promised to "end welfare as we know it." In 1996, Congress passed a law that put a five-year limit on getting cash payments, and shifted the emphasis to getting a job. The new program also offered job training, child care, and transportation so people could get work to support their families.

In areas where the president was unable to work with Congress, he accomplished a number of important goals by issuing executive orders. In this way, he set aside vast tracts of wilderness to be enjoyed by future generations, and put safety rules into effect for American workers.

A SECOND TERM

Although President Clinton attracted bitter opposition from some quarters, the American public largely approved of his performance as president. His two terms of office spanned the longest period of economic expansion in American history. Business flourished and the stock market skyrocketed. The booming economy in combination with a tight rein on government spending resulted in a balanced federal budget for the first time since the early 1960s.

Clinton won his second term in 1996 with ease. Increasingly, however, many disapproved of some of the president's personal behavior. Stories about his involvement with a White House intern turned into a scandal so huge that the House of Representatives actually **impeached** the president. Only Andrew Johnson, the vice president who succeeded Abraham Lincoln after Lincoln's assassination,

had been similarly impeached. Like Johnson, Clinton was not convicted by the Senate, but he did apologize to the American public.

FOREIGN AFFAIRS

Because Clinton came to office as former governor with no prior exposure to international politics, people were skeptical about Clinton's ability to represent the United States among foreign leaders. In fact, his quick mind and outgoing nature won him many friends, particularly Boris Yeltsin of Russia and Tony Blair of the United Kingdom. Although his strategies drew some criticism, he did authorize decisive military moves when he felt they were required. He ordered bombing of Iraq when that country refused to honor the "no fly zone" established at the end of the Gulf War, and he took on the cause of the Albanian minority in Kosovo who were being systematically murdered by the Serbian army. Another Arkansan, General Wesley Clark, commander of the American and other NATO forces in Europe, headed the military forces in this engagement.

Clinton also sought peace. He worked with the Irish and the English to end violence in Northern Ireland. He brought Israeli and Palestinian leaders together on several occasions, investing great personal effort in trying to help the two warring groups come to an agreement. If Clinton himself expressed any regrets about his time in America's highest office, it was his inability to bring peace to the Middle East.

In the presidential election of 2000, Clinton's vice president, Al Gore, lost to George W. Bush, the son of former president George H. W. Bush. Bush carried Arkansas easily, but nationally the election was so close that it was not settled until the Supreme

This is an artist's drawing of what the Clinton Presidential Library in Little Rock will look like. The glass and steel building stretching to the Arkansas River will house the museum and a large meeting space. Behind it and to the side, barely visible in this drawing, is a long, low building that will house the **archives***. The red stone building at the lower right, the nineteenth-century Choctow railroad station, will be remodeled to house the University of Arkansas academic program and the Clinton Presidential* **Foundation***. The abandoned railroad bridge on the left will become a walkway to the North Little Rock side of the river.* (Artwork by T. W. Schaller, courtesy of Polshek Partnership Architects and the William J. Clinton Presidential Foundation.)

Court ruled on the ballots in one state. And First Lady Hillary Clinton wrapped up her career in the White House by winning a Senate seat representing the state of New York. The Clintons bought a house in Westchester County, just outside New York City, and now live in New York.

A NEW GOVERNOR

Clinton's presidency indirectly contributed to more change in Arkansas state government. Among those the special prosecutor charged with a crime was Gov. Jim Guy Tucker, who had done business with the savings and loan association in the 1980s, while he was out of politics and involved in private business. In the summer of 1996, an Arkansas jury in federal court convicted Tucker of illegal business dealings. Tucker immediately announced that he would resign the governorship.

The new governor was Mike Huckabee, who acquitted himself well during a brief crisis on his first day. It appeared that Tucker might change his mind about giving up the governorship, but after a brief period of confusion, Tucker did complete his resignation. Huckabee had first been elected lieutenant governor in a special election in 1993 and was reelected in 1994 and 1998. Huckabee was a Republican, the third Republican governor in Arkansas in

The William J. Clinton Presidential Library But Don't Try to Check Out the Books

One of the legacies of the Clinton presidency will be the William J. Clinton Presidential Library on twenty-seven acres of park land on the Arkansas River in downtown Little Rock. The library is expected to open in 2004.

There are eleven other presidential libraries, one for each president since the 1930s. Private individuals and local governments provide the land and build the buildings, and the National Archives, a part of the federal government, operates the library. (At its offices in Washington, the National Archives also maintains millions of government records, including the original Constitution and Declaration of Independence.)

A presidential library isn't really a place where you can go to check out books. First, it's an **archive**, a place to store and protect original historical documents. It's also a museum, a visual and interactive record of the Clinton years in Arkansas and in the presidency. The museum is expected to be a major tourist attraction. Some of the other presidential libraries draw hundreds of thousands of people a year.

The **archive** is mostly useful to journalists and historians, although anyone can see the material. The amount of archival material in the Clinton Library is hard to visualize. It will have more than seventy-six million pages of printed and typed material, about forty million emails, and almost two million photographs. There are also seventy-five thousand material objects, mostly gifts to the president from foreign governments and ordinary American citizens. Some of them will be on display in the museum.

In addition, several universities in the University of Arkansas system will operate a joint masters degree program in public service, drawing on the resources of the **archive** and people associated with the Clinton administration. The Clinton Library will also have an apartment for the Clintons and offices for the Clinton Presidential **Foundation**, the private organization that helped to raise money for the library and continues to serve as headquarters for many of the former president's interests. There will also be a facility for meetings and study groups on Lake Hamilton in Hot Springs, on land originally owned by a member of the Clinton family.

And of course the Clinton Library will have a feature common to most presidential libraries—a reproduction of the president's oval office in the White House.

the twentieth century. Like Clinton a native of Hope, Arkansas, Huckabee was forty years old when he became governor. Ordained as a Baptist minister at the age of eighteen, he had been minister of churches in Pine Bluff and in Texarkana and operator of a Christian television station before entering public life. He was the author of several books, including one on violence among young people.

TERM LIMITS

One of the most important political changes in Arkansas was the enactment of term limits for legislators. The voters approved a state constitutional amendment that limited members of the state house of representatives to no more than three two-year terms, and members of the state senate to no more than two four-year terms. The governor and the other elected executive officers were limited to two four-year terms. The term limits would apply to anyone elected after January 1, 1993.

The first session of the legislature significantly affected by the new term-limits measure was in 1999, when there were fifty-seven new members among the one hundred members of the house of representatives. The house leadership conducted training programs and practice sessions for the newcomers. Many of the new members had served in city or county government, so their lack of experience was not a major factor. Politicians also discovered that when they used up their time in the house, they could run for election to the senate, or the other way around.

PARTY POLITICS

The Republican Party continued to make gains in Arkansas. Voters picked Democrats for most state and county offices and for the legislature, but in elections for statewide offices and for members of the U.S. Congress, they were as likely to choose Republicans. The booming northwest section of Fayetteville, Springdale, and Rogers, the area around Fort Smith, and parts of Little Rock produced a sizable Republican vote. In the state legislature elected in 2000, with positions opened up by term limits, thirty of the one hundred members of the house and eight of the thirty-five members of the senate were Republicans.

For a while in the late twentieth century, Arkansas's four members of the U.S. House of Representatives were half Democrat, half Republican. As the twenty-first century began, the two senators were one Democrat and one Republican.

The Republican was Tim Hutchinson, elected in 1996. Born in Gravette, he graduated from high school in Springdale, and before entering politics taught history at John Brown University and was co-owner of a radio station in Bentonville. For a time his brother, Asa Hutchinson, was the member of the House of Representatives from northwest Arkansas, until President George W. Bush appointed him to head the Federal Drug Enforcement Agency.

The Democratic senator was Blanche Lambert Lincoln of Helena, whose family had been Delta farmers for several generations. She had first been elected to the House of Representatives, then took two years off after the birth of twin boys. She was elected to the Senate in 1998, the youngest woman ever elected to the Senate. (And Arkansas's second woman senator, after Hattie Caraway.)

HUCKABEE AS GOVERNOR

In state public affairs, Huckabee was a Republican governor with Democratic majorities in the legislature. The major achievements during this period included cuts in the state income tax; a reduction in the number of people on **welfare;** the establishment of a college scholarship program; simplification of the process for registering cars and trucks; the creation of the ARKids program to provide health care for children; and a plan for improving the state's highways. The highway plan, which involved some state funds and a ten-to-one match in federal funds, was a one-billion-dollar project. Most of the work would be on the interstate highway system.

In the legislative session of 2001, the governor proposed and the legislature approved a $3,000 raise for teachers, but there was some fear that a decline in state income would delay the raises. That session also created a state holiday, shared with the Washington's Birthday holiday, to honor Daisy Bates, who had guided the African American students in the desegregation of Central High School in 1957–1958. In 1997, at the fortieth anniversary of the Central High crisis, Governor Huckabee made a gracious speech, then he and President Bill Clinton held open the door of Central High for the "Little Rock Nine."

INCREASING DIVERSITY

A major trend in Arkansas was an increasing diversity in the population. The two fastest-growing groups were Asians and Hispanics. The Vietnam War ended in 1975 when North Vietnam captured South Vietnam. Thousands of people from South Vietnam and the neighboring countries of Laos and Cambodia fled with the hope of reaching the United States. Many of them did get to America, sometimes after enduring extreme hardships. The federal government used Fort Chaffee as a relocation center. Many of the refugee families chose to stay in the area for a while. Their presence, plus the availability of jobs, attracted more Vietnamese.

The Asian population of Arkansas grew from 1,619 in 1970 to 21,386 in 2000, mostly Vietnamese. Most were drawn to Fort Smith, Little Rock, and the Fayetteville-Springdale-Rogers area of northwest Arkansas. Many worked in low-paying, unskilled labor jobs like those in the chicken processing plants. Others became professionals, store owners, and restaurant operators, giving Arkansans both a figurative and literal flavor of Southeast Asia. There were even places in Arkansas where you could rent a videotape in Vietnamese.

HISPANIC GROWTH

A later and larger wave, also drawn by the promise of jobs, was Hispanic. Beginning about 1990, people from Mexico, Central America, and the Latin areas of Texas and California began to move to Arkansas in large numbers. The Hispanic migration was a national trend, but the rate of growth in Arkansas was among the fastest in the country.

By the 2000 census, there were 86,860 people of Hispanic descent in the state, an increase in the previous ten years of 337 percent. They were in almost every county, but the largest numbers were in southwest Arkansas, around DeQueen and Texarkana, and in the Fort Smith area. They were originally attracted by jobs in the **poultry** industry, but soon began to spread to other areas of the economy. Most were in family groups who were clearly in Arkansas to stay.

There arose Spanish-language radio stations, grocery stores, newspapers, and other businesses. Anglo businesses, as well as the state and local governments, moved to make information available in Spanish to their new customers, and the governor had an aide of Hispanic descent. Some of the largest employers, like Tyson, offered English language classes to their employees. And everyone could enjoy the annual Cinco de Mayo festival, a holiday imported from Mexico.

THE FUTURE

Bill Clinton's presidency focused attention on Arkansas as nothing had done before. The beautiful land we know as our state had, until the 1990s, lived a sheltered life, rarely in the center of national or global affairs. Arkansas had moved through history a bit on the sidelines, a little bit removed. That was often a

In September 1997, Little Rock and Arkansas marked the fortieth anniversary of the desegregation crisis at Little Rock Central High School in 1957. Here on the front landing of the school are the "Little Rock Nine," all returned for the occasion. They are, from left to right, *Thelma Mothershed Wair, Minnijean Brown, Jefferson Thomas, Terrence Roberts, Carlotta Walls LaNier, Gloria Ray Karlmark, Ernest Green, Elizabeth Eckford, and Melba Pattillo Beals. Behind them are,* left to right, *Little Rock mayor Jim Dailey, Governor Mike Huckabee, and President Bill Clinton. After the picture was taken, Huckabee and Clinton held open the door to Central High for the "Little Rock Nine" to enter.* (Courtesy of A. C. Haralson, Arkansas Dept. of Parks and Tourism)

comfortable place; isolation can sometimes be protection.

In the past, being sheltered in the Arkansas hills and hollows and prairies meant isolation from one another, and it meant being cut off from the free flow of ideas in the United States and the world. Now Arkansas, for better or worse, was the focus of intense **scrutiny.** In addition, the smaller world of electronic communications required Arkansans to keep pace in the marketplace of both goods and ideas.

Working together, Arkansas's next generation, growing up in a new century, can fulfill this state's wonderful promise.

Thorncrown Chapel is the masterpiece of Arkansas architect E. Fay Jones. Made almost entirely of glass and wood, it sits in an undisturbed wooded area near Eureka Springs. The American Institute of Architects named it the fourth best American architectural design of the twentieth century. (Courtesy of A. C. Haralson, Arkansas Dept. of Parks and Tourism)

Natural Materials, Soaring Vision: the Architect Fay Jones

The American Institute of Architects has awarded its Gold Medal for lifetime achievement to only about sixty people. One of them is E. Fay Jones of Arkansas.

Jones was born in Pine Bluff in 1921 and reared in El Dorado. He liked to say that his first important building was a really good tree house. While he was in high school, he became fascinated with the work of the most famous American architect of his time, Frank Lloyd Wright. Wright's buildings were filled with light, and many of them were designed to fit in a natural setting.

When the University of Arkansas at Fayetteville started an **architecture** program, Jones was in its first graduating class in 1950. He did advanced study at Rice University, then was invited to join Wright as a student in his workshop in Wisconsin.

Jones returned to Arkansas and essentially never left. His career and most of his major works were in the state. He joined the faculty of the School of Architecture at the University of Arkansas at Fayetteville, serving for a time as dean. He eventually retired from the faculty to devote all of his time to his private architecture practice. A former student gave the university the money to create a professorship to honor Jones.

He built mostly houses and chapels. He used natural stone, wood, and glass to make structures that are tucked into the ground but soar above it. His best known work is Thorncrown Chapel, west of Eureka Springs. Jim Reed, a retired school teacher, owned the land and thought of building on it a small chapel open to everyone. Jones accepted the challenge. Thorncrown Chapel was completed in 1980. It's only twenty-four feet by sixty feet, but it reaches up forty-eight feet, more than four stories. The glass walls are supported by a wooden framework that leaves the building open all around. To avoid damaging the tress and plants on the site, Jones used standard lumber, in sizes that could be carried onto the site by hand.

More than four million people have visited Thorncrown Chapel. Jones built similar chapels elsewhere, including one at Bella Vista, Arkansas.

The American Institute of Architects selected Thorncrown Chapel as one of the ten best American designs of the twentieth century. It's fourth on the list; the building just before it is one of Frank Lloyd Wright's houses.

Thirty Years of Growth and Change

A comparison of the 1970 *census* and the 2000 census shows how the Arkansas population has gotten larger and more diverse over thirty years.

	1970	2000
Total	1,923,295	2,673, 400
White	1,565,915	2,100, 135
Black	352,445	416,615
Hispanic	*	86,866
Asian**	1,619	21,386
Am. Indian	2,014	16,702
Other	1,302	1,332
More than 1 category	—	30,364***

*The small Hispanic population was included in "Other."

**The category "Asian"here includes a small number of Pacific Island peoples, including people from Guam and Hawaii.

***Most people complete the census by filling out a form, which includes boxes to check for race or ethnicity. The U. S. Census Bureau accepts the category the individual chooses. The 2000 census, for the first time, allowed people to check more than one box for race or ethnicity (like white, Hispanic). People who listed two or more categories are reported in the census summary as "other."

VOCABULARY

amateur (AM-uh-TURE) one who does something for fun, rather than pay.

architecture (AR-ka-TEK-chur) the art and science of designing and building houses and other kinds of buildings; a style of design.

archive (AR-kive) a collection of original documents or records of historical interest; the place such records are kept.

average (AVE-er-ige), or mean (MEEN) in mathematics or statistics, the value obtained by dividing the total of a set of numerals by the number of numerals in the set. See also **median**.

census (SEN-sus) an official count of people or things, often with other kinds of information; the Constitution requires the U. S. government to conduct a national census every ten years.

consolidated (kon-SOL-uh-DATE) put together; a consolidated school district is one that has been created by joining several districts into one.

creationist (kree-AY-shun-ist) the idea, associated with fundamentalist Christianity, that the story of creation described in Genesis in the Bible is literally true; one who holds that concept.

curriculum (kur-RICK-u-LUM) all the courses offered by a school.

ethnic (ETH-nik) related to any large group of people who have a common cultural, racial, historical, or language background.

evolution (EV-oh-LOO-shun) the theory of the gradual change of a species over time to better adapt to existing environmental conditions.

foundation (foun-DA-shun) an organization for raising and spending money, usually devoted to a specific purpose.

historic preservation saving and restoring buildings erected in earlier times that represent a region's heritage and character.

hydroelectric (HI-dro-eh-LECK-trick) making electricity with the power of running water, such as water over a dam.

impeach (im-PEACH) the provision in the U.S. Constitution for removing a national executive or judicial figure from office. The House of Representatives decides if a person should be impeached, or sent to the Senate for trial. The Senate tries cases of impeachment, with the chief justice of the Supreme Court presiding if a president is involved. Thus President Clinton was impeached by the House, but not convicted by the Senate. Impeachment, the act of impeaching.

inauguration (in-OG-u-RAY-shun) the formal ceremony or act of taking office.

median the middle value in a distribution. Similar to average, usually used for things such as annual income figures; the median is the point at which half the population is above the figure, and half is below.

NCAA the National Collegiate Athletic Association, the organization that controls college and university athletic programs.

per capita (per KAP-i-ta) by unit of population, or per person; equally to each individual. The per capita income for Arkansas is the income each person would have if all the income in the state was given equally to every person.

poultry (POLE-tree) domestic birds, such as chickens, turkeys, ducks, or geese, raised for meat or eggs.

professional (pruh-FESH-uh-nul) keeping to the recognized standards of a career, or working for pay.

repertory (REP-uh-TOR-ee) a theater in which a resident group of actors present plays, often regularly repeating some plays.

Rhodes Scholar (ROHDZ SKAH-ler) one who wins a two- to three-year scholarship to Oxford University in England.

scrutiny (SKROOT-nee) detailed observation; a close, careful examination or study.

urban, urbanization (UR-bahn) concerning, or located in a city; to become urban.

Victorian (vic-TORE-ee-uhn) the term used to describe buildings constructed during the late nineteenth century, in the last part of Queen Victoria's reign in Great Britain; also any thing relating to Queen Victoria and her reign.

welfare (well-FAIR) the common name for any government program that gives financial aid to people. One of largest welfare programs, begun in the 1930s, provided financial aid to women with young children, and others. It's formal name was Aid to Families with Dependent Children.

STUDY QUESTIONS

1. What were the major population trends in Arkansas during this period?

2. Describe some of the elements in the cultural revival in Arkansas.

3. Why and how did Arkansans show an interest in historic preservation.

4. Describe the rise of the Republican Party in Arkansas in this period.

5. What were Bill Clinton's major accomplishments as governor?

6. Describe the major trends in Arkansas business, industry, and agriculture in the period.

7. What were the accomplishments and problems in public education in this period?

8. Evaluate the presidency of Bill Clinton.

9. Explain the origins and effects of the increasing Hispanic population.

10. Describe the major factors in party politics and public affairs in Arkansas during the last years of the twentieth century.

GOVERNORS OF ARKANSAS

1. James Sevier Conway, 1836–1840
2. Archibald Yell, 1840–1844
3. Thomas Stevenson Drew, 1844–1849
4. John Selden Roane, 1849–1852
5. Elias Nelson Conway, 1852–1860
6. Henry Massie Rector, 1860–1862
7. Harris Flanagin, 1862–1864
8. Isaac Murphy, 1864–1868
9. Powell Clayton, 1868–1871
   Ozro A. Hadley, 1871–1873*
10. Elisha Baxter, 1873–1874
11. Augustus Hill Garland, 1874–1877
12. William Read Miller, 1877–1881
13. Thomas James Churchill, 1881–1883
14. James Henderson Berry, 1883–1885
15. Simon P. Hughes, 1885–1889
16. James Philip Eagle, 1889–1893
17. William Meade Fishback, 1893–1895
18. James Paul Clarke, 1895–1897
19. Daniel Webster Jones, 1897–1901
20. Jeff Davis, 1901–1907
21. John Sebastian Little, 1907–1909
    Xenophon Overton Pindall, Acting
    Governor, 1907–1909**
22. George Washington Donaghey, 1909–1913

23. Joseph Taylor Robinson, 1913
24. George Washington Hays, 1913–1917
25. Charles Hillman Brough, 1917–1921
26. Thomas Chipman McRae, 1921–1925
27. Thomas Jefferson Terral, 1925–1927
28. John E. Martineau, 1927–1928
29. Harvey Parnell, 1928–1933
30. Junius Marion Futrell, 1933–1937
31. Carl Edward Bailey, 1937–1941
32. Homer Martin Adkins, 1941–1945
33. Benjamin Travis Laney, Jr., 1945–1949
34. Sidney Sanders McMath, 1949–1953
35. Francis Adams Cherry, 1953–1955
36. Orval Eugene Faubus, 1955–1967
37. Winthrop Rockefeller, 1967–1971
38. Dale Leon Bumpers, 1971–1975
39. David Hampton Pryor, 1975–1979
40. William Jefferson "Bill" Clinton,
    1979–1981
41. Frank Durwood White, 1981–1983
42. William Jefferson "Bill" Clinton,
    1983–1993
43. Jim Guy Tucker, 1993–1996
44. Mike Huckabee, 1996–

*Ozro Hadley became governor after Powell Clayton became a U.S. senator. Hadley served from March 17, 1871 to January 6, 1873. There were other Arkansas political figures who were acting governors for shorter periods of time.

**From May 14, 1907 until 1909, Xenophon Overton Pindall served as acting governor for John Little, who served only from January 1907 until February 11, 1907. John Isaac Moore served from February 11, 1907 until May 14, 1907, when Pindall took over the governorship.

INDEX

(Items that are in italic, *like this,* are in the maps, illustrations, or captions.)

Bella Vista, 355
Bemis family, 204
Bendix Transcontinental Air Race, 251
Benton County, 105
Bentonville, *251*, 351
"Big Bear of Arkansas, The," 84
Big Mulberry, 59
Bigelow, 203
Bigelow Brothers and Walker Company, 202
bilious fever, 60
Bird, J. & N., *86*
Black, Etta, *201*
Black, James, 107
Black River, 55, 74, *174*
Black Rock, *299*
blacks or African Americans: on De Soto's expedition, 29; at Arkansas Post, 44, 47; in Santo Domingo rebellion, 49; at Battle of New Orleans, 62; and slavery, at time of Missouri Compromise, 65–67; population, 1830–1860, 95; population distribution, 1860, *112;* in plantation slavery system, 93, 98–102; free blacks, 101; proposal to arm slaves during Civil War, 124; in Union army, 125, *127*, 135, *137, 143;* during Civil War, 138; and end of slavery, 141–44; in Reconstruction, 148, 153–54; and the Ku Klux Klan, 150; population, 1870–1900, 163; in farmers' revolt, 165, 166; and voter discrimination, segregation, 167–69; and lynching, 169; in late nineteenth century, 170–72; and education, late nineteenth century, 171–72; and fraternal societies, 172; and prison system, 188; population, 1900–1920, 198; and labor unions, 205; in World War I, 211, 212; and Elaine race riots, 212–15; and Ku Klux Klan of 1920s, 229; and education in the 1920s, 234; and tuberculosis sanatorium, 234; and sharecropping, 154, 237; in Great Depression, 243, *244;* and Southern Tenant Farmers' Union, 254–55; and New Deal, 259; and shift to Democratic Party, 259; population, 1920–1940, 260; at St. Bartholomew's School, *266;* and World War II, 269, 271, 281–83; in McMath administration, 285–86; in colleges, late 1940s, 288; population, 1940 and 1950, 292; and school desegregation, 301–10; and Winthrop Rockefeller, 312–13; appointments to state boards, 316; and voting, membership in General Assembly, 316; population, 1970–2000, 355. *See also* civil rights
Blair, Tony, 348
Blakely Town, 57
Blease, Cole, 184
"Blissville," *143*
Blitzkrieg, 267
Blossom, Virgil, 302, 305
Blossom Plan, 302, 303
Blue Mountain, 272

blues music, *282*
Blunt, General James G., 132
Blytheville, 273
Board of Education, state, 192
Board of Health, 196
boll weevil, 238
Bolshevik Revolution, 212
Bond, Scott, 178, 214
Booker, Joseph A., 215
Boone County, 254
Booneville, 197
Borland, Solon, 107, 109
Boston Mountains, 128, 132
"Bounce," 96
bow and arrow, 15
Bowie, Jim, 107
Bowie knife, 88, 107, 123
Bowie Lumber Company, 204
Brady School, Little Rock, *195*
Branch Normal College, 171, *191. See also* Arkansas AM&N; University of Arkansas at Pine Bluff
Branton, Wiley, 303
Breckinridge, John C., 119, 120
"Brindletails," 157
Brinkley, *199*
Britt, Lieutenant Governor Maurice L. "Footsie," 270, 271, *274*
Brooks, Dr. Ida Jo, 200
Brooks, Joseph, 156–57
Brooks-Baxter War, 157, *158*
Brotherhood of Sleeping Car Porters, 281
Brotherhood of Timber Workers, 205
Brough, Governor Charles H., 189, 191, 197, 215, 228, 247
Brown, Bobby, *314*
Brown, Dee, 329, *330*
Brown, Floyd. 234
Brown, Minnijean, *353*
Brown, Wilson N., 105
Brown vs. Topeka Board of Education, 301, 302, 303, 305
Broyles, Frank, 322, *323*
Bryan, William Jennings, 167, *183*, 230
Buena Vista, Battle of, 109, *110*
buffalo, 26, 50, 59, 61
Buffalo River, 205, 249, 332, 328
Bull Run, First Battle of, 123, 124, 126. *See also* Manassas, First Battle of
Bull Shoals Lake, 316
Bumpers, Betty, 333
Bumpers, Governor/Senator Dale, 328, 332–33, *334*
Bureau of Immigration and State Lands, 151
Burns, Bob, 228
Burr, Aaron, 71
Bury My Heart at Wounded Knee, 329
Bush, John E., 172
Bush, President George H. W., 345, 346, 348

and Louisiana Purchase, 48–50; and World
War I, 209–10; and John Gould Fletcher, 258;
and World War II, 266–67
Franklin, Battle of, 124, 134
Franklin, Tennessee, 124
Franklin County, 205, 211
Fredericksburg, Battle of, 134
Freedmen's Bureau, 144, 150
French, Alice (Octave Thanet), 174
French and Indian War, 47
Frisco railroad, 161
fruit growing, *207, 239, 241*
Fugitives, 258
Führer, 267
Fulbright, Senator J. William, 284, 287, *310,* 319,
328, 333, 343
Fulton, Governor/Senator William S., 72, 90, 93
fundamentalism, 230
Furbush, W. H., 157
"furnish," 237
Futrell, Governor Marion, 244–45, 259

gambling, 311, 313
Game and Fish Commission, 325
"Game of the Century," 322
Gammon, John, 313
Gammonville, 313
Gannett Company, 343
Garland, Augustus Hill, 157, 159
Garner, William Wakefield, 132
Gator Bowl, 293
Gazette. See Arkansas Gazette
General Assembly: of Arkansas Territory, 68;
composition, early statehood period, 87; knife
fight in first session as state, 1836, 88; chooses
U.S. Senators, 90; and education, 93; and
secession, 120–21; composition, 1865, 148;
refusal to accept Fourteenth Amendment,
148; and Reconstruction programs, 151; after
Reconstruction, 159–60; and segregation,
voter discrimination, 167–69; and Jeff Davis,
187; and road building, 194; and state flower,
flag, 197; and voting for women, 200; and
prohibition, 201; and new capitol, 202;
changes state motto, 228; and theory of evolution, 230; and road building in 1920s, 231;
and funding for medical school, 234; and
Great Depression, 244; and New Deal, 259;
and McMath administration, 287; and industrial development, 298; and *Brown* ruling,
303; and Faubus administration, 304–5, 311;
and segregation, 309; and Rockefeller administration, 313; African American members,
1980s, 316; and Equal Rights Amendment,
323; and Bumpers administration, 333; and
community colleges, 338; effect of term limits, 351
Genesis, 230, 335
Georgia, 120, 177, 184, 229, 283, 305, 335

Germany: immigration from, *129,* 140, 162, *195;*
and World War I, 209–10; and World War II,
266–69, 270, 272, 285; prisoners of war, 278–79
Gettysburg, Battle of, 134
Gibbs, Mifflin W., 154, *156*
G. I. Bill, 287
Gifted and Talented education, 338
G. I. Revolt, 285–87
Goff, Norris, 227, *228*
Golden City steamboat, *162*
Gold Lake, *182*
Gold Rush, 111, 220
goosefoot, 8
Gore, Vice President Al, 345, 346, 347, 348
gourds, 8
Governor's Council on Human Resources, 316
Grand Prairie, 6
Grangers, 165
Grant, General/President Ulysses S., 124, 126,
134, 136, 144, 157
Gravette, 211, 351
Great Britain. *See* England
Great Depression, 220, 236, 239–43, 245, 259,
265, 266, 328, 344
Great Society, 316
Great War. *See* World War I
Greek Revival style, 79
Green, Ernest, 309, *353*
Greenback Party, 165
Greene County, 132
Greer's Ferry Dam and Reservoir, 315
Greer's Ferry Lake, 316
Gregory, *205*
Grey, William H., 153
Grider, John McGravock, 211
Griffin, Governor Marvin, 305
Gulf Coastal Plain, 5
Gulf War. *See* Persian Gulf War
Gunther, John, 287
Guthridge, Amis, 302
gypsies, 267

Hall, C. G. "Crip," *321*
Hall High School, 302, 310
Hamilton, Alexander, 71
Hammond, John, *96*
Hammond, William H., *96*
"Hanging Judge," the, 174, 177
Harrington, Donald, 329
Harris, Charlaine, 329
Harrison, 254–55
Harrison, Bill, 329
Harvard University, 258
Harvey, W. H. "Coin," 194
Hatfield, Ken, 322
Hawaiian Islands, 269
Hawthorne, Nathaniel, 67
Hays, Congressman Brooks, 259, 301, 308
Hays, George W., 189

War II, 273, 282–83; and Jehovah's Witnesses, 280–81; in 1946, 287; changes in segregation, 1950s, 301; and Governor Faubus, 304; effect of Central High crisis, 1957, 311; and Civil Rights Movement, 315–16; and Interstate Highway System, 317; population changes, late twentieth century, 327; and historic preservation, 331–32; in modern times, 342; newspapers, 343; headquarters for Clinton presidential campaign, 1992, 345, 346; site of Clinton Presidential Library, *349,* 350; and Republican vote, 351; and Asian population, 352; and fortieth anniversary of Central High crisis, *353*
"Little Rock Nine," the, *306,* 307, 308, 352, *353*
Livingston, Robert, 49
loess, 7
logging. *See* timber industry
London, 258
Long, Governor/Senator Huey, 247
Longview, Texas, 214
Lonoke, 166, 208, 231, 244, 245, 270, 238
Louis XIV, *39,* 40, 42
Louisiana, 120, 189, 205, 227, 246, 247, 283
Louisiana Purchase, 48–50, 53, 62, 63, 67, 328
Louisiana Purchase Historical Monument, *49*
Louisiana Purchase Historical State Park, 63
Lum and Abner, 227–28
lumbering. *See* timber industry
lynching, 169
Lyon, General Nathan, 127

MacArthur, General Douglas, *289*
MacArthur Knitting Club, 271
MacArthur Museum of Arkansas Military History, 91, *113*
Madagascar, 154
Madison, 93
Madison County, 123, 290
Magnolia, 192
Main Street Arkansas, 332
malaria, 60, 138, 195–96
Mammoth Springs, 55
Manassas, First Battle of, 123, 124, 126, 134. *See also* Bull Run
Manassas, Second Battle of, 134
Manchuria, 267
manganese, 205
"Manifest Destiny," 107
Manila, 211
Mann, Mayor Woodrow, 308
Mansfield, Louisiana, 135
Maple Valley schoolhouse, *233*
Marche, 162
march elder, 8
Marett, Lieutenant Samuel H., 270
Marianna, *240*
Marine Corps, U.S., 285
Marinoni, Rosa, 200

Marks' Mill, Battle of, 134, 136
Marley, Florence, 201
Marquette, Father Jacques, 34–38
Marshall, 345
Marshall, Justice Thurgood, 283
martial law, 131, 150
Martineau, Governor John E., 231, 233
Marvell, 63, *309*
Maryland, 190
Mary Woods II, 75
Masons, 103
mastodon, *2, 3, 7*
math and science high school, 338
Maumelle, 272
Maumelle River, 5
McBeth, Dr. Francis, 329
McBride, Bill, 223
McCauley, John, *106*
McCauley, Mrs. Nancy Fletcher O'Kelly, *106*
McClarty, Thomas F. "Mack," 346
McClellan, Senator John L., 284, *320, 321,* 333
McClellan-Kerr Arkansas River Navigation Project, 316
McCulloch, General Ben, 127, 128
McIlroy Farm, 152
McKennon, Major Pierce, 270
McLaughlin, Mayor Leo P., 285
McMath, Governor Sidney S., 285–87, *288,* 289–90
McRae, Governor Thomas C., 231, 234
measles, 94, 138
"Meatless Tuesdays," 210
Medal of Honor, 125, 241, 270, 271, *274*
Memphis, *30,* 31, 73, 93, 140, *162,* 316
Memphis, Battle of, 134
Mena, 227, 246, 247, 290
Mental Retardation, Division of, 313
Merrimac, 134
Methodist church, 105, 171, 234
Mexican War, 106–11, 128
Mexico, 11, 26, 27, 34, 352. *See also* Mexican War
Mexico City, 109
Michigan, 84, 86, 202
Middle East, 348
Military Cross, British, 270
Military Road, 73
Miller, A. H., *173*
Miller, Daisy, *201*
Miller, Governor James, 67, 70
Miller, John E., 284, 303
Miller, Oscar Franklin, 211
"million dollar race," 284
Mills, Representative Wilbur, 284
minimum wage, 259
minimum-wage law, state, 313
mining, 205–7
"Minstrels," 156
Missionary Ridge, Battle of, 124
Mississippi, 55, 72, 93, 119, 120, 142, 184, 190, 215, 227, 242, 283, 338

United Nations, 288
University of Arkansas, Fayetteville, 151, 152, 185, 189, 190, *191*, 234, 270, *276*, 284, 288, 303, *308*, 322, 343, 355
University of Arkansas at Pine Bluff (UAPB), 171, 234. *See also* Branch Normal College, Arkansas AM&N
University of Arkansas Medical School, 200, 203, 234, 288
University of Arkansas Press, 331
University of Arkansas system, *349*, 350
University of Central Arkansas, 193
University of Chicago, 283
University of Illinois, 152
University of Texas, 322
Uplands, 3
urbanization, 177, 219, 260, 327
Urban League, 301
USA Today, 343
Utah, 190

Van Buren, 102, 109, 111, 152, 332
Van Buren, President Martin, 84, 86
Van Dalsem, Paul, 322
Vanderbilt Law School, 185
Vanderbilt University, 258
Van Dorn, General Earl, 128–30
Vardaman, James K., 184
Venegar, E. T., 215
Vermont, 66
Vicksburg, 130, 133, 134
victory gardens, 271
Vietnam Veterans Memorial, 322
Vietnam War, 319, *320*, 322, 345, 352. *See also* North Vietnam; South Vietnam
Villiers, Balthazar de, 48
Virginia, 34, 97, 122, 126, 136, 283
Vital Statistics, Bureau of, 196
Vocational Technical Educational Program, 298
vocational-technical schools, 338

Wabbaseka, 197
Wager's Mills, 105
Wair, Thelma Mothershed, *353*
Walker, David, 87, 121, 122
Wallace, George, 319
Wal-Mart, 328, 338
Walnut Ridge, 273
Walton, Sam, 328, 338, 344
war bonds, 210, 270
Ward Bus Company, *248*
War Eagle, 105
War Memorial Building, 203
War of 1812, 62–63, 67, 68
War on Poverty, 316
Warren, Anne, 99
Warren, Nathan, 101, *103*
Washburn, Abbe, 77
Washburn, Cephas, 77

Washington, Arkansas, 107, 139, *339, 341*
Washington, Booker, T., 170, 188, *214*, 215
Washington County, 90, 105, 141, 152, 193
Washington, D. C., 202, 214, 346
Washington, George, 47
Washington, state, 239
watermelons, 255
Watson, Tom, 184
WEHCO company, 343
welfare reform, 347, 352
"We Shall Overcome," 316
West Fork, 190
West Memphis, 57, 93, 259, 291, *317*
West Point, 128, 272
"Wheatless Mondays," 210
Whetstone, Pete. *See* "Pete Whetstone"
Whig Party: origins in Arkansas, 70; and *Arkansas Advocate,* Albert Pike, 72; leadership and supporters, 1830s and 1840s, 87; breaks apart, 117; in election of 1860, 120; role of former members, 139, 149, 159
White, Gay, *335*
White, Governor Frank, 335–36
White, J. T., *173*
White Citizens' Council, 303, 305
White County, *106*
White River, 6, 31, 46, 55, 74, 84, *246, 256, 299,* 347
"Whitewater" investigation, 347
Whittington, Hiram, 74
Wilkerson, Lieutenant James, 53
Williams, Lucinda, 331
Williams, Miller, 329–31
Wilson, 258
Wilson, John, 88
Wilson, President Woodrow, 190, 207
Wilson's Creek, Battle of, 127, 134
Winn, Martha, *201*
Winn, Oscar, 281
Winn, Stella, *201*
Winslow, *72,* 190, *201*
Winthrop, *311*
Wisconsin, 202
Witt, James Lee, 346
Wolf, John Quincy, 166
Wolf House, *58*
women: at Arkansas Post, 45; in Territorial Arkansas, 74; frontier life, 94–95; in Civil War, 138; activism in late nineteenth century, 172–73, 197; and Federation of Women's Clubs, 173, 197, 234; and right to vote, 200–201; Winslow's "petticoat government," *201;* election of Senator Hattie Caraway, 247; as aviators, *251;* in World War II, 271, *274;* defense industries, 275; in Central High crisis, *309,* 310; "barefoot and pregnant," 322; in 1960s and 1970s, 322–23
Women's Army Corps, *271*
Women's Christian Temperance Union, 201